P9-DIJ-170

Modern Imperialism
Western Overseas Expansion
and Its Aftermath, 1776-1965

STUDIES IN HISTORY AND POLITICS

Under the editorial direction of Gerald E. Stearn

RUSSIA AND THE WEST FROM PETER TO KHRUSHCHEV

Edited by L. Jay Oliva, New York University

CHURCH AND STATE IN AMERICAN HISTORY

John F. Wilson, Princeton University

THE AMERICAN IMAGE,

PAST AND PRESENT

Edited by G. D. Lillibridge, Chico State College

SOLDIERS AND STATES

CIVIL-MILITARY RELATIONS IN MODERN EUROPE

Edited by David B. Ralston, Massachusetts Institute of Technology

THE DEVELOPMENT OF THE COMMUNIST BLOC

Edited by Roger Pethybridge, University College, Swansea

BRITISH POLITICS

PEOPLE, PARTIES AND PARLIAMENTS

Edited by Anthony King, University of Essex

FRENCH POLITICS

Edited by Martin Harrison, University of Keele

THE POLITICS OF AMERICAN FEDERALISM

Edited by Daniel J. Elazar, Temple University

MODERN IMPERIALISM

WESTERN OVERSEAS EXPANSION AND ITS AFTERMATH, 1776-1965

Edited by Ralph A. Austen, University of Chicago

AGRARIANISM IN AMERICAN HISTORY

Edited by Louis H. Douglas, Kansas State University

Other volumes in preparation

STUDIES IN HISTORY AND POLITICS

Modern Imperialism

Western Overseas Expansion and Its Aftermath 1776–1965

Edited with an introduction by

Ralph A. Austen

University of Chicago

D. C. HEATH AND COMPANY
A Division of Raytheon Education Company
Lexington, Massachusetts

Copyright © 1969 by Raytheon Education Company

All rights reserved. No part of this publication may be reproduced or transmitted in any form or by any means, electronic or mechanical, including photocopy, recording, or any information storage or retrieval system, without permission in writing from the publisher.

Printed in the United States of America

Library of Congress Number: 71-80474

Table of Contents

Introduction

The student of imperialism in the mid-twentieth century suffers the handicap of approaching a subject whose very name has become less a descriptive term than an ideological battle cry. For almost any liberal or radical, the word "imperialism" primarily evokes western oppression of the nonwestern world. The reaction of many conservatives to being labelled imperialists is to defend the right and duty of civilized nations to impose their values upon less enlightened peoples.

In presenting the following selection of documents and commentaries, the hope is to demonstrate that the process of modern western overseas expansion was far too complex to be susceptible to a single moral judgment. At the same time, it should become clear that imperialism has played a key role in creating the close ties which bind together almost all parts of the present day world. Thus, no meaningful attitude towards contemporary international politics can either ignore or oversimplify the motives, forces, and conditions which created and characterized colonial empires.

If morality must remain somewhat selective, historical interpretation can still look for unifying themes. The various factors combining to produce the extension of western power over the rest of the world share, first of all, an easily identified practical effect. Asia, Africa, and Latin America have, in the last two centuries, undergone a "modernization" resulting almost entirely from western initiatives, however much or little the West has been able to control the process. Secondly, the relations between West and non-West have been, and continue to be, shaped by the *idea* of western domination. This concept, even when exaggerated or misapplied, is as much a part of imperialism as the tangible realities of change and control.

While the overseas expansion dealt with here is not the beginning of western world hegemony, it nevertheless represents the extension of this power to a degree unprecedented in the history of any empire. The builders of the Old Colonial System from the Renaissance to the eighteenth century are distinguished from their successors of the postindustrial age by both a greater conscious dedication to imperial power and a lesser capability of transforming the non-European world. The Old Colonial System was the creation of absolutist or would-be absolutist monarchies who frankly expressed their concern for strict control over all overseas possessions. Mercantilist doctrine also made clear the vital but subordinate function of colonies in strengthening the economy of the mother country. The objects of such colonialism, however, remained limited to strategic commercial centers and relatively vacant plantation areas; direct control over substantial non-European populations was neither sought nor, in most instances, attained.

Europeans, in the first phase of their overseas expansion, possessed only a limited technological advantage over other peoples, mainly in regard to seafaring. Even here, the slowness of communication by sailing vessel restricted home government control over colonies. Moreover, despite the economic importance of colonies, conditions of life overseas and an abundance of domestic opportunities meant that—with the possible exception of the Spaniards—few Europeans of high social or intellectual standing chose to follow colonial careers.

Paradoxically, it is with the fall of the Old Colonial System, where this volume begins, that the fullest European domination of the world first gets under way. Imperialism has been viewed by both critics and defenders as a process through which western "rationalism" overcame the traditional values of nonwestern societies; yet, in regard to immediate European needs of the modern era, imperialism itself may be seen as irrational.

Where the absolutist state and the mercantilist economy had relished centralized control over the inflow of colonial goods, the parliamentary state and the industrial economy of the nineteenth and early twentieth centuries put relatively little value on either extending governmental responsibilities overseas or acquiring tropical commodities and markets. As the following selections should indicate, imperialism in this period is less the result of a deliberate expansive *will* than the effect of a vast increase in expansive *capacity*.

Thus the examples of political interest in colonies presented here form a rather sporadic pattern, largely subsumed by more serious rivalries within Europe; but the ability of small forces with modern weapons and transport to rapidly establish claims to colonial tracts was both astounding and, until the rise of anticolonial nationalism, irreversible. Economically, the tropical commercial centers which became the nuclei of new colonies must also be seen as peripheral to industrial needs. The massive availability of cheap European goods and the force of even marginal European capital undermined traditional society in these areas to a point where colonial rule sometimes offered the only means of maintaining order.

The tools of expansion—steamships, railroads, telegraphy, and rapid-fire weapons—were products of industrialism developed for, and mainly dedicated to, internal European needs. But this technology came into the hands of not only the industrial classes but also those sectors of the western elite who found their status undermined by industrialism. For the displaced military officer, clergyman, and country squire, the colonies offered a career combining the traditionalist heirarchy of the Old Regime with the materialist progress of the new.

The opening selections in this volume illustrate an ideological opposition to imperialism. This opposition accompanied the fall of the Old Colonial System and never disappeared for any extended period in the modern era. While liberalism, in its various forms, stressed the wastefulness and authoritarianism of overseas dependencies, socialists and communists pointed to the exploitative nature of the colonial relationship. The expressions of widespread enthusiasm for imperialism are limited to a few decades at the end of the nineteenth century, and, as will be seen, they immediately inspired an equally spirited counterattack.

Nevertheless, the reality of empire managed to survive all of these onslaughts, and European overseas possessions increased steadily from the early nineteenth century to the end of World War I. Even the postindependence 1960s are still characterized by "spheres of influence" in which western powers exercise economic control, sometimes reinforced by political manipulation and military intervention. To the political left everywhere, anti-imperialism thus remains a lively and useful issue. The efforts of the Soviet Union and Communist China to form alliances with excolonial states are based upon their identification of United States' policies with imperialism.

However ambivalent in its own attitudes, the United States has undoubtedly fallen heir to part of the role played in the past by self-confessed European colonial empires. In evaluating the motives and achievements of those who dominate the world, however, it is not sufficient simply to demonstrate the fact that they do so. It is hoped that the present volume will assist such an evaluation by showing both the historical continuities of modern empire and the particular problems that empire has presented to the powers responsible for both its growth and decay.

Chronology of Major Political Events

1776   American Declaration of Independence.

1784   Pitt India Act initiates parliamentary control over British East India Company.

1788   Britain claims and begins colonization of Australia.

1798   Napoleon conquers Egypt.

1807   Britain abolishes its slave trade.

1815   Peace of Vienna: (1) all western European nations abandon slave trade; (2) dismantling of first French overseas empire completed; (3) Britain takes South Africa and a foothold in Southeast Asia.

1806-25   Latin America gains independence from Spain and Portugal but without internal unity.

1830   France conquers Algiers.

1837   Great Trek of Dutch-speaking South Africans to escape paternalistic British native policy at the Cape of Good Hope.

1837-40   Canadian revolt and reforms preparing way for self-government.

1840   Britain claims New Zealand.

1839-41   Eastern crisis as Mohammed Ali of Egypt is checked by Britain in attempt to gain control of the Ottoman Empire.

1841-42   Opium War: first of many European impositions of free trade upon the Chinese Empire.

1858   Indian Mutiny: final abolition of British East India Company's political authority.

1858   France occupies Saigon.

1861-67   French troops occupy Mexico and impose Emperor Maximilian.

1869   Opening of the Suez Canal.

1870   Reform of abusive "Culture System" in Dutch East Indies (Indonesia).

1881   France occupies Tunisia.

1882   Britain occupies Egypt.

1884-85   Berlin Conference sanctions new British, French, German, and Belgian (King Leopold) expansion in tropical Africa.

1896   Ethiopians defeat Italians at Adua.

1896   Germans occupy Kiaochow initiating new imperialist competition for Chinese concessions.

1898   Spanish-American War.

1898-99 Fashoda crisis: Britain forces France to abandon the Nile Valley.

1899-01 United States enunciates "Open Door" policy in China and Chinese attack Europeans in "Boxer Rebellion."

1899-02 Anglo-Boer War in South Africa.

1904-05 Russo-Japanese War.

1905,11 First and Second Morocco crises: Germany antagonizes Britain and France by protesting as latter establishes protectorate in Morocco.

1907   Anglo-Russian agreement on rival interests in Persia, Afghanistan, and Turkish Straits.

1914-18 Collapse of Ottoman Empire, Germany loses colonies, Balfour Declaration on Jewish National Home in Palestine, constitutional reforms, and nationalist agitation in British India.

1919   Versailles Peace: (1) German and Ottoman dependencies redistributed as mandates; (2) Japan expands in the Pacific and makes extreme demands upon China.

1923   Egypt granted qualified independence.

1923   Britain declares that colonial policy in settler-infested East Africa is "Native Paramountcy."

1935   Italy invades Ethiopia.

1940-42 Japan overruns French Indochina, Indonesia, the Philippines, Malaya, Burma, and various Pacific Islands held by the United States.

1945   San Francisco Conference establishes United Nations Organization with anti-colonial United States, Soviet Union, and Nationalist China in major positions and effective Trusteeship Council.

1947   British India receives independence as separate states of India and Pakistan.

1948   British abandonment of Palestine leads to warfare between newly created Israel and surrounding Arab states.

1949   Indonesian independence from Holland.

1954   France withdraws from Indochina, leaving new South Viet-Nam Republic under informal United States protection.

1955   Bandung Asian-African Conference.

1956   Suez crisis: Israel, Britain, and France attack Egypt after Nasser nationalizes the Suez Canal.

1957   Ghana is first tropical African colony to achieve independence.

1960-61 Congo crisis.

1961 Abortive invasion of Cuba by anti-Castro forces supported by the United States.

1963 Algeria, after prolonged warfare, granted independence thus completing emancipation of former French Africa.

1965 Escalation of Viet-Nam War with United States bombing of north and increased troop commitments.

1965 Rhodesia Unilateral Declaration of Independence from Britain.

I.   *Expansion in the Era of Free Trade: 1776-1875*

The first century of the industrial age witnessed the emergence of two mutually contradictory developments which together constitute the core paradox of modern imperialism: a systematic denunciation of the concept of imperial domination and an uncontrollable growth in the substance of empire.

The key to this paradox was Great Britain, which had emerged from its eighteenth-century wars with France as the first power of the Old Colonial System. But victory over its main rival was soon followed by dissension within the British Empire as North American settlers utilized the ideology of British parliamentarianism and the weakness of imperial control to throw off their subjugation to the mother country (1). Yet the American Revolution caused little real damage to British world hegemony, a development predicted in advance by the new liberal school of British economics, which deplored colonialism along with all other mercantilist restrictions on the natural flow of goods and services (2). By the end of the Napoleonic Wars, when an independence movement had broken out in Spanish America, revolutionaries like Simon Bolivar (3) could look upon Britain as their ally against any restoration of European rule.

Relying upon the power of its fleet and the marketability of its new industrial goods, Britain became the advocate of free competition rather than colonial monopoly throughout the non-European world. Such an attitude limited state control over expansion, but it reflected also a vast increase throughout Europe in the technological and economic capacity for penetrating alien societies.

Thus, in the most elemental sense of colonization, European populations, whose size grew enormously during the period of the Industrial Revolution, began migrating overseas in unprecedented numbers. Even opponents of mercantilism could be in favor of having these departing compatriots settle in territories which would remain loyal to the mother country (4). In a larger sense, however, the flow of excess population from Europe hardly affected the growth of colonialism; most of the emigrants went to already independent areas in North and South America, while even formal British dependencies like Canada, Australia, New Zealand, and South Africa were seen as moving towards some kind of autonomy (5).

The main contribution of the liberal era to increased European control over non-European populations occurred through informal political and economic expansion beyond the perimeters of official colonial possessions. Political expan-

1

sion, insofar as it was a liberal policy, sought only to maintain the neutrality of areas, such as the eastern Mediterranean, considered strategically important to the routes of trade and the protection of British India (6). The complex relationship between this entire trading system and imperial policy was never apparent to any contemporary policymakers and has only recently begun to be appreciated by historians (7, 16).

Despite the tight control which middle-class liberal parliamentarians were able to maintain over budgetary appropriations for colonial ventures, certain attitudes of old regime imperialism managed to find new life in the nineteenth-century institutions of national armies and national monarchies. It was the restored Bourbon monarchy in France, abortively seeking to stabilize its position by a quick gain of prestige, which brought France into Algeria in 1830; with the overthrow of the Bourbons by the July Revolution of that same year, Algeria became a virtually exclusive project of the French army (8). The steady expansion of British rule in India throughout this period was the result also of military initiatives which came to operate on an almost self-sustaining and even bloodless basis (9). One of the ways by which Napoleon III of France attempted to recapture the glory of his uncle was through a series of vaguely conceived colonial enterprises, including the particularly sensational and disastrous establishment of a puppet empire in Mexico (10).

If all the expansion of the free trade era produced relatively little in the way of new European territorial claims, it set the stage for the later peak of formal empire by the transformation of existing holdings into a new type of overseas dependency: the paternalist colony. Under the Old Colonial System, colonial possessions were classified as either "plantations," areas in which a transplanted European population directly exploited local resources, or "factories," stations by which a European power monopolized trade with a politically independent indigenous population. The fall of this entire system was characterized not only by the breaking away of the plantation colonies from their mother countries but also by a severe moral critique in the metropole of the factory colonies. While the effectiveness of this critique was not unrelated to the decline of the entire economic system within which such colonies had flourished, control over the areas in question did not slacken, but instead was intensified. Although their populations remained essentially indigenous, the rulers at all levels came more and more to be European or European-trained officials whose task was to develop these parts of the world as tropical counterparts of European society.

The first and most significant of the new model colonies was British India, for which the London government took increasing responsibility from the end of the eighteenth century (11). West Africa was affected less positively by the new climate since critics of the factory colonial system there felt that the substitution of "legitimate" trade for the slave trade would bring economic and social reforms without the need for administrative intervention (12). In South Africa, however, the danger of native exploitation by white settlers provoked a relatively early call for closer imperial control (13). Within the French colonial empire, the cause of antislavery and paternalism found its most effective exponents among soldier-administrators such as Faidherbe (14). By the second half of the nineteenth century even the Dutch East Indies, always the most remote and ruthlessly commercial of European colonial holdings, were touched by the movement for paternalistic reform (15).

THE DISSOLUTION OF THE OLD COLONIAL SYSTEM

Thomas Paine

1. AMERICAN INDEPENDENCE

The grievances of the rebellious British colonies in North America were also the classic indictment of the Old Colonial System. In a pamphlet which greatly influenced the ultimate declaration of United States independence, Thomas Paine (1737–1809), himself only a year out of his native England, condemns the existing imperial arrangements on three counts: their incompatibility with current liberal political doctrine, their economic exploitation of the colonies, and their premise of homogeneity between what had become two very different societies.

THOUGHTS ON THE PRESENT STATE OF AMERICAN AFFAIRS

In the following pages I offer nothing more than simple facts, plain arguments, and common sense; and have no other preliminaries to settle with the reader than that he will divest himself of prejudice and prepossession, and suffer his reason and his feelings to determine for themselves; that he will put on, or rather that he will not put off, the true character of a man, and generously enlarge his views beyond the present day.

Volumes have been written on the subject of the struggle between England and America. Men of all ranks have embarked in the controversy, from different motives and with various designs; but all have been ineffectual, and the period of debate is closed. Arms as the last resource decide the contest; the appeal was the choice of the king, and the continent has accepted the challenge.

It has been reported of the late Mr. Pelham (who, though an able minister, was not without his faults) that, on his being attacked in the House of Commons on the score that his measures were only of a temporary kind, replied, "they will last my time." Should a thought so fatal and unmanly possess the colonies in the present contest, the name of ancestors will be remembered by future generations with detestation.

The sun never shined on a cause of greater worth. 'Tis not the affairs of a city, a county, a province, or a kingdom, but of a continent—of at least one-eighth part of the habitable globe. 'Tis not the concern of a day, a year, or an age; posterity are virtually involved in the contest, and will be more or less affected even to the end of time by the proceedings now. Now is the seedtime of continental union, faith, and honor. The least fracture now will be like a name engraved with the point of a pin on the tender rind of a young oak; the wound would en-

Common Sense (first published 1776).

large with the tree, and posterity read it in full-grown characters.

By referring the matter from argument to arms, a new era for politics is struck — a new method of thinking has arisen. All plans, proposals, etc., prior to the nineteenth of April, i.e., to the commencement of hostilities, are like the almanacs of the last year, which, though proper then, are superseded and useless now. Whatever was advanced by the advocates on either side of the question then terminated in one and the same point, viz., a union with Great Britain; the only difference between the parties was the method of effecting it — the one proposing force, the other friendship; but it has so far happened that the first has failed, and the second has withdrawn her influence.

As much has been said of the advantages of reconciliation, which, like an agreeable dream, has passed away and left us as we were, it is but right that we should examine the contrary side of the argument and inquire into some of the many material injuries which these colonies sustain, and always will sustain, by being connected with and dependent on Great Britain. To examine that connection and dependence on the principles of nature and common sense; to see what we have to trust to, if separated, and what we are to expect, if dependent.

I have heard it asserted by some that, as America has flourished under her former connection with Great Britain, the same connection is necessary toward her future happiness and will always have the same effect. Nothing can be more fallacious than this kind of argument. We may as well assert that because a child has thrived upon milk that it is never to have meat, or that the first twenty years of our lives is to become a precedent for the next twenty. But even this is admitting more than is true; for I answer roundly that America would have flourished as much, and probably much more, had no European power had anything to do with her. The commerce by which she has enriched herself are the necessaries of life and will always have a market while eating is the custom of Europe.

But she has protected us, say some. That she has engrossed us is true, and defended the continent at our expense as well as her own is admitted; and she would have defended Turkey from the same motive, viz., for the sake of trade and dominion.

Alas! we have been long led away by ancient prejudices and made large sacrifices to superstition. We have boasted the protection of Great Britain without considering that her motive was *interest,* not *attachment;* and that she did not protect us from *our enemies* on *our account* but from *her enemies* on *her own account*, from those who had no quarrel with us on any *other account* and who will always be our enemies on the *same account.* Let Britain waive her pretensions to the continent or the continent throw off the dependence, and we should be at peace with France and Spain, were they at war with Britain. The miseries of Hanover's last war ought to warn us against connections.

It has lately been asserted in Parliament that the colonies have no relation to each other but through the parent country, i.e., that Pennsylvania and the Jerseys, and so on for the rest, are sister colonies by the way of England; this is certainly a very roundabout way of proving relationship, but it is the nearest and only true way of proving enemyship, if I may so call it. France and Spain never were, nor perhaps ever will be, our enemies as *Americans,* but as our being the *subjects of Great Britain.*

But Britain is the parent country, say some. Then the more shame upon her conduct. Even brutes do not devour their young nor savages make war upon their families; wherefore the assertion, if true, turns to her reproach; but it happens not to be true, or only partly so, and the phrase "parent" or "mother country" has been jesuitically adopted by the king and his parasites with a low papistical design of gaining an unfair bias on the credulous weakness of our minds. Europe, and not England, is the parent country of America. This New World has been the asylum for the persecuted lovers of civil and religious liberty from *every part* of Europe. Hither have they fled, not from the tender embraces of the mother, but from the cruelty of the monster; and it is so far true of England that the same tyranny which drove the first emigrants from home pursues their descendants still.

In this extensive quarter of the globe, we forget the narrow limits of three hundred and sixty miles (the extent of England) and carry our friendship on a larger scale; we claim brotherhood with every European Christian, and triumph in the generosity of the sentiment.

It is pleasant to observe by what regular gradations we surmount the force of local prejudices as we enlarge our acquaintance with the world. A man born in any town in England divided into parishes will naturally associate most with his fellow parishioners (because their interests in many cases will be common) and distinguish him by the name of "neighbor"; if he meet him but a few miles from home, he drops the narrow idea of a street and salutes him by the name of "townsman"; if he travel out of the county and meet him in any other, he forgets the minor division of street and town, and calls him "countryman," i.e., "county-man"; but if in their foreign excursions they should associate in France, or any other part of *Europe,* their local remembrance would be enlarged into that of "Englishmen." And by a just parity of reasoning, all Europeans meeting in America, or any other quarter of the globe, are "countrymen"; for England, Holland, Germany, or Sweden, when compared with the whole, stand in the same places on the larger scale which the divisions of street, town, and county do on the smaller ones—distinctions too limited for continental minds. Not one third of the inhabitants, even of this province, are of English descent. Wherefore I reprobate the phrase of parent or mother country applied to England only as being false, selfish, narrow, and ungenerous.

But, admitting that we were all of English descent, what does it amount to? Nothing. Britain, being now an open enemy, extinguishes every other name and title; and to say that reconciliation is our duty is truly farcical. The first king of England of the present line (William the Conqueror) was a Frenchman, and half the peers of England are descendants from the same country; wherefore, by the same method of reasoning, England ought to be governed by France.

Much has been said of the united strength of Britain and the colonies, that in conjunction they might bid defiance to the world. But this is mere presumption; the fate of war is uncertain, neither do the expressions mean anything; for this continent would never suffer itself to be drained of inhabitants to support the British arms in either Asia, Africa, or Europe.

Besides, what have we to do with setting the world at defiance? Our plan is commerce, and that, well attended to, will secure us the peace and friendship of all Europe; because it is the interest of all Europe to have America a free port. Her trade will always be a protection, and her barrenness of gold and silver secure her from invaders.

I challenge the warmest advocate for reconciliation to show a single advantage that this continent can reap by being connected with Great Britain. I repeat the challenge; not a single advantage is derived. Our corn will fetch its price in any market in Europe, and our imported goods must be paid for, buy them where we will.

But the injuries and disadvantages we sustain by that connection are without number, and our duty to mankind at large, as well as to ourselves, instruct us to renounce the alliance; because any submission to or dependence on Great Britain tends directly to involve this continent in European wars and quarrels and sets us at variance with nations who would otherwise seek our friendship and against whom we have neither anger nor complaint. As Europe is our market for trade, we ought to form no partial connection with any part of it. It is the true interest of America to steer clear of European contentions, which she never can do while, by her dependence on Britain, she is made the makeweight in the scale of British politics.

Adam Smith

2. COLONIES VERSUS FREE TRADE ECONOMICS

The Wealth of Nations by the Scotsman Adam Smith (1732–1790) was first published in England during the American Revolution and within a few decades had become the virtual Bible of classic liberal economic thought. While Smith's advocacy of emancipation for all colonies found little practical and only limited theoretical support among his many followers, the basic ideas of free trade helped maintain middle-class opposition to colonialism up to the end of the nineteenth century.

The policy of Europe has very little to boast of, either in the original establishment or, so far as concerns their internal government, in the subsequent prosperity of the colonies of America.

Folly and injustice seem to have been the principles which presided over and directed the first project of establishing those colonies; the folly of hunting after gold and silver mines, and the injustice of coveting the possession of a country whose harmless natives, far from having ever injured the people of Europe, had received the first adventurers with every mark of kindness and hospitality.

The adventurers, indeed, who formed some of the later establishments, joined to the chimerical project of finding gold and silver mines other motives more reasonable and more laudable; but even these motives do very little honour to the policy of Europe.

The English Puritans, restrained at home, fled for freedom to America, and established there the four governments of New England. The English Catholics, treated with much greater injustice, established that of Maryland; the Quakers, that of Pennsylvania. The Portuguese Jews, persecuted by the inquisition, stripped of their fortunes, and banished to Brazil, introduced by their example some sort of order and industry among the transported felons and strumpets by whom that colony was originally peopled, and taught them the culture of the sugar-cane. Upon all these different occasions it was not the wisdom and policy, but the disorder and injustice of the European governments which peopled and cultivated America.

In effectuating some of the most important of these establishments, the different governments of Europe had as little merit as in projecting them. The conquest of Mexico was the project, not of the council of Spain, but of a governor of Cuba; and it was effectuated by the spirit of the bold adventurer to whom it was entrusted, in spite of everything which that governor, who soon repented of having trusted such a person, could do to thwart it. The conquerors of Chile and Peru, and of almost all the other Spanish settlements upon the continent of America, carried out with them no other public encouragement, but a general permission to make settlements and conquests in the name of the king of Spain. Those adventures were all at the private risk and expense of the adventurers. The government of Spain contributed scarce anything to any of them. That of England contributed

An Inquiry into the Nature and Causes of the Wealth of Nations (first published 1776), Book IV, Chapter IV, Parts 2,3.

as little towards effectuating the establishment of some of its most important colonies in North America.

When those establishments were effectuated, and had become so considerable as to attract the attention of the mother country, the first regulations which she made with regard to them had always in view to secure to herself the monopoly of their commerce; to confine their market, and to enlarge her own at their expense, and, consequently, rather to damp and discourage than to quicken and forward the course of their prosperity. In the different ways in which this monopoly has been exercised consists one of the most essential differences in the policy of the different European nations with regard to their colonies. The best of them all, that of England, is only somewhat less illiberal and oppressive than that of any of the rest.

In what way, therefore, has the policy of Europe contributed either to the first establishment, or to the present grandeur of the colonies of America? In one way, and in one way only, it has contributed a good deal. *Magna virûm Mater!* It bred and formed the men who were capable of achieving such great actions, and of laying the foundation of so great an empire; and there is no other quarter of the world of which the policy is capable of forming, or has ever actually and in fact formed such men. The colonies owe to the policy of Europe the education and great views of their active and enterprising founders; and some of the greatest and most important of them, so far as concerns their internal government, owe to it scarce any thing else.

* * *

OF THE ADVANTAGES WHICH EUROPE HAS
DERIVED FROM THE DISCOVERY OF AMERICA,
AND FROM THAT OF A PASSAGE TO THE EAST
INDIES BY THE CAPE OF GOOD HOPE

Such are the advantages which the colonies of America have derived from the policy of Europe.

What are those which Europe has derived from the discovery and colonisation of America?

Those advantages may be divided, first, into the general advantages which Europe, considered as one great country, has derived from those great events; and, secondly, into the particular advantages which each colonising country has derived from the colonies which particularly belong to it, in consequence of the authority or dominion which it exercises over them.

The general advantages which Europe, considered as one great country, has derived from the discovery and colonisation of America, consist, first, in the increase of its enjoyments; and, secondly, in the augmentation of its industry.

The surplus produce of America, imported into Europe, furnishes the inhabitants of this great continent with a variety of commodities which they could not otherwise have possessed; of productive labour than what can have been thrown out of employment by the revulsion of capital from other trades of which the returns are more frequent. If the colony trade, however, even as it is carried on at present, is advantageous to Great Britain, it is not by means of the monopoly, but in spite of the monopoly.

It is rather for the manufactured than for the rude produce of Europe that the colony trade opens a new market. Agriculture is the proper business of all new colonies; a business which the cheapness of land renders more advantageous than any other. They abound, therefore, in the rude produce of land, and instead of importing it from other countries, they have generally a large surplus to export. In new colonies, agriculture either draws hands from all other employments, or keeps them from going to any other employment. There are few hands to spare for the necessary, and none for the ornamental manufactures. The greater part of the manufactures of both kinds they find it cheaper to purchase of other countries than to make for themselves. It is chiefly by encouraging the manufactures of Europe that the colony trade indirectly encourages its agriculture. The manufactures of Europe, to whom that trade gives employment, constitute a new market for the produce of the land; and the most advantageous of all markets, the home market for the corn and cattle, for the bread and butcher's meat of Europe, is thus greatly extended by means of the trade to America.

* * *

If the manufactures of Great Britain, however, have been advanced, as they certainly have, by the colony trade, it has not been by means of the monopoly of that trade but in spite of the monopoly. The effect of the monopoly has been, not to augment the quantity, but to alter the quality and shape of a part of the manufactures of Great Britain, and to accommodate to a market, from which the returns are slow and distant, what would otherwise have been accommodated to one from which the returns are frequent and near. Its effect has consequently been to turn a part of the capital of Great Britain from an employment in which it would have maintained a greater quantity of manufacturing industry to one in which it maintains a much smaller, and thereby to diminish, instead of increasing, the whole quantity of manufacturing industry maintained in Great Britain.

The monopoly of the colony trade, therefore, like all the other mean and malignant expedients of the mercantile system, depresses the industry of all other countries, but chiefly that of the colonies, without in the least increasing, but on the contrary diminishing that of the country in whose favour it is established.

* * *

It is thus that the single advantage which the monopoly procures to a single order of men is in many different ways hurtful to the general interest of the country.

To found a great empire for the sole purpose of raising up a people of customers may at first sight appear a project fit only for a nation of shopkeepers. It is, however, a project altogether unfit for a nation of shop-

keepers; but extremely fit for a nation whose government is influenced by shopkeepers. Such statesmen, and such statesmen only, are capable of fancying that they will find some advantage in employing the blood and treasure of their fellow-citizens to found and maintain such an empire. Say to a shopkeeper, Buy me a good estate, and I shall always buy my clothes at your shop, even though I should pay somewhat dearer than what I can have them for at other shops; and you will not find him very forward to embrace your proposal. But should any other person buy you such an estate, the shopkeeper would be much obliged to your benefactor if he would enjoin you to buy all your clothes at his shop. England purchased for some of her subjects, who found themselves uneasy at home, a great estate in a distant country. The price, indeed, was very small, and instead of thirty years' purchase, the ordinary price of land in the present times, it amounted to little more than the expense of the different equipments which made the first discovery, reconnoitred the coast, and took a fictitious possession of the country. The land was good and of great extent, and the cultivators having plenty of good ground to work upon, and being for some time at liberty to sell their produce where they pleased, became in the course of little more than thirty or forty years (between 1620 and 1660) so numerous and thriving a people that the shopkeepers and other traders of England wished to secure to themselves the monopoly of their custom. Without pretending, therefore, that they had paid any part, either of the original purchase-money, or of the subsequent expense of improvement, they petitioned the parliament that the cultivators of America might for the future be confined to their shop; first, for buying all the goods which they wanted from Europe; and, secondly, for selling all such parts of their own produce as those traders might find it convenient to buy. For they did not find it convenient to buy every part of it. Some parts of it imported into England might have interfered with some of the trades which they themselves carried on at home. Those particular parts of it, therefore, they were willing that the colonists should sell where they could — the farther off the better; and upon that account purposed that their market should be confined to the countries south of Cape Finisterre. A clause in the famous act of navigation established this truly shopkeeper proposal into a law.

The maintenance of this monopoly has hitherto been the principal, or more properly perhaps the sole end and purpose of the dominion which Great Britain assumes over her colonies. In the exclusive trade, it is supposed, consists the great advantage of provinces, which have never yet afforded either revenue or military force for the support of the civil government, or the defence of the mother country. The monopoly is the principal badge of their dependency, and it is the sole fruit which has hitherto been gathered from that dependency. Whatever expense Great Britain has hitherto laid out in maintaining this dependency has really been laid out in order to support this monopoly. The expense of the ordinary peace establishment of the colonies amounted, before the commencement of the present disturbances, to the pay of twenty regiments of foot; to the expense of the artillery, stores, and extraordinary provisions with which it was necessary to supply them; and to the expense of a very considerable naval force which was constantly kept up, in order to guard, from the smuggling vessels of other nations, the immense coast of North America, and that of our West Indian islands. The whole expense of this peace establishment was a charge upon the revenue of Great Britain, and was, at the same time, the smallest part of what the dominion of the colonies has cost the mother country. If we would know the amount of the whole, we must add to the annual expense of this peace establishment the interest of the sums which, in consequence of her considering her colonies as provinces subject to her dominion, Great Britain has upon different occasions laid out upon their defence. We must add to it, in

particular, the whole expense of the late war, and a great part of that of the war which preceded it. The late war was altogether a colony quarrel, and the whole expense of it, in whatever part of the world it may have been laid out, whether in Germany or the East Indies, ought justly to be stated to the account of the colonies. It amounted to more than ninety millions sterling, including not only the new debt which was contracted, but the two shillings in the pound additional land tax, and the sums which were every year borrowed from the sinking fund. The Spanish war, which began in 1739, was principally a colony quarrel. Its principal object was to prevent the search of the colony ships which carried on a contraband trade with the Spanish main. This whole expense is, in reality, a bounty which has been given in order to support a monopoly. The pretended purpose of it was to encourage the manufactures, and to increase the commerce of Great Britain. But its real effect has been to raise the rate of mercantile profit, and to enable our merchants to turn into a branch of trade, of which the returns are more slow and distant than those of the greater part of other trades, a greater proportion of their capital than they otherwise would have done; two events which, if a bounty could have prevented, it might perhaps have been very well worth while to give such a bounty.

Under the present system of management, therefore, Great Britain derives nothing but loss from the dominion which she assumes over her colonies.

To propose that Great Britain should voluntarily give up all authority over her colonies, and leave them to elect their own magistrates, to enact their own laws, and to make peace and war as they might think proper, would be to propose such a measure as never was, and never will be adopted, by any nation in the world. No nation ever voluntarily gave up the dominion of any province, how troublesome soever it might be to govern it, and how small soever the revenue which it afforded might be in proportion to the expense which it occasioned.

Such sacrifices, though they might frequently be agreeable to the interest, are always mortifying to the pride of every nation, and what is perhaps of still greater consequence, they are always contrary to the private interest of the governing part of it, who would thereby be deprived of the disposal of many places of trust and profit, of many opportunities of acquiring wealth and distinction, which the possession of the most turbulent, and, to the great body of the people, the most unprofitable province seldom fails to afford. The most visionary enthusiast would scarce be capable of proposing such a measure with any serious hopes at least of its ever being adopted. If it was adopted, however, Great Britain would not only be immediately freed from the whole annual expense of the peace establishment of the colonies, but might settle with them such a treaty of commerce as would effectually secure to her a free trade, more advantageous to the great body of the people, though less so to the merchants, than the monopoly which she at present enjoys. By thus parting good friends, the natural affection of the colonies to the mother country which, perhaps, our late dissensions have well nigh extinguished, would quickly revive. It might dispose them not only to respect, for whole centuries together, that treaty of commerce which they had concluded with us at parting, but to favour us in war as well as in trade, and, instead of turbulent and factious subjects, to become our most faithful, affectionate, and generous allies; and the same sort of parental affection on the one side, and filial respect on the other, might revive between Great Britain and her colonies, which used to subsist between those of ancient Greece and the mother city from which they descended.

Simon Bolivar

3. EUROPE AND LATIN AMERICAN INDEPENDENCE

When considering nineteenth-century imperialism, the significance of the independence movement in Latin America lies less in the blow it struck at an already decrepit Spanish empire than in the opportunity it afforded for British — and later for United States — informal economic domination. Simon Bolivar (1783 – 1830), "The Liberator" of South America, sought both to overthrow foreign rule and to create a continent-wide Colombian Federation on the model of the U.S.A. While unsuccessful in the latter aim, Bolivar in the article below correctly predicted the role that Britain would play in preventing any restoration of Spanish power in the Americas. During the subsequent Latin American wars of liberation, various forms of British support proved useful to the rebels, and after 1823 Britain tacitly backed the United States' Monroe Doctrine, which officially declared that the western hemisphere was barred to European colonial endeavors.

At last, the second of the two great problems that have caused the flow of so much blood on the European continent appears to be approaching a solution. Since the conti-

---

"Thoughts on the Present State of Europe with Relation to America" (*Gaceta de Caracas*, June 9, 1814), in *Selected Writings of Bolivar*, trans. Lewis Bertrand (New York: Colonial Press, 1951), pp. 76-80, with omissions.

nental system of Napoleon was destroyed when the present coalition of the north erected an impenetrable barrier against his power, there only remains to be seen whether he who established that system and briefly maintained it by extremes of outrage and violence is to remain tranquilly on the throne of France.

Interests of the most complex character have powerfully influenced these important transactions. On the one hand, the allies, it appears, sought only to check the power of France to the point of freeing themselves from the dictatorial and imperious tone with which her agents addressed the other courts; while, on the other hand, the English government, whose keen foresight could not foresee anything good from the French *caudillo*, was determined not to end the conflict until the empire that he had erected upon the ruins of the Republic had been completely razed. The first of these intentions is clearly revealed in the public declaration of Frankfort, and the second may be regarded as certain from the results obtained by the visit of Lord Castlereagh to the General Headquarters of the Allies.

According to the latest advices, we are assured that Great Britain has completely triumphed over her enemies. A combination of circumstances, perhaps unforeseen by the allies, has carried them in triumph into Paris, where the inhabitants have received them more as deliverers than as conquerors. An event so astonishing must, without doubt, be the harbinger of general peace, for the white cockade frequently seen in the streets of that affluent capital shows a positive determination [on the part of the people] to entrust themselves to the discretion of the former dynasty.

Turning our eyes now toward this vast continent, let us weigh the consequences that these European events may have in store for us. If the continental Europeans, weary of so many political experiments, return to what they previously rejected as evil; if, rueful of so many errors and excesses, they seek to restore all that formerly existed, they may well stifle our political existence in

its cradle. Some say that the Bourbons are returning to gain their lost influence; if so, their family alliances will multiply the number of our enemies and end all that we have accomplished.

But it is very easy to convince some men, especially those who choose to interpret events according to their personal inclinations, that the current European situation particularly favors our best interests and is, therefore, the very one to help consolidate our liberty and independence promptly.

To be sure, neither the interests of the princes or ruling families, nor those of any one nation alone determine the course of European politics. These are usually only secondary causes which merely contribute to the furthering of primary interests; we often see flare up, on pretext of avenging a wrong done to one sovereign and for the benefit of another, a war that injures the well-being of his people.

The so-called rights of the Bourbons, about which the English long have had so much to say, have been nothing more than the ostensible objects of their policy. The real aim of this policy is to establish English maritime preponderance by destroying the immense power which sooner or later might result in its ruination. The diligence with which they have proceeded to dissolve whatever coalitions were formed against Spain clearly demonstrates the true object of their concern. But, to their good fortune, the man who controlled the continent was the one best calculated to bring about their triumph in a most rare and extraordinary manner. Bonaparte's despotism and arbitrariness is the motif they have adopted in order to achieve this victory.

One of the necessary consequences of this new order of things will be the reëstablishment of the political balance of power among the nations of the continent. I say among these nations, because such an equilibrium does not now exist, nor can it come into existence for a long time with respect to Great Britain. Great Britain has won her maritime supremacy in glorious battles brought on by the disorders of Europe; and

11

it cannot be imagined that she will, by a display of extraordinary disinterestedness not to be found in British history where commercial interests have been involved, now voluntarily place herself on a par with the other nations that previously were her equals in naval power.

American independence, therefore, owes its first advances to this balance of power. France aided North America with troops and warships, not out of philanthropy or for love of the American people, but because it became necessary that she, having lost her holdings in Canada, deprive her rival of the other provinces of the north and thereby reduce Great Britain's weight in the balance of power. Otherwise, why should France have set such a fatal example for her colonial possessions? How could Spain herself have acquiesced as she did, in what the ministry of Saint-Cloud was doing in that regard? But England, on her part, fomented the insurrection of Santo Domingo, and her plans to grant liberty to the Spanish colonies have long been known.

If we agree, then, as we must, that even with the establishment of this new European balance of power, the interests of Great Britain are entirely opposed to those of the continental powers, who can be so mad as to believe that, with England today the first maritime nation of the world, she would support a renewed effort of Spain to assert her control in America? Even assuming that Spain should conclude with Great Britain treaties favorable to her commerce, would the mere pledge of these treaties be a sufficient guarantee of their observance?

It is not necessary to know the far-sighted genius of the British Cabinet in order to entertain such conjectures. Now that the power of Bonaparte has been destroyed, could not another leader be found to oppose Britain's predominance? Perhaps Emperor Alexander, who today has put himself at the head of the Holy Alliance in order to destroy that power, will tomorrow promote a continental coalition, more powerful than any formed in the past. Amidst such vicissitudes of European politics, will England

wish to see America the permanent dependency of some continental power, thereby adding American wealth and population to the reserves of the power that may resist her?

For this reason the emancipation of America has always entered into the calculations of the English Cabinet. Great Britain, situated between the old continent and the new, will, by virtue of this new universal equilibrium, attain the ultimate in greatness and power, to which no people of the world have ever dared aspire.

The remaining question of control of the seas is for profounder analysts to ponder. We can only envision for the future a Great Britain, perplexed and bowed under the enormous weight of her wealth, forming, with America, the most powerful empire on earth.

Our revolution, on the other hand, has made such significant strides that it cannot be crushed by force. Mexico, Perú, Chile, Buenos Aires, New Granada, and Venezuela, today, through the identity of their principles and sentiments, constitute a formidable league which cannot be destroyed, despite the intention of its enemies.

If we had to consider the fate of these areas separately, we might calculate differently. Let it be a great consolation to us to know that any outrage committed against the smallest segment of Colombian soil will be avenged by an endless number of brother peoples spread over this new hemisphere.

But let us suppose that Europe as a whole should wish to subjugate us. In this case, it is necessary to assume that civil war will cause even greater havoc throughout our continent and will destroy whatever industries and arts it may have cultivated during the past three centuries. To admit the possibility of such an episode is to overlook the extent to which the wealth and the products of the New World have influenced the customs and the politics of Europe. Properly understood, it is to the interests of all nations, and particularly to the British, to expedite the channels of commerce and to prevent a war that would consume the resources which could materially develop their industry.

America, moreover, is fortunately situated, for she does not inspire apprehension in those who thrive on commerce and industry. For a long time to come, we cannot be anything but an agricultural people capable of supplying the markets of Europe with the most valuable products. The agricultural group, therefore, is the one best calculated to promote friendly relations with merchants and manufacturers. With our independence recognized, and with our countries opened to all foreigners without discrimination, we can hardly foresee how rapidly public demand will increase from year to year. Articles of export will increase and multiply indefinitely, and imports will always seek a balance of trade with our products. When we consider this aspect of our future destiny we can at once conclude that the emancipation of America

must bring about, in luxuries, in the wealth of nations, in short, in the habits of the human race, a revolution far more amazing than that ushered in by its discovery.

If, then, it is well established that the independence of the United States is of greater benefit to England than was their dependence, what shall we say of our countries, whose political importance will never compare with that of the United States? The results of United States independence set such a clear example for all to see that, without doing violence to reason, it is impossible to imagine that England would prefer to adopt conservative ideas which have always resulted in misery and oppression.

If we were not loath to make ourselves boring, we should point out many other things to banish the fears of some of our friends. Let us, therefore, look forward to another more opportune occasion when we shall develop and coordinate our ideas in a manner more appropriate to what we ourselves have in mind.

THE SHAPING OF LIBERAL EMPIRE

Gibbon Wakefield

4. LIBERAL COLONIZATION

Edward Gibbon Wakefield (1796–1862), a publicist generally identified with the radical wing among British Liberals, advocated reforms in the existing British colonial empire and government encouragement for the foundation of new overseas settlements. Through his writings and his contact with responsible figures, Wakefield influenced policy toward Canada (see next selection), Australia, and New Zealand. Emigration to these areas was encouraged by British government subsidies, which owed much to Wakefield's urging. Official policy, however, was more liberal—and indifferent—than Wakefield in refusing to control land sales through the "sufficient price" whose necessity he argues in the second selection below. Wakefield, who had never visited any colony when he began his writing on colonization, finally settled and died in a New Zealand community which had been established under his guidance.

If an Englishman who ardently desires the greatest good of his country—Mr. Wilmot Horton, for instance—were offered the gratification of one wish, however extravagant, for what would he ask? For an immense gold mine? For the destruction of his natural enemies, the French? For an earthquake to swallow up troublesome Ireland? Oh no!—for none of these would he ask. If his character were more remarkable for justice than humanity, he might, perhaps, be tempted to wish for a straightforward Catholic Relief Bill; but, on the whole, he would, I think, wish for the power to increase the territory of Britain according to the wants of the people. And, in making this choice of blessings, he would not be actuated by any ambitious views with reference to the territorial extent of his country. His sole object would be to put an end to that portion of crime and misery which in Britain is produced by an excess of people in proportion to territory; and he would not care, therefore, whether the increase of territory, having that effect, should take place near to or at a distance from Britain.

The colonies . . . would no longer be new societies, strictly speaking. They would be so many *extensions* of an old society. Pursue that idea, and you will see that emigration from Britain would not be confined to Paupers, passing by the free bridge. We (I speak in the name of the colonists) should acquire wealth rapidly. Such of us are landowners must have good incomes, without trouble; for remember that, though the tax upon rent would take something from us, it would only take a part from what it would first bestow! How many readymade articles, both useful and ornamental, should we import from England, for which, now, we have not the means to pay? Let me enumerate a few of them—farming bailiffs, surveyors, builders, architects and engineers; min-

A Letter from Sidney (1829), 180-81, 186-88, 196-99.
England and America (1834), 159.

eralogists, practical miners, botanists and chemists; printers, schoolmasters and schoolmistresses, booksellers, authors, publishers, and even reviewers; merchants, to supply us with English goods, and to take our surplus produce; bankers, underwriters, life-insurers, and clerks innumerable; actors, surgeons, and physicians; lawyers, clergymen, singers, music and dancing masters, milliners and other female artists, and at least, one good Political Economist at each settlement, to prevent us from devising an Australasian tariff. Most of these emigrants would call themselves ladies and gentlemen, and would object to pass by the bridge of charity. Consequently we could not force them to preserve an equal sexual proportion; but if an excessive number of males should emigrate, they would create, here, a demand for females, and a supply would immediately follow by the bridge. Moreover, as the value of all land purchased of the government must necessarily rise somewhat above the amount of the purchase-money; and as portions, on or near to which towns would grow up, must rise in value considerably above the government price, the purchase of waste land would be an excellent employment of capital. Much of the surplus capital of Britain, therefore, might be so invested, instead of being given away to monks in Spain and to Tartars in South America. Some of the persons, who should invest their money in this manner, would emigrate along with it, in order to become the leading men of civilized Australasia.

Though some of the above speculations may be doubtful, they might perhaps be carried much farther without extravagance. This, however, admits of no uncertainty either way, being positive and self-evident —namely, that the system in question would tend more than anything to preserve an intimate connection between the colony and the mother country. In fact, the mother country and the colony would become partners in a new trade — the creation of happy human beings; one country furnishing the raw material — that is, the land, the dust of which man is made; the other furnishing the machinery — that is, men and women, to convert the unpeopled soil into living images of God. In this honourable and, we may say, even glorious co-partnership, the interest of the mother country would be greater than that of the colony; and a rupture of their connection would, therefore, be most injurious to the former. If the system of free migration should be destroyed by a war of independence, the colony might still pursue the system of restriction, and so preserve all the desirable attributes of an old people; but in that case, the mother country would lose a given portion of the means by which she had enjoyed the one great good that belongs to new countries — the power of supplying a constant increase of territory according to the wants of the people. The mother country, therefore, in governing the colony, would consult the greatest advantage of the colonists, in order to preserve their friendship; and the colonists, having much to lose, and being incapable of dispersion, would feel a wholesome dread of war. The colonists, being an instructed and civilized people, would be as well qualified to govern themselves as the people of Britain; and, being a wealthy people, they would be able, without going to war, to assert the birth-right of all British subjects — to enforce in the British Parliament, against a bad British ministry, their claim to equality before the law. Qualified, entitled, and powerful to govern themselves, they might either take a share in framing the general laws of the empire, by means of their representatives in the British Parliament; or, if a mean jealousy on the part of Englishmen should prevent such an arrangement, they might frame their own laws, in a Colonial Assembly, under the eye of a viceroy, incapable of wrong, and possessing a veto like the king of England, but whose secretaries, like the ministers of England, should be responsible to the people! At all events, they must be governed, by whatever machinery, with a view to their good and their contentment, which is the greatest good, instead of to the satisfaction of their governors only. This would render them happy in a most intimate connexion with their mother country; and the American war of independence would no longer be a favourite theme in the still dependent colonies of Britain. Mutual dependence would prevent oppression on the one part, and on the other, a wish for independence; reciprocity of interest would occasion mutual good will; there would no longer be injurious distinctions, or malignant jealousies, or vulgar hatred between British subjects, wherever born; and Britain would become the centre of the most extensive, the most civilized, and, above all, the happiest empire in the world.

DISPOSAL OF WASTE LAND

The second objection is, that into a colony, where new land was not obtainable except by purchase, neither capitalists nor labourers would be disposed to immigrate, but that, on the contrary, from such a colony both classes would be disposed to emigrate to other colonies not far off, where new land was obtainable for nothing.

We cannot decide this point by reference to facts; because in no colony has that price ever been required for new land, which, together with perfect liberty of appropriation, would ensure the greatest productiveness of industry or, in other words, the highest profits and wages. But there are some facts which tend to show, that the attractive power of a colony would be increased by putting a sufficient price upon all new land. Why have so many English and Irish labourers, who had emigrated to Canada, removed from Canada to the United States? from a colony where land was cheaper to one where it was dearer. The only rational answer is, because employment was more regular, with higher wages, where the people were in some degree kept together than where they were carefully dispersed.

5. THE DURHAM REPORT: CANADIAN SELF-GOVERNMENT

John George Lambton, Earl of Durham (1792—1840), a leading Liberal politician, was appointed Governor General of Canada in 1838 with a special commission to deal with a recent series of rebellions there. Under the influence of such men as Wakefield (see selection above), he produced a report which, when finally accepted in practice, laid the foundation for a Commonwealth in the British Empire, based on mutual ties between the mother country and the Dominions, whose autonomy would soon exceed even the limits proposed here.

The preceding pages have sufficiently pointed out the nature of those evils, to the extensive operation of which I attribute the various practical grievances, and the present unsatisfactory condition of the North American Colonies. It is not by weakening, but strengthening the influence of the people on its Government; by confining within much narrower bounds than those hitherto allotted to it, and not by extending the interference of the imperial authorities in the details of colonial affairs, that I believe that harmony is to be restored, where dissension has so long prevailed; and a regularity and vigour hitherto unknown, introduced into the administration of these Provinces. It needs no change in the principles of government, no invention of a new constitutional theory, to supply the remedy which would, in my opinion, completely remove the existing political disorders. It needs but to follow out consistently the principles of

---

The Report of The Earl of Durham, H. M. High Commissioner and Governor General of British North America (1839).

the British constitution, and introduce into the Government of these great Colonies those wise provisions, by which alone the working of the representative system can in any country be rendered harmonious and efficient. We are not now to consider the policy of establishing representative government in the North American Colonies. That has been irrevocably done; and the experiment of depriving the people of their present constitutional power, is not to be thought of. To conduct their Government harmoniously, in accordance with its established principles, is now the business of its rulers; and I know not how it is possible to secure that harmony in any other way, than by administering the Government on those principles which have been found perfectly efficacious in Great Britain. I would not impair a single prerogative of the Crown; on the contrary, I believe that the interests of the people of these Colonies require the protection of prerogatives, which have not hitherto been exercised. But the Crown must, on the other hand, submit to the necessary consequences of representative institutions; and if it has to carry on the Government in unison with a representative body, it must consent to carry it on by means of those in whom that representative body has confidence.

* * *

I know that it has been urged, that the principles which are productive of harmony and good government in the mother country, are by no means applicable to a colonial dependency. It is said that it is necessary that the administration of a colony should be carried on by persons nominated without any reference to the wishes of its people; that they have to carry into effect the policy, not of that people, but of the authorities at home; and that a colony which should name all its own administrative functionaries, would, in fact, cease to be dependent. I admit that the system which I propose would, in fact, place the internal government of the colony in the hands of the colonists themselves; and that we should thus

leave to them the execution of the laws, of which we have long entrusted the making solely to them. Perfectly aware of the value of our colonial possessions, and strongly impressed with the necessity of maintaining our connection with them, I know not in what respect it can be desirable that we should interfere with their internal legislation in matters which do not affect their relations with the mother country. The matters, which so concern us, are very few. The constitution of the form of government — the regulation of foreign relation, and of trade with the mother country, the other British Colonies, and foreign nations — and the disposal of the public lands, are the only points on which the mother country requires a control. This control is now sufficiently secured by the authority of the Imperial Legislature; by the protection which the Colony derives from us against foreign enemies; by the beneficial terms which our laws secure to its trade; and by its share of the reciprocal benefits which would be conferred by a wise system of colonization. A perfect subordination, on the part of the Colony, on these points, is secured by the advantages which it finds in the continuance of its connection with the Empire. It certainly is not strengthened, but greatly weakened, by a vexatious interference on the part of the Home Government, with the enactment of laws for regulating the internal concerns of the Colony, or in the selection of the persons entrusted with their execution. The colonists may not always know what laws are best for them, or which of their countrymen are the fittest for conducting their affairs; but, at least, they have a greater interest in coming to a right judgment on these points, and will take greater pains to do so than those whose welfare is very remotely and slightly affected by the good or bad legislation of these portions of the Empire. If the colonists make bad laws, and select improper persons to conduct their affairs, they will generally be the only, always the greatest, sufferers; and, like the people of other countries, they must bear the ills which they bring on themselves, until they choose to apply the remedy. But it surely cannot be the duty or the interest of Great Britain to keep a most expensive military possession of these Colonies, in order that a Governor or Secretary of State may be able to confer colonial appointments on one rather than another set of persons in the Colonies. For this is really the only question at issue. The slightest acquaintance with these Colonies proves the fallacy of the common notion, that any considerable amount of patronage in them is distributed among strangers from the mother country. Whatever inconvenience a consequent frequency of changes among the holders of office may produce, is a necessary disadvantage of free govern-ment, which will be amply compensated by the perpetual harmony which the system must produce between the people and its rulers. Nor do I fear that the character of the public servants will, in any respect, suffer from a more popular tenure of office. For I can conceive no system so calculated to fill important posts with inefficient persons as the present, in which public opinion is too little consulted in the original appointment, and in which it is almost impossible to remove those who disappoint the expectations of their usefulness, without inflicting a kind of brand on their capacity or integrity.

6. LORD PALMERSTON ON THE EASTERN QUESTION

The combination of liberal principles and bullying imperialist behavior among British statesmen of this period is best exemplified by the figure of Henry John Temple, Viscount Palmerston (1784–1865), who frequently served as Foreign Secretary during the middle of the nineteenth century. The steady decline of the Ottoman Empire created at this time an endemic "Eastern Question," that is, a struggle over the division of influence in the Balkans and the Eastern Mediterranean. Among the various powers involved, Russia constantly threatened European and Anatolian Turkey, France promoted the interests of an independent Egypt, and Britain tried to restrain both by supporting the Ottoman Sultanate as a harmless buffer state on the route to India. The first of the following letters refers to a French-supported effort by Mohammed Ali of Egypt to annex Syria and Palestine. The other letters concern schemes for increased Franco-British involvement in the affairs of Egypt and North Africa which, despite Palmerston's various objections, all came to pass later in the century.

PALMERSTON TO COLONEL CAMPBELL
(BRITISH REPRESENTATIVE IN EGYPT)
July 7, 1838

Her Majesty's Government have received the Communication made through You of the Intention of the Pasha of Egypt to throw off his Allegiance to the Sultan, and to declare himself the Independent Sovereign of those Provinces of the Turkish Empire, which he has been appointed by the Sultan to govern.

The British Government have received this announcement with extreme Regret; and You are instructed to express to the Pasha the deep concern which this Intelligence has occasioned them, but at the same

Harold Temperly and Lilian M. Penson, eds., *Foundations of British Foreign Policy* (New York, 1938), 124–126. Reprinted by permission of Cambridge University Press.
Evelyn Ashley, *The Life of Viscount Palmerston*, Vol. II (London, 1876), 125–126, 325–328.

time to state that Her Majesty's Government do not yet abandon the hope that fuller Consideration of the subject, and more mature Reflection, both upon the nature of the contemplated step, and upon its inevitable consequences, may lead the Pasha to come to a more just and prudent Resolution.

Two Motives are represented as impelling the Pasha thus to rebel against his Sovereign and to attempt to dismember the Turkish Empire. The one is a Regard for his own Fame, the other an anxiety for the future Fate of his Family. — But, in the opinion of Her Majesty's Government, both these Motives ought on the contrary strongly to operate to dissuade the Pasha from adopting the contemplated Course.

For, with respect to his own Fame, he ought to recollect that if he has hitherto risen progressively in the esteem of the Nations of Europe, it has been in consequence of the Pains he has taken to establish the authority of the Law among the People whom he has governed, and by reason of his successful exertions to give the ascendancy to Justice in all the Transactions between Man and Man, so as to secure to every man the Possession and enjoyment of what rightfully belongs to him.

But if now the Pasha should himself set all these Principles at naught, and should give to the world by his own Conduct a signal example of violent Injustice and of wrong deliberately done, instead of leaving behind him a name to be respected by future ages, he will tarnish the Reputation he has already acquired, and be included in the List of Men who, according to the extent of their means, have, upon a larger or smaller scale, endeavoured to appropriate to themselves by Force Things which belonged of Right to others.

But equally erroneous would be the expectation that by such an attempt he would improve the Condition of his Family. Far different would be the Result. For, success in such an enterprize being impossible, He would only involve his Family in the inevitable Ruin which He would bring upon Himself; and thus He would destroy those very Persons for whose future welfare He feels so strong an Interest.

Her Majesty's Gov[ernmen]t at once and decidedly pronounce the successful execution of the attempt to be impossible; and its inevitable Consequence to be Ruin to the Pasha; because they know that the Conflict which must necessarily be brought on by such an attempt, would not be between the Pasha and the Sultan singlehanded, but between the Pasha and the Sultan aided and supported by all the Powers of Europe.

Were the Contest indeed to lie between the Turkish and Egyptian Forces left to themselves, it would not in the present state of Things be safe for the Pasha to reckon upon obtaining the same success as that which attended his arms in 1832; But it is needless to say that if the Great Powers of Europe shall determine to assist and uphold the Sultan, the Result of the Contest must be the overthrow and expulsion of the Pasha.

The British Government, however, speaks only for itself; but feels itself bound, in return for the frank and unreserved Communication which it has received from the Pasha, to declare to him, in a manner equally unreserved and explicit, that, if He should unfortunately proceed to execute his announced Intentions; and if Hostilities should (as they indisputably would) break out thereupon between the Sultan and the Pasha, The Pasha must expect to find Great Britain taking Part with the Sultan in order to obtain Redress for so flagrant a Wrong done to the Sultan, and for the Purpose of preventing the Dismemberment of the Turkish Empire; and the Pasha would fatally deceive himself if he were to suppose that any Jealousies among the Powers of Europe would prevent those Powers from affording to the Sultan, under such Circumstances, every assistance which might be necessary for the Purpose of upholding, enforcing, and vindicating his just and legitimate Rights.

Piccadilly, March 1, 1857.

My dear Clarendon,

As to the Emperor's [Napoleon III of

France] schemes about Africa, the sooner Cowley sends in his grounds of objection the better. It is very possible that many parts of the world would be better governed by France, England, and Sardinia than they are now; and we need not go beyond Italy, Sicily, and Spain for examples. But the alliance of England and France has derived its strength not merely from the military and naval power of the two states, but from the force of the moral principle upon which that union has been founded. Our union has for its foundation resistance to unjust aggression, the defence of the weak against the strong, and the maintenance of the existing balance of power. How, then, could we combine to become unprovoked aggressors, to imitate, in Africa, the partition of Poland by the conquest of Morocco for France, of Tunis and some other state for Sardinia, and of Egypt for England? and, more especially, how could England and France, who have guaranteed the integrity of the Turkish Empire, turn round and wrest Egypt from the Sultan? A coalition for such a purpose would revolt the moral feelings of mankind, and would certainly be fatal to any English Government that was a party to it. Then, as to the balance of power to be maintained by giving us Egypt. In the first place, we don't want to have Egypt. What we wish about Egypt is that it should continue attached to the Turkish empire, which is a security against its belonging to any European Power. We want to trade with Egypt, and to travel through Egypt, but we do not want the burthen of governing Egypt, and its possession would not, as a political, military, and naval question, be considered, in this country, as a set-off against the possession of Morocco by France. Let us try to improve all these countries by the general influence of our commerce, but let us all abstain from a crusade of conquest which would call down upon us the condemnation of all the other civilised nations.

This conquest of Morocco was the secret aim of Louis Philippe, and is one of the plans deposited for use, as occasion may offer, in the archives of the French Government. . . .

94, Piccadilly, December 8, 1861.
My dear Russell,

The proposal of a French, English, and Austrian commission to inquire into the practicability of the Suez Canal sounds fair and plausible, but would be a dangerous measure.

There are three aspects under which this scheme may be looked at. First, as to the commercial advantage of it, if completed; secondly, as to the engineering and financial practicability of executing; thirdly, as to the political effect of the canal, if completed.

* * *

Well, then, we come to the last point, namely, the political objects of the enterprise; and these are hostility to England in every possible modification of the scheme.

It requires only a glance at the map of the world to see how great would be the naval and military advantage to France in a war with England to have such a short cut to the Indian seas, while we should be obliged to send ships and troops round the Cape. Thouvenel proposes, indeed, that the passage of ships-of-war should be forbidden as at the Dardanelles, but I presume he does not expect us to receive such a proposal except with a decently suppressed smile. Of course the first week of a war between France and England would see 15,000 or 20,000 Frenchmen in possession of the canal, to keep it open for them and shut for us. But then, moreover, so strong a military barrier between Syria and Egypt would greatly add to the means of the Pacha for the time being to declare himself independent of Turkey, which would mean his being a dependent of France; and lastly, if the canal should never be made, the French company are to have a large grant of land in the centre of Egypt, and would establish in Egypt a colony whose complaints against the Egyptian Government, well or ill-founded, would give the French Government pretences for interfering in all the internal affairs of the country.

I should say, therefore, on the whole, that it would be best for the French and English Governments to leave this scheme as a commercial and engineering question to be settled by the result of experience and the money markets of Europe; and that, as regards the political question, all we ask of the French Government is not to interfere in the matter, but to let all questions between the Sultan and the Pacha be settled according to the mutual rights and reciprocal obligations of those two parties.

Yours sincerely,
Palmerston.

J. Gallagher and R. Robinson

7. INFORMAL EMPIRE

The following article has played a major role in turning the historical interpretation of modern imperialism away from a fixation on the 1880s and 1890s towards an appreciation of continuous expansion throughout the nineteenth century. To Gallagher and Robinson, "informal empire" is the classic form of overseas expansion for industrial Europe, and formal colonial administration was revived only under conditions of panic and failure. The authors are both British historians attached, respectively, to Oxford and Cambridge Universities.

I

It ought to be a commonplace that Great Britain during the nineteenth century expanded overseas by means of "informal empire" as much as by acquiring dominion in the strict constitutional sense. For purposes of economic analysis it would clearly be unreal to define imperial history exclusively as the history of those colonies coloured red on the map. Nevertheless, almost all imperial history has been written on the assumption that the empire of formal dominion is historically comprehensible in itself and can be cut out of its context in British expansion and world politics. The conventional interpretation of the nineteenth-century empire continues to rest upon study of the formal empire alone, which is rather like judging the size and character of icebergs solely from the parts above the water-line.

The imperial historian, in fact, is very much at the mercy of his own particular concept of empire. By that, he decides what facts are of "imperial" significance; his data are limited in the same way as his concept, and his final interpretation itself depends largely upon the scope of his hypothesis. Different hypotheses have led to conflicting conclusions. Since imperial historians are writing about different empires and since they are generalizing from eccentric or isolated aspects of them, it is hardly surprising that these historians sometimes contradict each other.

The orthodox view of nineteenth-century imperial history remains that laid down from the standpoint of the racial and legalistic concept which inspired the Imperial Federation movement. Historians such as Seeley and Egerton looked on events in the formal empire as the only test of imperial

John Gallagher and Ronald Robinson, "The Imperialism of Free Trade," *The Economic History Review*, Second Series, VI (1953), 1–13, with omissions.

activity; and they regarded the empire of kinship and constitutional dependence as an organism with its own laws of growth. In this way the nineteenth century was divided into periods of imperialism and anti-imperialism, according to the extension or contraction of the formal empire and the degree of belief in the value of British rule overseas.

Ironically enough, the alternative interpretation of "imperialism," which began as part of the radical polemic against the Federationists, has in effect only confirmed their analysis. Those who have seen imperialism as the high stage of capitalism and the inevitable result of foreign investment agree that it applied historically only to the period after 1880. As a result they have been led into a similar preoccupation with formal manifestations of imperialism because the late-Victorian age was one of spectacular extension of British rule. Consequently, Hobson and Lenin, Professor Moon and Mr Woolf have confirmed from the opposite point of view their opponents' contention that late-Victorian imperialism was a qualitative change in the nature of British expansion and a sharp deviation from the innocent and static liberalism of the middle of the century. This alleged change, welcomed by one school, condemned by the other, was accepted by both.

*   *   *

The trouble with this argument is that it leaves out too many of the facts which it claims to explain. Consider the results of a decade of "indifference" to empire. Between 1841 and 1851 Great Britain occupied or annexed New Zealand, the Gold Coast, Labuan, Natal, the Punjab, Sind and Hong Kong. In the next twenty years British control was asserted over Berar, Oudh, Lower Burma and Kowloon, over Lagos and the neighbourhood of Sierra Leone, over Basutoland, Griqualand and the Transvaal; and new colonies were established in Queensland and British Columbia. Unless this expansion can be explained by "fits of absence of mind," we are faced with the paradox that it occurred despite the determination of the imperial authorities to avoid extending their rule.

This contradiction arises even if we confine our attention to the formal empire, as the orthodox viewpoint would force us to do. But if we look beyond into the regions of informal empire, then the difficulties become overwhelming. The normal account of South African policy in the middle of the century is that Britain abandoned any idea of controlling the interior. But in fact what looked like withdrawal from the Orange River Sovereignty and the Transvaal was based not on any *a priori* theories about the inconveniences of colonies but upon hard facts of strategy and commerce in a wider field. Great Britain was in South Africa primarily to safeguard the routes to the East, by preventing foreign powers from acquiring bases on the flank of those routes. In one way or another this imperial interest demanded some kind of hold upon Africa south of the Limpopo River, and although between 1852 and 1877 the Boer Republics were not controlled formally for this purpose by Britain, they were effectually dominated by informal paramountcy and by their dependence on British ports. If we refuse to narrow our view to that of formal empire, we can see how steadily and successfully the main imperial interest was pursued by maintaining supremacy over the whole region, and that it was pursued as steadily throughout the so-called anti-imperialist era as in the late-Victorian period. But it was done by shutting in the Boer Republics from the Indian Ocean: by the annexation of Natal in 1843, by keeping the Boers out of Delagoa Bay in 1860 and 1868, out of St Lucia Bay in 1861 and 1866, and by British intervention to block the union of the two Republics under Pretorius in 1860. Strangely enough it was the first Gladstone Government which Schuyler regards as the climax of anti-imperialism, which annexed Basutoland in 1868 and Griqualand West in 1871 in order to ensure "the safety of our South African Possessions." By informal means if possible, or by formal annexations when necessary, British paramountcy was steadily upheld.

Are these the actions of ministers anxious to preside over the liquidation of the British Empire? Do they look like "indifference" to an empire rendered superfluous by free trade? On the contrary, here is a continuity of policy which the conventional interpretation misses because it takes account only of formal methods of control. It also misses the continuous grasp of the West African coast and of the South Pacific which British sea-power was able to maintain. Refusals to annex are no proof of reluctance to control. As Lord Aberdeen put it in 1845: ". . . it is unnecessary to add that Her Majesty's Government will not view with indifference the assumption by another Power of a Protectorate which they, with due regard for the true interests of those [Pacific] islands, have refused."

Nor can the obvious continuity of imperial constitutional policy throughout the mid- and late-Victorian years be explained on the orthodox hypothesis. If the granting of responsible government to colonies was due to the mid-Victorian "indifference" to empire and even a desire to be rid of it, then why was this policy continued in the late-Victorian period when Britain was interested above all in preserving imperial unity? The common assumption that British governments in the free-trade era considered empire superfluous arises from overestimating the significance of changes in legalistic forms. In fact, throughout the Victorian period responsible government was withheld from colonies if it involved sacrificing or endangering British paramountcy or interests. Wherever there was fear of a foreign challenge to British supremacy in the continent or subcontinent concerned, wherever the colony could not provide financially for its own internal security, the imperial authorities retained full responsibility, or, if they had already devolved it, intervened directly to secure their interests once more. In other words, responsible government, far from being a separatist device, was simply a change from direct to indirect methods of maintaining British interests. By slackening the formal political bond at the appropriate time, it was possible to rely on economic dependence and mutual good-feeling to keep the colonies bound to Britain while still using them as agents for further British expansion.

The inconsistency between fact and the orthodox interpretation arises in yet another way. For all the extensive anthologies of opinion supposedly hostile to colonies, how many colonies were actually abandoned? For instance, the West Africa Committee of 1865 made a strong and much quoted case for giving up all but one of the West African settlements, but even as they sat these settlements were being extended. The Indian empire, however, is the most glaring gap in the traditional explanation. Its history in the "period of indifference" is filled with wars and annexations.

Moreover, in this supposedly *laissez-faire* period India, far from being evacuated, was subjected to intensive development as an economic colony along the best mercantilist lines. In India it was possible, throughout most of the period of the British Raj, to use the governing power to extort in the form of taxes and monopolies such valuable primary products as opium and salt. Furthermore, the characteristics of so-called imperialist expansion at the end of the nineteenth century developed in India long before the date (1880) when Lenin believed the age of economic imperialism opened. Direct governmental promotion of products required by British industry, government manipulation of tariffs to help British exports, railway construction at high and guaranteed rates of interest to open the continental interior — all of these techniques of direct political control were employed in ways which seem alien to the so-called age of *laissez-faire*. Moreover, they had little to do, particularly in railway finance, with the folk-lore of rugged individualism. "All the money came from the English capitalist" as a British official wrote, "and, so long as he was guaranteed five per cent on the revenues of India, it was immaterial to him whether the funds which he

23

lent were thrown into the Hooghly or converted into bricks and mortar."

To sum up: the conventional view of Victorian imperial history leaves us with a series of awkward questions. In the age of "anti-imperialism" why were all colonies retained? Why were so many more obtained? Why were so many new spheres of influence set up? Or again, in the age of "imperialism," as we shall see later, why was there such reluctance to annex further territory? Why did decentralization, begun under the impetus of anti-imperialism, continue? In the age of *laissez-faire* why was the Indian economy developed by the state?

These paradoxes are too radical to explain as merely exceptions which prove the rule or by concluding that imperial policy was largely irrational and inconsistent, the product of a series of accidents and chances. The contradictions, it may be suspected, arise not from the historical reality but from the historians' approach to it. A hypothesis which fits more of the facts might be that of a fundamental continuity in British expansion throughout the nineteenth century.

II

The hypothesis which is needed must include informal as well as formal expansion, and must allow for the continuity of the process. The most striking fact about British history in the nineteenth century, as Seeley pointed out, is that it is the history of an expanding society. The exports of capital and manufactures, the migration of citizens, the dissemination of the English language, ideas and constitutional forms, were all of them radiations of the social energies of the British peoples. Between 1812 and 1914 over twenty million persons emigrated from the British Isles, and nearly 70 per cent of them went outside the Empire. Between 1815 and 1880, it is estimated, £1,187,000,000 in credit had accumulated abroad, but no more than one-sixth was placed in the formal empire. Even by 1913, something less than half of the £3,975,000,000 of foreign investment lay inside the Empire. Similarly, in no year of the century did the Empire buy much more

than one-third of Britain's exports. The basic fact is that British industrialization caused an ever-extending and intensifying development of overseas regions. Whether they were formally British or not, was a secondary consideration.

Imperialism, perhaps, may be defined as a sufficient political function of this process of integrating new regions into the expanding economy; its character is largely decided by the various and changing relationships between the political and economic elements of expansion in any particular region and time. Two qualifications must be made. First, imperialism may be only indirectly connected with economic integration in that it sometimes extends beyond areas of economic development, but acts for their strategic protection. Secondly, although imperialism is a function of economic expansion, it is not a necessary function. Whether imperialist phenomena show themselves or not, is determined not only by the factors of economic expansion, but equally by the political and social organization of the regions brought into the orbit of the expansive society, and also by the world situation in general.

It is only when the polities of these new regions fail to provide satisfactory conditions for commercial or strategic integration and when their relative weakness allows, that power is used imperialistically to adjust those conditions. Economic expansion, it is true, will tend to flow into the regions of maximum opportunity, but maximum opportunity depends as much upon political considerations of security as upon questions of profit. Consequently, in any particular region, if economic opportunity seems large but political security small, then full absorption into the extending economy tends to be frustrated until power is exerted upon the state in question. Conversely, in proportion as satisfactory political frameworks are brought into being in this way, the frequency of imperialist intervention lessens and imperialist control is correspondingly relaxed. It may be suggested that this willingness to limit the use of paramount power to establishing security for trade is the distinctive feature of the British imperialism of free trade in the nineteenth century, in contrast to the mercantilist use of power to obtain commercial supremacy and monopoly through political possession.

On this hypothesis the phasing of British expansion or imperialism is not likely to be chronological. Not all regions will reach the same level of economic integration at any one time; neither will all regions need the same type of political control at any one time. As the British industrial revolution grew, so new markets and sources of supply were linked to it at different times, and the degree of imperialist action accompanying that process varied accordingly. Thus mercantilist techniques of formal empire were being employed to develop India in the mid-Victorian age at the same time as informal techniques of free trade were being used in Latin America for the same purpose. It is for this reason that attempts to make phases of imperialism correspond directly to phases in the economic growth of the metropolitan economy are likely to prove in vain. The fundamental continuity of British expansion is only obscured by arguing that changes in the terms of trade or in the character of British exports necessitated a sharp change in the process.

From this vantage point the many-sided expansion of British industrial society can be viewed as a whole of which both the formal and informal empires are only parts. Both of them then appear as variable political functions of the extending pattern of overseas trade, investment, migration and culture. If this is accepted, it follows that formal and informal empire are essentially interconnected and to some extent interchangeable. Then not only is the old, legalistic, narrow idea of empire unsatisfactory, but so is the old idea of informal empire as a separate, non-political category of expansion. A concept of informal empire which fails to bring out the underlying unity between it and the formal empire is sterile. Only within the total framework of expansion is nineteenth-century empire intelligi-

ble. So we are faced with the task of re-fashioning the interpretations resulting from defective concepts of organic constitutional empire on the one hand and Hobsonian "imperialism" on the other.

The economic importance — even the preeminence — of informal empire in this period has been stressed often enough. What was overlooked was the inter-relation of its economic and political arms; how political action aided the growth of commercial supremacy, and how this supremacy in turn strengthened political influence. In other words, it is the politics as well as the economics of the informal empire which we have to include in the account. Historically, the relationship between these two factors has been both subtle and complex. It has been by no means a simple case of the use of gunboats to demolish a recalcitrant state in the cause of British trade. The type of political lien between the expanding economy and its formal or informal dependencies, as might be expected, has been flexible. In practice it has tended to vary with the economic value of the territory, the strength of its political structure, the readiness of its rulers to collaborate with British commercial or strategic purposes, the ability of the native society to undergo economic change without external control, the extent to which domestic and foreign political situations permitted British intervention, and, finally, how far European rivals allowed British policy a free hand.

Accordingly, the political lien has ranged from a vague, informal paramountcy to outright political possession; and, consequently, some of these dependent territories have been formal colonies whereas others have not. The difference between formal and informal empire has not been one of fundamental nature but of degree. The ease with which a region has slipped from one status to the other helps to confirm this. Within the last two hundred years, for example, India has passed from informal to formal association with the United Kingdom and, since World War II, back to an informal connexion. Similarly, British West Africa

25

has passed through the first two stages and seems to-day likely to follow India into the third.

III

Let us now attempt, tentatively, to use the concept of the totality of British expansion described above to restate the main themes of the history of modern British expansion. We have seen that interpretations of this process fall into contradictions when based upon formal political criteria alone. If expansion both formal and informal is examined as a single process, will these contradictions disappear?

The growth of British industry made new demands upon British policy. It necessitated linking undeveloped areas with British foreign trade and, in so doing, moved the political arm to force an entry into markets closed by the power of foreign monopolies.

British policy, as Professor Harlow has shown, was active in this way before the American colonies had been lost, but its greatest opportunities came during the Napoleonic Wars. The seizure of the French and Spanish West Indies, the filibustering expedition to Buenos Aires in 1806, the taking of Java in 1811, were all efforts to break into new regions and to tap new resources by means of political action. But the policy went further than simple house-breaking, for once the door was opened and British imports with their political implications were pouring in, they might stop the door from being shut again. Raffles, for example, temporarily broke the Dutch monopoly of the spice trade in Java and opened the island to free trade. Later, he began the informal British paramountcy over the Malacca trade routes and the Malay peninsula by founding Singapore. In South America, at the same time, British policy was aiming at indirect political hegemony over new regions for the purposes of trade. The British navy carried the Portuguese royal family to Brazil after the breach with Napoleon, and the British representative there extorted from his grateful clients the trade treaty of 1810 which left British imports paying a lower tariff than the goods of the mother country. The thoughtful stipulation was added "that the Present Treaty shall be unlimited in point of duration, and that the obligations and conditions expressed or implied in it shall be perpetual and immutable."

From 1810 onwards this policy had even better chances in Latin America, and they were taken. British governments sought to exploit the colonial revolutions to shatter the Spanish trade monopoly, and to gain informal supremacy and the good will which would all favour British commercial penetration. As Canning put it in 1824, when he had clinched the policy of recognition: "Spanish America is free and if we do not mismanage our affairs sadly she is *English.*" Canning's underlying object was to clear the way for a prodigious British expansion by creating a new and informal empire, not only to redress the Old World balance of power but to restore British influence in the New. He wrote triumphantly: "The thing is done . . . the Yankees will shout in triumph: but it is they who lose most by our decision . . . the United States have gotten the start of us in vain; and we link once more America to Europe." It would be hard to imagine a more spectacular example of a policy of commercial hegemony in the interests of high politics, or of the use of informal political supremacy in the interests of commercial enterprise. Characteristically, the British recognition of Buenos Aires, Mexico and Colombia took the form of signing commercial treaties with them.

In both the formal and informal dependencies in the mid-Victorian age there was much effort to open the continental interiors and to extend the British influence inland from the ports and to develop the hinterlands. The general strategy of this development was to convert these areas into complementary satellite economies, which would provide raw materials and food for Great Britain, and also provide widening markets for its manufactures. This was the period, the orthodox interpretation would have us believe, in which the political arm of expansion was dormant or even withered. In fact, that alleged inactivity is seen to be a delusion if we take into account the development in the informal aspect. Once entry had been forced into Latin America, China and the Balkans, the task was to encourage stable governments as good investment risks, just as in weaker or unsatisfactory states it was considered necessary to coerce them into more co-operative attitudes.

*   *   *

The types of informal empire and the situations it attempted to exploit were as various as the success which it achieved. Although commercial and capital penetration tended to lead to political co-operation and hegemony, there are striking exceptions. In the United States, for example, British business turned the cotton South into a colonial economy, and the British investor hoped to do the same with the Mid-West. But the political strength of the country stood in his way. It was impossible to stop American industrialization, and the industrialized sections successfully campaigned for tariffs, despite the opposition of those sections which depended on the British trade connexion. In the same way, American political strength thwarted British attempts to establish Texas, Mexico and Central America as informal dependencies.

Conversely, British expansion sometimes failed, if it gained political supremacy without effecting a successful commercial penetration. There were spectacular exertions of British policy in China, but they did little to produce new customers. Britain's political hold upon China failed to break down Chinese economic self-sufficiency. The Opium War of 1840, the renewal of war in 1857, widened the inlets for British trade but they did not get Chinese exports moving. Their main effect was an unfortunate one from the British point of view, for such foreign pressures put Chinese society under great strains as the Taiping Rebellion unmistakably showed. It is important to note that this weakness was regarded in London

as an embarrassment, and not as a lever for extracting further concessions. In fact, the British worked to prop up the tottering Pekin regime, for as Lord Clarendon put it in 1870, "British interests in China are strictly commercial, or at all events only so far political as they may be for the protection of commerce." The value of this self-denial became clear in the following decades when the Pekin government, threatened with a scramble for China, leaned more and more on the diplomatic support of the honest British broker.

The simple recital of these cases of economic expansion, aided and abetted by political action in one form or other, is enough to expose the inadequacy of the conventional theory that free trade could dispense with empire. We have seen that it did not do so. Economic expansion in the mid-Victorian age was matched by a corresponding political expansion which has been overlooked because it could not be seen by that study of maps which, it has been said, drives sane men mad. It is absurd to deduce from the harmony between London and the colonies of white settlement in the mid-Victorian age any British reluctance to intervene in the fields of British interests. The warships at Canton are as much a part of the period as responsible government for Canada; the battlefields of the Punjab are as real as the abolition of suttee.

Far from being an era of "indifference," the mid-Victorian years were the decisive stage in the history of British expansion overseas, in that the combination of commercial penetration and political influence allowed the United Kingdom to command those economies which could be made to fit best into her own. A variety of techniques adapted to diverse conditions and beginning at different dates were employed to effect this domination. A paramountcy was set up in Malaya centred on Singapore; a suzerainty over much of West Africa reached out from the port of Lagos and was backed up by the African squadron. On the east coast of Africa British influence at Zanzibar, dominant thanks to the exertions of

Consul Kirk, placed the heritage of Arab command on the mainland at British disposal.

But perhaps the most common political technique of British expansion was the treaty of free trade and friendship made with or imposed upon a weaker state. The treaties with Persia of 1836 and 1857, the Turkish treaties of 1838 and 1861, the Japanese treaty of 1858, the favours extracted from Zanzibar, Siam and Morocco, the hundreds of anti-slavery treaties signed with crosses by African chiefs — all these treaties enabled the British government to carry forward trade with these regions.

Even a valuable trade with one region might give place to a similar trade with another which could be more easily coerced politically. The Russian grain trade, for example, was extremely useful to Great Britain. But the Russians' refusal to hear of free trade, and the British inability to force them into it, caused efforts to develop the grain of the Ottoman empire instead, since British pressure at Constantinople had been able to hustle the Turk into a liberal trade policy. The dependence of the commercial thrust upon the political arm resulted in a general tendency for British trade to follow the invisible flag of informal empire.

Since the mid-Victorian age now appears as a time of large-scale expansion, it is necessary to revise our estimate of the so-called "imperialist" era as well. Those who accept the concept of "economic imperialism" would have us believe that the annexations at the end of the century represented a sharp break in policy, due to the decline of free trade, the need to protect foreign investment, and the conversion of statesmen to the need for unlimited land-grabbing. All these explanations are questionable. In the first place, the tariff policy of Great Britain did not change. Again, British foreign investment was no new thing and most of it was still flowing into regions outside the formal empire. Finally the statesmens' conversion to the policy of extensive annexation was partial, to say the most of it. Until 1887, and only occasionally after that date,

party leaders showed little more enthusiasm for extending British rule than the mid-Victorians. Salisbury was infuriated by the "superficial philanthropy" and "roguery" of the "fanatics" who advocated expansion. When pressed to aid the missions in Nyasaland in 1888, he retorted: "It is not our duty to do it. We should be risking tremendous sacrifices for a very doubtful gain." After 1888, Salisbury, Rosebery and Chamberlain accepted the scramble for Africa as a painful but unavoidable necessity which arose from a threat of foreign expansion and the irrepressible tendency of trade to overflow the bounds of empire, dragging the government into new and irksome commitments. But it was not until 1898 that they were sufficiently confident to undertake the reconquest of so vital a region as the Sudan.

Faced with the prospect of foreign acquisitions of tropical territory hitherto opened to British merchants, the men in London resorted to one expedient after another to evade the need of formal expansion and still uphold British paramountcy in those regions. British policy in the late, as in the mid-Victorian period preferred informal means of extending imperial supremacy rather than direct rule. Throughout the two alleged periods the extension of British rule was a last resort — and it is this preference which has given rise to the many "anti-expansionist" remarks made by Victorian ministers. What these much quoted expressions obscure, is that in practice mid-Victorian as well as late-Victorian policy makers did not refuse to extend the protection of formal rule over British interests when informal methods had failed to give security. The fact that informal techniques were more often sufficient for this purpose in the circumstances of the mid-century than in the later period when the foreign challenge to British supremacy intensified, should not be allowed to disguise the basic continuity of policy. Throughout, British governments worked to establish and maintain British paramountcy by whatever means best suited the circumstances of their diverse regions of interest. The aims of the mid-

Victorians were no more "anti-imperialist" than their successors', though they were more often able to achieve them informally; and the late-Victorians were no more "imperialist" than their predecessors, even though they were driven to annex more often. British policy followed the principle of extending control informally if possible and formally if necessary. To label the one method "anti-imperialist" and the other "imperialist," is to ignore the fact that whatever the method British interests were steadily safeguarded and extended. The usual summing up of the policy of the free trade empire as "trade not rule" should read "trade with informal control if possible; trade with rule when necessary." This statement of the continuity of policy disposes of the over-simplified explanation of involuntary expansion inherent in the orthodox interpretation based on the discontinuity between the two periods.

* * *

One principle then emerges plainly: it is only when and where informal political means failed to provide the framework of security for British enterprise (whether commercial, or philanthropic or simply strategic) that the question of establishing formal empire arose. In satellite regions peopled by European stock, in Latin America or Canada, for instance, strong governmental structures grew up; in totally non-European areas, on the other hand, expansion unleashed such disruptive forces upon the indigenous structures that they tended to wear out and even collapse with use. This tendency in many cases accounts for the extension of informal British responsibility and eventually for the change from indirect to direct control.

Marshal Bugeaud

8. MILITARY COLONIZATION OF ALGERIA

The easy French victory over the Turkish forces of the Dey of Algiers in 1830 was paid for by two subsequent decades of warfare against the Arab-Berber tribesmen of the Algerian hinterland. The French army was successfully adapted to these mobile desert conditions by Marshal Thomas-Robert Bugeaud de la Piconnerie (1784–1849) who became also Governor of the new colony. Although civilian settlers (many not originally French) were brought into Algeria from the beginning of the occupation, the following selection from a pamphlet published by Bugeaud well before the completion of the conquest indicates the extent to which the French military viewed North Africa as their own exclusive field of endeavor.

CONCLUSION TO SECOND SECTION
THE CONSTITUTION OF THE LEGIONS

... What the Government has brought to light up to today is only a military occupation; what it has not shown is the goal which it plans to attain thereby. Now or never is the time to indicate this *goal* in the fullest sense; instead of expressing it in half phrases, it is necessary to speak out frankly; it is necessary to declare that the only way to bring about any results from a sterile and endless occupation is through military colonies. Thus, what the Government has not said, has not done, it must say and above all it must do; the matter is urgent. To nourish the hope that we will conquer the Arabs simply by the gentility of our customs, by persuasion, by the advantages of our civilization, this is an enormous deception and nothing more. While such language circulates in books, in drawing rooms, sometimes even on public platforms, let us look at what is happening in Africa: the Arabs reply to sentiments with rifle shots. And even when the Arabs are finally conquered, will they present you with guarantees for the future? Could you give up your conquest to them and withdraw your army? No. With only them as colonists you would always have to remain strong, you would not be able to withdraw a single soldier, and then what danger for us in Europe! You thus require a loyal population.

But military colonies will only make the occupation disappear little by little? Agreed; but as quickly as they settle themselves in, a part of the task will be accomplished and each thousand men who return will leave in Africa an equal number of established cultivators. Can an occupation offer as much?

If military colonies were tried from the beginning on a large scale it is more than probable that the Arabs among and around them would be submissive and come to live peacefully in our midst. The passage of years, good conduct, military policy, and organization would see to it that the work would be accomplished.

T. R. Bugeaud, *De l'establissement de legions de colons militaires dans les possessions francaises du Nord de l'Afrique suivi d'un projet d'ordonnance. Adressé au Gouvernement et aux Chambres* (Paris, 1838).

In this new course, only the first steps will be difficult; but, once these first steps are taken, the others will be easier, and, once confronted with the first success, everyone will take heart for the task. We know that colonization demands a population which is active, warlike, agricultural, and organized somewhat on Arab lines. But we must know how to attract such a population. As long as we have in the Regency [of Algeria] only Turks, Arabs, Moors, and Jews, we will be forced to keep the army of conquest there if we do not want the colony to be lost the first time that there is a war in Europe.

Lord Dalhousie

9. BRITISH SUPREMACY IN INDIA

British entanglement in the internal affairs of India began under the Old Colonial System when successful warfare against France, together with the crumbling of the indigenous Moghul Empire, left the British East India Company as the main military and political power on the subcontinent. The defense and consolidation of this position led the Company's servants to extend their power still further until, under the 1848–1856 Governor Generalship of the Earl (later Marquis) of Dalhousie (1812–1860), British control covered all of present day India and Pakistan as well as parts of Burma. Dalhousie brought the policy of military expansion to a climax by both the various wars over which he presided and the "doctrine of lapse," enunciated in the following minute, which justified peaceful annexation of independent Indian states. Dalhousie's disregard for the traditional political system of India contributed to the unrest which, in the 1857 Sepoy Rebellion, led Indian troops of the British Company to attempt a restoration of Moghul rule.

THE RAJ OF SATTARA

1. The death of his highness Shreemunt Mabaraj, the Sovereign of Sattara, has rendered it necessary for the British Government to determine the important question, whether the State of Sattara shall be continued as an independent sovereignty, or whether it shall be held to have lapsed to the paramount state, and shall henceforth form an integral part of the British Empire in India. . . .

5. His highness Shreemunt Mabaraj has died leaving no heirs natural, but having, in accordance with Hindoo custom, adopted one of his kinsmen as his heir a few hours before his death.

6. The questions for decision are

First: Is the British Government bound, as a matter of justice and of right, to recognize the boy just adopted as being actually the successor of the late Raja and heir to the throne of Sattara?

Second: If not as a matter of justice and of right, ought the British Government to approve of the succession of this boy as a matter of wisdom and sound policy? . . .

14. It is on these grounds [legal argument in paragraphs 7–13] that I found my conviction that the British Government is not

Minute of August 30, 1848. (Printed in House of Commons, Accounts and Papers, 1849, Volume XXXIX.)

bound, as a matter of justice and of right, to recognize this boy as actually the heir to the sovereignty of Sattara, but is free in this, as it has been in others, to confer or to refuse its sanction as it may think fit.

15. This power it possesses by virtue of its authority as the sovereign state over Sattara, a position which it holds equally as the successor of the emperors of Delhi, as the successor by conquest of the Peishwas, the virtual sovereigns of the Rajas of Sattara, and, lastly, especially as the creator of the raj of Sattara under the treaty of 1819. . . .

20. The assumption of the raj by the British will cause no ferment or discontent among other native powers, though it must, of necessity, be obnoxious to the pride and to the feelings of those who have lived and held influence within its bounds.

21. While therefore I do not presume to doubt the wisdom of creating the raj in 1819, I conceive that the same reasons prevail for its reconstitution now, when it is again placed by events at our disposal. . . .

24. While I find no sufficient reasons for the reconstitution of Sattara, either in the considerations which led to the original foundation of its government or in the manner in which that government has lately been administered, I conceive that many powerful arguments may be advanced in favor of its ceasing to be a separate state, and being resumed as a portion of the British territories.

25. I take this fitting occasion of recording my strong and deliberate opinion that, in the exercise of a wise and a sound policy, the British Government is bound not to put aside or to neglect such rightful opportunities of acquiring territory or revenue as may from time to time present themselves, whether they rise from the lapse of subordinate states, by failure of all heirs of every description whatsoever, or from the failure of heirs natural, where the succession can be sustained only by the sanction of the Government being given to the ceremony of adoption according to Hindoo law.

26. The Government is bound, in duty as well as in policy, to act on every such an occasion with the purest integrity, and in the most scrupulous observance of good faith. Where even a shadow of a doubt can be shown, the claim should at once be abandoned.

27. But where the right to territory, by lapse, is clear, the Government is bound to take that which is justly and legally its due, and to extend to that territory the benefits of our sovereignty, present and prospective.

28. In like manner, while I would not seek to lay down any inflexible rule with respect to adoption, I hold that on all occasions, where heirs natural shall fail, the territory should be made to lapse, and adoption should not be permitted, excepting in those cases where some strong political reason may render it expedient to depart from this general rule.

29. There may be conflict of opinion as to the advantage or the propriety of extending our already vast possessions beyond their present limits. No man can more sincerely deprecate than I do any extensions of the frontiers of our territory which can be avoided, or which may not become indispensably necessary, from conditions of our own safety, and of the maintenance of the tranquility of our provinces.

But I cannot conceive it possible for anyone to dispute the policy of taking advantage of every just opportunity which presents itself for consolidating the territories that already belong to us, by taking possession of states in the midst of them; for thus getting rid of those petty intervening principalities which may be made a means of annoyance, but which can never, I venture to think, be a source of strength, for adding to the resources of the public treasury, and for extending the uniform application of our system of government to those whose best interests, we sincerely believe, will be promoted thereby.

10. NAPOLEON III SEEKS A MEXICAN EMPIRE

The image of French grandeur pursued by Louis Napoleon Bonaparte (1808–1873, President and Emperor, 1848–1870) led him to take an active, if ambiguous, interest in a number of overseas efforts including reforms in Algeria, expansion of French West Africa, punitive expeditions and protectorates in Indochina, and, finally, the sponsorship of a Mexican empire under the Austrian Habsburg Archduke Maximilian. Napoleon's intentions as outlined in the following letter were ultimately carried out, but without English and Spanish participation. At the conclusion of the American Civil War, Napoleon withdrew his own troops from Mexico, thus abandoning Maximilian to capture and execution by the restored indigenous regime of Benito Juarez.

TO THE COMTE DE FLAHAULT IN LONDON

Palace of Compiègne, October 1861
My dear Comte de Flahault,

Hearing from Mr. Thouvenel that our convention on the subject of Mexico is making no progress, I wish to express my ideas to you frankly, so that you may communicate them to Lord Palmerston. When the Prime Minister is informed of the intentions with which I approach this affair I hope he will be so good as to tell you equally clearly what is in his mind, and that the result will be an understanding and common action. There is no need for me to enlarge upon the common interest which we in Europe have in seeing Mexico pacified and endowed with a stable government. Not only has that country, which enjoys every natural advantage, attracted much of our capital and many of our fellow-countrymen, whose existence is subjected to a continual menace, but, if it were regenerated, it would form an impassable barrier to the encroachments of North America, it would afford an important opening for English, Spanish, and French trade, while exploiting its own wealth, and lastly it would render great services to our manufactories by extending its cultivation of cotton. The consideration of its various advantages, as well as the spectacle of one of the finest countries in the world given over to anarchy and threatened with impending ruin, such are the motives which have always given me a keen interest in the fate of Mexico. For many years past important persons from that country have waited upon me in order to draw a picture of their unfortunate condition and ask for my help, saying that a monarchy alone could restore order in a country rent by factions; they also, I believe, approached England, but at that time I could only indulge in fruitless wishes. In spite of my sympathy, I replied that I had no pretext for intervention in Mexico; that in America, above all, my course of action was closely bound up with that of England; that I thought it would be difficult to arrive at an agreement with the Cabinet of St. James's for the purpose which they proposed; that we should risk falling out with the United States; and that it was therefore necessary to wait for better days. Today unexpected events have arisen and

Reprinted by permission of the publisher from *Maximilian and Charlotte of Mexico*, Vol. I, by Egon Cesor Count Corti, translated by Catherine Alison Phillips, pp. 361–363. Copyright, 1928 by Alfred A. Knopf, Inc.

changed the face of affairs. The American war has made it impossible for the United States to interfere in the matter, and, what is more, the outrages committed by the Mexican Government have provided England, Spain, and France with a legitimate motive for interference in Mexico. What direction ought this intervention to take? That is the question. I can quite understand that the convention between the three powers which will send forces to America should lay down as the ostensible object of our intervention nothing but the redress of our legitimate grievances, but we must foresee what may possibly happen, and not gratuitously tie our hands in such a way as to prevent a solution which would be to the interest of all. According to the information I have received, as soon as the squadrons arrive off Vera Cruz, a considerable party in Mexico is prepared to seize the supreme power, summon a national assembly, and proclaim the monarchy. I was asked confidentially who would be my candidate in the event of this happening. I declared that I had none, but that, should the occasion arise, it would be necessary to choose a prince informed with the spirit of the age, endowed with sufficient intelligence and firmness to found a durable order of things in a country disturbed by so many revolutions; and lastly that it was necessary that this choice should not wound the susceptibilities of the great naval powers; and I put forward the name of the Archduke Maximilian. This idea was joyfully accepted by the little committee resident in Paris. The Prince's personal qualities, his connexion through his wife with the King of the Belgians, the natural link between France and England, and the fact that he belongs to a great non-maritime power, appeared to me to meet all desirable conditions. For my part, I confess, I thought it was in good taste for me to propose as candidate, in certain contingencies, a prince belonging to a dynasty with which I had recently been at war. The Mexicans, who naturally show more eagerness in the matter than I do, and are impatient to see events move quickly, have had the Cabinet of Vienna sounded, and according to the information I have received, it has accepted the overture, subject to two conditions: firstly, that the Prince should have the support of France and England, and secondly, that the wishes of the people should be frankly and fairly expressed to me.

Such is the position of affairs. You see, my dear Monsieur de Flahault, that I have only one object in this whole question; namely, to see to it that French interests are in future protected and safeguarded by an organization which should rescue Mexico from devastation by the Indians or an American invasion. I am moreover very glad to show that, far from having any selfish preferences or unjust dislikes, I seek nothing but good, convinced that to try to make a people prosperous is to work effectively for the prosperity of all.

To sum up, I ask nothing better than to sign a convention with England and Spain, in which the ostensible object of our intervention shall be the redress of our grievances, but it would be impossible, without a breach of good faith, and knowing the state of affairs as I do, to bind myself not to lend at least moral support to a change which I desire with all my heart, because it is in the interest of the whole of civilization.

Be assured of my sincere friendship.

Napoleon.

11. EDMUND BURKE ON BRITISH RESPONSIBILITIES IN INDIA

Along with his well-known liberal defense of the American Revolution and conservative attack upon the French Revolution, Edmund Burke (1729–1797) also turned his great political and theoretical gifts to the questions raised by British rule in India. The first of the two speeches cited below was made in defense of a bill to increase parliamentary control over the hitherto privately managed British East India Company. The second selection forms part of the indictment of Warren Hastings, a Governor of India eventually found innocent by both the Court of the House of Lords and modern historians of the specific crimes charged against him by Burke and his party. Both speeches, however, helped set a tone of moral concern which was to govern both metropolitan British attitudes towards India and British administration within India itself for the duration of imperial rule.

SPEECH ON MR. FOX'S EAST INDIA BILL
December 1, 1783

I therefore freely admit to the East India Company their claim to exclude their fellow-subjects from the commerce of half the globe. I admit their claim to administer an annual territorial revenue of seven millions sterling, to command an army of sixty thousand men, and to dispose (under the control of a sovereign, imperial discretion, and with the due observance of the natural and local law) of the lives and fortunes of thirty millions of their fellow-creatures. All this they possess by charter, and by Acts of Parliament, (in my opinion,) without a shadow of controversy.

Those who carry the rights and claims of the Company the furthest do not contend for more than this; and all this I freely grant. But, granting all this, they must grant to me, in my turn, that all political power which is set over men, and that all privilege claimed or exercised in exclusion of them, being wholly artificial, and for so much a derogation from the natural equality of mankind at large, ought to be some way or other exercised ultimately for their benefit.

If this is true with regard to every species of political dominion and every description of commercial privilege, none of which can be original, self-derived rights, or grants for the mere private benefit of the holders, then such rights, or privileges, or whatever else you choose to call them, are all in the strictest sense *a trust*: and it is of the very essence of every trust to be rendered *accountable*,— and even totally to *cease*, when it substantially varies from the purposes for which alone it could have a lawful existence.

This I conceive, Sir, to be true of trusts of power vested in the highest hands, and of such as seem to hold of no human creature. But about the application of this principle to subordinate *derivative* trusts I do not see how a controversy can be maintained. To whom, then, would I make the East India Company accountable? Why, to Parliament, to be sure,—to Parliament, from whom their trust was derived,—to Parliament, which alone is capable of comprehending the magnitude of its object, and its abuse, and

Speech on Mr. Fox's East India Bill, December 1, 1783. Speech in Opening the Impeachment of Warren Hastings, February 15, 1788, Esq., Late Governor of Bengal.

alone capable of an effectual legislative remedy. The very charter, which is held out to exclude Parliament from correcting malversation with regard to the high trust vested in the Company, is the very thing which at once gives a title and imposes a duty on us to interfere with effect, wherever power and authority originating from ourselves are perverted from their purposes, and become instruments of wrong and violence.

SPEECH IN OPENING IMPEACHMENT OF
WARREN HASTINGS
February 15, 1788

Your Lordships see here a regular series of gradation, which requires eleven years before any persons can arrive at the highest trusts and situations. You will therefore be astonished, when so long a probationary service was required, that effects very different from those to be expected from long probation have happened, and that in a much shorter time than those eleven years you have seen persons returning into this kingdom with affluent, with overbearing fortunes. It will be a great part of your inquiry, when we come before your Lordships to substantiate evidence against Mr. Hastings, to discover how that order came to be so completely broken down and erased that scarce a trace of it for any good purpose remains. Though I will not deny that that order, or that any order in a state, may be superseded by the ruling power, when great talents, upon pressing exigencies, are to be called forth, yet I must say the order itself was formed upon wise principles. It furnished the persons who were put in that course of probation with an opportunity (if circumstances enabled them) of acquiring experience in business of revenue, trade, and policy. It gave to those who watched them a constant inspection of their conduct through all their progress. On the expectants of office it imposed the necessity of acquiring a character in proportion to their standing, in order that all which they had gained by the good behavior of years should not be lost by the misconduct of an

hour. It was a great substantial regulation. But scarce a trace of the true spirit of it remains to be discovered in Mr. Hastings's government; for Mr. Hastings established offices, nay, whole systems of offices, and especially a system of offices in 1781, which being altogether new, none of the rules of gradation applied to them; and he filled those offices in such a manner as suited best, not the constitution nor the spirit of the service, but his own particular views and purposes. The consequence has been, that persons in the most immature stages of life have been appointed to conduct affairs which required the greatest maturity of judgment, the greatest possible temper and moderation. Effects naturally consequent have followed upon it. — I shall not trouble your Lordships with any further observations on this system of gradation.

I must, however, remark, before I go further, that there is something in the representation of the East India Company in their Oriental territory different from that, perhaps, of any other nation that has ever transported any part of its power from one country to another. The East India Company in India is not properly a branch of the British nation: it is only a deputation of individuals. When the Tartars entered into China, when the Arabs and Tartars successively entered into Hindostan, when the Goths and Vandals penetrated into Europe, when the Normans forced their way into England, indeed, in all conquests, migrations, settlements, and colonizations, the new people came as the offset of a nation. The Company in India does not exist as a national colony. In effect and substance nobody can go thither that does not go in its service. The English in India are nothing but a seminary for the succession of officers. They are a nation of placemen; they are a commonwealth without a people; they are a state made up wholly of magistrates. There is nothing to be in propriety called people, to watch, to inspect, to balance against the power of office. The power of office, so far as the English nation is concerned, is the sole power in the country: the consequence of which is, that, being a kingdom of magistrates, what is commonly called the *esprit du corps* is strong in it. This spirit of the body predominates equally in all its parts; by which the members must consider themselves as having a common interest, and that common interest separated both from that of the country which sent them out and from that of the country in which they act. No control upon them exists,—none, I mean, in persons who understand their language, who understand their manners, or can apply their conduct to the laws. Therefore, in a body so constituted, confederacy is easy, and has been general. Your Lordships are not to expect that that should happen in such a body which never happened in any body or corporation,—that is, that they should, in any instance, be a proper check and control upon themselves. It is not in the nature of things. The fundamental principle of the whole of the East India Company's system is monopoly, in some sense or other. The same principle predominates in the service abroad and the service at home; and both systems are united into one, animated with the same spirit, that is with the corporate spirit. The whole, taken together, is such as has not been seen in the examples of the Moors, the Portuguese, the Spaniards, the Romans,—in no old, in no recent examples. The Dutch may resemble it, but they have not an empire properly so denominated. By means of this peculiar circumstance it has not been difficult for Mr. Hastings to embody abuse, and to put himself at the head of a regular system of corruption.

Another circumstance in that service is deserving of notice. Except in the highest parts of all, the emoluments of office do not in any degree correspond with the trust, nor the nature of the office with its name. In other official systems, the style, in general, is above the function; here it is the reverse. Under the name of junior merchant, senior merchant, writer, and other petty appellations of the counting-house, you have magistrates of high dignity, you have administrators of revenues truly royal, you have judges, civil, and in some respects criminal, who pass judgment upon the greatest properties of a great country. The legal public emoluments that belong to them are very often so inadequate to the real dignity of the character, that it is impossible, almost absolutely impossible, for the subordinate parts of it, which, though subordinate, are stations of power, to exist, as Englishmen, who look at a fortune to be enjoyed at home as their ultimate object, and to exist in a state of perfect incorruption in that service.

In some parts of Europe, it is true that the greatest situations are often attended with but little emolument; yet still they are filled. Why? Because reputation, glory, fame, the esteem, the love, the tears of joy which flow from happy sensibility, the honest applauses of a grateful country, sometimes pay the cares, anxieties, and toils which wait on great situations in the commonwealth; and in these they pay in money what cannot be paid in fame and reputation. It is the reverse in the service of the India Company.

Thomas Fowell Buxton

12. THE AFRICAN SLAVE TRADE AND ITS REMEDY

Under its late eighteenth-century leadership in Britain, France, and the United States, the movement against slave trading had been mainly concerned with the abolition of a very apparent colonial evil. When in 1807 Britain finally took the step of outlawing the trade, its erstwhile opponents were faced with the necessity of justifying the enforcement of this prohibition in economic as well as moral terms. Thomas Fowell Buxton (1786–1845), a leading abolitionist as well as a wealthy brewer, not only attempted, in the book cited below, to convince his countrymen that Africa offered great commercial opportunities, but invested much of his energies and fortune in dispatching an expedition to open up steam-ship trade on the Niger River in 1841. The effects of malaria brought about the total failure of this first effort, although Nigerian commerce was eventually established, with more complex political results than Buxton had anticipated.

But what is the true remedy? It cannot be too deeply engraven upon the minds of British statesmen, that it is beyond our power to rescue Africa, if the burthen is to fall wholly and permanently on ourselves. It is not the partial aid, lent by a distant nation, but the natural and healthy exercise of her own energies, which will ensure success. We cannot *create* a remedy; but, if it be true that this remedy already exists, and that nothing is wanting but its right application —if Africa possesses within herself vast, though as yet undeveloped resources—we may be competent to achieve the much less onerous task of calling forth her powers, and enabling her to stand alone, relying upon the strength of her own native sinews. The work will be done, when her population shall be sufficiently enlightened to arrive at the conviction, (grounded on what their eyes see, and their hands handle,) that the wealth readily to be obtained from peaceful industry, surpasses the slender and precarious profits of rapine.

Our system hitherto has been to obtain the co-operation of European powers, while we have paid very little attention to what might be done in Africa itself, for the suppression of the Slave Trade. Our efforts in that direction have been few, faint, and limited to isolated spots, and those by no means well chosen. To me it appears that the converse of this policy would have offered greater probabilities of success; that, while no reasonable expectations can be entertained of overturning this gigantic evil through the agency and with the concurrence of the civilized world, there is a well-founded hope, amounting almost to a certainty, that this object may be attained through the medium and with the concurrence of Africa herself. If, instead of our expensive and fruitless negotiations with Portugal, we had been, during the last twenty

The African Slave Trade and its Remedy (London, 1840), 264–69.

years, engaged in extending our intercourse with the nations of Africa, unfolding to them the capabilities of her soil, and the inexhaustible store of wealth which human labor might derive from its cultivation, and convincing them that the Slave Trade alone debars them from enjoying a vastly more affluent supply of our valuable commodities, and if we had leagued ourselves with them to suppress that baneful traffic, which is their enemy even more than it is ours, there is reason to believe that Africa would not have been what Africa is, in spite of all our exertions — one universal den of desolation, misery, and crime.

Why do I despair of winning the hearty co-operation of those European powers who now encourage or connive at the Slave Trade? I answer, because we have no sufficient bribe to offer. The secret of their resistance is the 180 per cent profit which attaches to the Slave Trade. This is a temptation which we cannot outbid. It has been, and it will be, the source of their persevering disregard of the claims of humanity, and of their contempt for the engagements, however solemn, which they have contracted with us.

But why do I entertain a confident persuasion that we may obtain the cordial concurrence of the African powers? Because the Slave Trade is not their gain, but their loss. It is their ruin, because it is capable of demonstration, that, but for the Slave Trade, the other trade of Africa would be increased fifty or a hundred-fold. Because central Africa now receives in exchange for all her exports, both of people and productions, less than half a million of imports, one-half of which may be goods of the worst description, and a third made up of arms and ammunition. What a wretched return is this, for the productions of so vast, so fertile, so magnificent a territory! Take the case of central Africa; the insignificance of our trade with it is forcibly exhibited by contrasting the whole return from thence, with some single article of no great moment which enters Great Britain. The feathers received at Liverpool from Ireland reach an amount exceeding all the productions of central Africa; the eggs from France and Ireland exceed one-half of it; while the value of pigs from Ireland into the port of Liverpool is three times as great as the whole trade of Great Britain in the productions of the soil of central Africa. What an exhibition does this give of the ruin which the Slave Trade entails on Africa! Can it be doubted that, with the extinction of that blight, there would arise up a commerce which would pour into Africa European articles of a vastly superior quality, and to a vastly superior amount?

If it be true that Africa, would be enriched, and that her population would enjoy, in multiplied abundance, those commodities, for the acquisition of which she now incurs such intense misery, the one needful thing, in order to induce them to unite with us in repressing the Slave Trade, is, to convince them that they will gain by selling the productive labor of the people, instead of the people themselves.

My first object, then, is to show that Africa possesses within herself the means of obtaining, by fair trade, a greater quantity of our goods than she now receives from the Slave Trade; and, secondly, to point out how this truth may be made plain to the African nations. I have further to prove, that Great Britain, and other countries (for the argument applies as much to them as to us), have an interest in the question only inferior to that of Africa, and that if we cannot be persuaded to suppress the Slave Trade for the fear of God, or in pity to man, it ought to be done for the lucre of gain.

The importance of Africa, as a vast field of European commerce, though it has been frequently adverted to, and its advantages distinctly pointed out by those who have visited that part of the world, has not hitherto sufficiently engaged public attention, or led to any great practical results. It is, perhaps, not difficult to account for the apathy which has been manifested on this subject — Africa has a bad name; its climate is represented, and not altogether unjustly, as pestilential, and destructive of European life; its population as barbarous and ignorant, indolent and cruel—more addicted to predatory warfare than to the arts of peace; and its interior as totally inaccessible to European enterprise. With the exception of a few spots, such as Sierra Leone, the Gambia, the Senegal, &c., its immensely extended line of coast is open to the ravages and demoralization of the Slave Trade, and the devastating incursions of pirates. The difficulties connected with the establishment of a legitimate commerce with Africa may be traced principally to these circumstances; and could they be removed, by the removal of their cause, the obstacles arising from climate—the supposed character of its people—and the difficulty of access to the interior, would be easily overcome.

Legitimate commerce would put down the Slave Trade, by demonstrating the superior value of man as a laborer on the soil, to man as an object of merchandise; and if conducted on wise and equitable principles, might be the precursor, or rather the attendant, of civilization, peace, and Christianity, to the unenlightened, warlike, and heathen tribes who now so fearfully prey on each other, to supply the slave-markets of the New World. In this view of the subject, the merchant, the philanthropist, the patriot, and the Christian, may unite; and should the Government of this country lend its powerful influence in organizing a commercial system of just, liberal, and comprehensive principles—guarding the rights of the native on the one hand, and securing protection to the honest trader on the other,—a blow would be struck at the nefarious traffic in human beings, from which it could not recover; and the richest blessings would be conferred on Africa, so long desolated and degraded by its intercourse with the basest and most iniquitous part of mankind.

The present condition of Africa in relation to commerce is deplorable.

The whole amount of goods exported direct from Great Britain to all Africa is considerably within one million sterling.

In the year 1835, the declared value of British and Irish produce and manufactures exported to the whole of Africa was £917,726.

Central Africa possesses within itself everything from which commerce springs. No country in the world has nobler rivers, or more fertile soil; and it contains a population of fifty millions.

This country, which ought to be amongst the chief of our customers, takes from us only to the value of £312,938 of our manufactures, £101,104 of which are made up of the value of arms and ammunition, and lead and shot.

John Philip

13. PROTECTION OF SOUTH AFRICAN NATIVES

While domestic antislavery advocates such as Buxton and later missionary-explorers of Africa like David Livingstone saw no conflict between liberal expansion and philanthropy, for humanitarians in already established colonies like Algeria, Australia, and South Africa, the conflict between settler and native interests was all too apparent. John Philip (1775–1851), chief representative of the fundamentalist London Missionary Society (to which Livingstone also belonged) in South Africa, became notorious for his defense of the local Bantu population (here referred to by the not yet derogatory term, "Caffres") against both British and Afrikaner settlers. In a period of dogmatic laissez-faire beliefs, Philip makes quite clear his desire for more direct government intervention beyond the existing South African frontiers.

On the subject of it being desirable that the Caffres should be retained as British subjects, I have long made up my mind. The question is not with me what might be, had we such men as Governor as William Penn, but what kind of Governor we have to expect in the ordinary course of things, and as the affairs of our Colony have been managed, and will be managed for a long time to come. *The Caffres cannot otherwise be saved from annihilation.* Were the Colony surrounded by belts of Native Tribes under the British Government, nations would get time to form beyond us, but no Tribes will be allowed time to rise into civilization and independence on our borders, if they are in immediate contact with our colonists. We never could have done anything with the Griquas, if it had not been that our work had arrived at a certain point before the Colony was extended to the Great River, and even notwithstanding their distance from us, nothing but a peculiar combination of circumstances could have saved, or can even now save, them. . . .

Contiguous nations never can be independent of each other without a balance of power, and there can be no such balance betwixt this Colony and the uncivilized tribes upon our borders. This fact must be obvious to any man acquainted with the Philosophy of History, and may be seen with half an eye by any one who is accustomed to look at men and things in the Colony as they are. Barbarous nations may rise to civilization and independence situated in the midst of nations in similar circumstances with themselves, and even in that case it must require long periods of time, and they must work their way to those points through great difficulties and much bloodshed; but in immediate contact with civilized nations—never! It may do very well to produce a momentary excitement on an English platform to talk of raising up civil Governments in Africa, as a man

Letter from Philip to James Read, October 19, 1835, from W. M. MacMillan, *Bantu, Boer and Briton* (Oxford, 1963), pp. 165–166. Reprinted by permission of the Clarendon Press, Oxford.

would light one candle by the gleam of another; but woe to the cause of missions and humanity in Africa if our missionaries beyond a certain point have no better light to guide them in their labours. When Mr. Campbell one day told me that Kok and the Griquas promised to keep his laws, and he wondered that they did not keep their promise, I asked him how long the Israelites kept their promise made at the foot of Mount Sinai—"all these things will we do." . . .

The more silent we are on the present state of things on the frontier the better; the question has become now so complicated that it will require more evidence than certain persons possess to know what should be done. Your wisdom now is to be careful to note down facts, and to avoid giving opinions. An experiment has been set up, and we must confine our attention to the results. . . .

Yours very truly,

John Philip

Louis Faidherbe

14. A HUMANITARIAN REGIME IN FRENCH SENEGAL

By training a military engineer, by experience in Algeria and the West Indies a colonialist, and by ideology a crusader against slavery, Louis Léon César Faidherbe (1818–1889) was the first major exponent outside British India of the new school of authoritarian-humanitarian imperialism. During his ten years (1854–1864) as Governor of Senegal in West Africa, Faidherbe expanded the areas and means of French control, established an export economy based upon free African peasant growers, and initiated a system of native education. The following letter, threatening resignation, was written in 1858 when Faidherbe learned that the Paris government planned to recruit Senegalese Africans by force as indentured laborers for the West Indies. The measure was repealed and Faidherbe remained in Senegal.

To the Minster of the Navy and Colonies:

During two months at Medina I have exhausted all my remaining physical and moral strength in order to put the affairs of the colony back in order.

Today I am no longer in a position to remain at my post and I consequently have the honor to ask you to allow me to be relieved as Governor of Senegal. I trust that I leave the colony in a reasonably satisfactory condition, and I am persuaded that France will derive both pride and material benefits from its possession, providing that the rule of conduct continues to be the interest of the natives. For this it is necessary that there be governors who have neither repugnance, aversion, nor scorn for these races which, as little as they are favored by nature from the viewpoint of human perfection, still merit some sympathy and who can, without being forced by means contrary to justice and humanity, produce on their own soil that which will amply recompense the European peoples and merchants who are really interested in them, who protect them, and who direct them with charity.

Louis Faidherbe, *Sénégal, la France dan l' Afrique Occidental* (Paris, 1889), 386.

Eduard Douwes Dekker

15. MAX HAVELAAR: A NOVEL OF PROTEST ON DUTCH INDONESIA

Generally in Europe the literary cult of the "noble savage" belongs to the later eighteenth century and was often associated with the antislavery movement. *Max Havelaar* (1860) by Multatuli ("I have suffered much"), pseudonym for Eduard Douwes Dekker (1820–1887), belongs stylistically to this genre, especially in its sentimental subplot about two youthful Javanese lovers, the epilogue of which is presented here. Douwes Dekker, a former Indonesian administrator, did, however, know what he was talking about, and his book, apart from becoming a best seller in several languages, helped bring about more humanitarian intervention by the Dutch colonial authorities into the harsh, forced cultivation system of Indonesia.

I have made the conclusion of the story of *Saïdyah* shorter than I might have done if I had felt inclined to a description of horrors. The reader will note how I dwelt on the account of my hero's watch under the *ketapan*, as though I feared the approach of the grievous dénouement, on which aversion made me touch only lightly. And yet this was not my intention when I began to write about *Saïdyah*. For at the outset I feared that I should need stronger colouring to move the reader with the description of such strange conditions. But little by little I realized that it would be an insult to my public to believe that I ought to have spilt more blood on my picture.

And yet I might have done so, for I have before me documents ... but no: I will rather make a confession.

Yes, a confession, reader! I do not know whether *Saïdyah* loved *Adinda*. Nor whether he went to *Batavia*. Nor whether he was murdered in the *Lampongs* with Dutch bayonets. I do not know whether his father succumbed in consequence of the *rattan*-scourging he received for having left *Badoor* without a passport. I do not know whether *Adinda* counted the moons by notches in her rice-block. . . .

All this I do *not* know!

But I know *more* than all this. I know *and I can prove* that there were many *Adindas* and many *Saïdyahs*, and that *what is fiction in a particular case is truth in general*. I have said that I can give the names of persons who, like the parents of *Saïdyah* and *Adinda*, were driven out of their country by oppression. It is not my object to give in this work statements such as would be required before a Court of Justice sitting to pronounce a verdict on the manner in which Dutch authority is exercised in India, statements that would only have force as evidence for those who had the patience to read them through with attention and interest, which cannot be expected from a public that reads for di-

Reprinted by permission of the publisher from Max Havelaar by Multatuli, translated by I. W. Siebenhaar, pp. 268–270. Copyright, 1927 by Alfred A. Knopf, Inc. Renewed, 1954.

version. For this reason, instead of dry names of persons and places, with dates, instead of a copy *of the list of thefts and extortions which lies before me*, instead of these I have endeavoured to give a sketch of what *may* pass in the hearts of the poor people who are robbed of that which has to serve for their maintenance, or I have even only allowed this to be guessed, fearing that I might be too greatly mistaken in delineating emotions which I never experienced.

But as to the *main point*? Oh, that I were but summoned to prove what I have written! Oh, that they might say: "You have invented this *Saïdyah* . . . he never sang that song . . . no *Adinda* ever lived at *Badoor!*" But then also, might it be said with the power and the desire to do justice, as soon as I had given the proofs that I am not a slanderer!

Is the parable of the good Samaritan a lie, because perhaps no robbed traveller was ever received in a Samaritan house? Is the parable of the Sower a lie, because no husbandman would cast his seed on a rock? Or —coming down to a level nearer my book— may one deny the truth which is the main point in *Uncle Tom's Cabin*, because perhaps there never was an *Evangeline*? Shall it be said to the writer of that immortal plea— immortal, not on account of art or talent, but because of its *tendency* and the *impression* made by it—shall it be said to her: "You have lied, the slaves are not ill-treated, for . . . there is untruth in your book: it is a novel"? Was not she also compelled to give, instead of an enumeration of dry facts, a story that clothed those facts, so that the realization of the need of reform might penetrate to the hearts? Would her book have been read, if she had given it in the form of a court-case? Is it her fault—or mine—that the truth, in order to gain access, has so often to borrow the guise of a lie?

And to others who will perhaps contend that I have idealized *Saïdyah* and his love, I must put the question: "How can you know

this?" For is it not a fact that only very few Europeans consider it worth while to condescend to an observation of the emotions of the coffee- and sugar-producing machines we call "Natives"? But even suppose their remarks were well-founded, he that adduces such considerations as a proof against the main tendency of my book gives me a great victory. For, translated, these considerations are as follows: "The evil you combat does not exist, or not in so high a degree, *because* the Native is not like your *Saïdyah* . . . there is in the ill-treatment of the Javanese not so great an evil as would be the case if you had drawn your *Saïdyah* more accurately. This Soondanese does not sing such songs, loves not thus, feels not thus, and therefore. . . ."

No, Minister for the Colonies, no, Governor-General retired from active service, it is not *that* which you have to prove! You have to prove that the population is not ill-treated, apart from the question whether or no there are sentimental *Saïdyahs* among the population. Or would you dare maintain that it was lawful to steal buffaloes from people who do *not* love, who sing *no* melancholy songs, who are *not* sentimental?

If an attack were made from a literary point of view, I should defend the accuracy of my drawing of *Saïdyah*; but as a question of politics I would at once concede any strictures on this accuracy, in order to prevent the main argument from being shifted to wrong premises. It is all the same to me whether I am considered an incompetent artist, provided the admission be made that the ill-treatment of the native is: OUT-RAGEOUS! For that is the word used in the note of Havelaar's predecessor, and shown to Controller Verbrugge: *a note which I have in front of me*.

But I have other proof! And this is fortunate, for even Havelaar's predecessor might have been mistaken.

Alas! if *he* was mistaken, he was severely punished for his mistake. He was *murdered*.

A MODERN SUMMARY

Duignan and Gann

16. IMPERIALISM IN THE MIDDLE OF THE NINETEENTH CENTURY

Along similar but broader lines than Robinson and Gallagher (see selection 7 above), the authors of the following passage attempt to explain how a weak European interest in colonies during the liberal era could nevertheless maintain and even increase the substance of empire. While Duignan and Gann do not directly defend imperialism, they strike back at some modern anti-imperialists by pointing out how even the most radical and humanitarian thinkers of the mid-nineteenth century endorsed the imposition of European values upon alien peoples. Both these authors are members of the Hoover Institution of Stanford University, where they have specialized in the history of European penetration of Africa.

The first of the great social issues in the colonies that exercised the minds of Europe was slavery. The abolitionist movement revealed many features which characterized subsequent imperial reform campaigns. Abolitionism was linked to a growing interest in social welfare at home, to a new spirit of sensitivity to evils long taken for granted, to social conflicts within the metropolitan countries, and to rivalries among the European powers. The campaign began with an attack against the legality of the seaborne slave trade. Denmark made an honorable start by outlawing slave traffic in 1792. After a long struggle the British prohibited slave traffic to their subjects in 1807 and subsequently used their diplomatic and naval influence to prevent foreigners from making profits from the trade.

The Humanitarians then turned upon slavery as a domestic institution. The abolitionists now had a good deal of published material to draw on; they started their campaign at a time when conditions in the slave islands were not quite as bad as they had been in the past. Helped by a new climate of opinion, the British abolitionists won all along the line, and in the 1830s slavery was eliminated from all British possessions. The British compensated slaveholders in the West Indies and the Cape; they also made extensive grants to Spain and Portugal in return for engagements to end the traffic from their dominions south of the Equator, shouldered heavy financial responsibilities in founding Sierra Leone as a settlement for freemen, and disbursed vast amounts of money to patrol the coasts of Africa.

British policy backed philanthropy with cash and played a major share in putting an end to slave commerce. France followed suit in 1848, when the newly established republic abolished slavery in all French territories. The final elimination of seaborne slave traffic resolved more and more into diplomatic negotiations concerning the right of

From P. Duignan and L. H. Gann, *Burden of Empire: An Appraisal of Western Colonialism in Africa South of the Sahara* (New York, 1967), pp. 6–9, with omissions. Reprinted by permission of Frederick A. Praeger, Inc. and the Pall Mall Press Ltd. (London, 1968).

search and maritime policing, an issue too technical to arouse the same fervor that abolitionism occasioned in the past.

In the 1830s and 1840s the problems of white-settlement territories moved more into the intellectual foreground. Many Victorian reformers thought of such countries as Canada, Australia, and New Zealand in terms of solving Britain's domestic difficulties. Great Britain was supposedly overpopulated; future generations would not be able to feed all the surplus mouths at home. Britain possessed a more numerous working class without property than any other country. Revolution seemed to lurk round the corner. In 1834 Edward Gibbon Wakefield, a hardheaded middle-class optimist, predicted that "if it were to come to a trial of strength between the two parties [the rich and the poor] in open warfare (which God forbid!), the result must inevitably be favourable to the great majority."

There were, of course, also military factors of a more technical kind which seemed to favor the cause of insurrection at the time. Town-bred insurgents, armed with muskets and entrenched in narrow, winding streets, formed a greater potential threat against organized armies than they did toward the end of the century, when superior staff work and transportation, repeating rifles, and better artillery swept away the European revolutionary's barricades as effectively as the African warrior's wood-and-mud stockade. Wakefield, a Radical reformer, thus thought of settlement colonies as a kind of safety valve for a mother country threatened by potential popular violence. . . . Colonization, however, would succeed only under a limited form of self-government. Remote control from London, feebly and incompetently exercised, would never work. Privileged officials appointed from home (the "mother country") might give themselves the airs of demigods; but they could not in fact vie with the better class of settler in qualities of mind, manners, and morals.

These ideas exercised great influence in Britain; they seemed to dovetail with the need for economy and even appealed to the very people whom the "colonial reformers" lampooned as "Little Englanders." The British subsidized overseas settlement. They also moved away from older policies of imperial centralization which their fathers derived from the supposed lesson of the American War of Independence—that concessions to colonists only encourage revolution. In 1837 an abortive rising in Canada discredited traditional policies, and reform became the order of the day.

Responsible government probably saved the empire. But the influence of the reformers should not be exaggerated. Their activities were confined to a few years, their idea of limited local self-government to some extent miscarried, and the remnants of imperial control over such things as crown lands and tariffs crumbled away. Colonies moreover seemed expensive. The British, preoccupied with expanding their industries at home, aimed at low taxation, laissez-faire, and limited public expenditure, but this policy could never be fully carried out. The needs of economy conflicted with humanitarian demands and the ambitions of local governors in, say, Hong Kong or the Gold Coast. Slavery was put down, but slave owners required compensation and naval patrols to track down slave traders proved expensive. Subsidized emigration was expected to solve domestic problems, but few operations cost more money than settling farmers on a strange soil. The frontier, whether in New Zealand or South Africa, also produced perennial military problems. The British treasury consistently advocated retrenchment in West and South Africa and the restriction of imperial power to strategically vital areas. Many missionaries and traders, on the other hand, wanted the imperial power to assert its authority in the distant interior; in South Africa, for instance, missionaries called for men and money to protect the African tribes inland against Boer settlers and also against the depredations of other African raiders. The British thus careened between these two opposing policies, with the result that imperial taxpayers in the end had to disburse even bigger funds.

* * *

In 1833, argued an early Victorian economist, the annual cost of empire stood at over £2,300,000. British government revenue during the 1830s and 1840s never exceeded £50 million a year, and every class in society was clamoring against what it regarded as the excessive weight of taxation. Yet, continued the expert, Britain owed none of its prosperity to colonial possessions. The country derived infinitely more advantage from its intercourse with the United States. The American trade had no drawbacks; Britain was not obliged to purchase American commodities which it could obtain more cheaply elsewhere, nor was it forced to keep up armaments for the protection of extensive regions on the other side of the Atlantic.

Britain, confident in its industrial and maritime superiority, thus turned toward free trade. . . . and the British settler colonies began to lose popularity when they departed from this principle.

On the Continent public interest in overseas territories remained even slighter. The French old colonial empire owed too much to the Bourbons' desire for prestige and royal dignity, to past efforts of the Catholic Church, and to an outworn doctrine of mercantilist control to command the loyalty of the nation. Although the French Revolutionary and Napoleonic wars deprived France of the bulk of its transmaritime possessions, these blows injured none but a small group of shipowners, merchants, and planters. The great majority of Frenchmen, preoccupied with political struggles at home and military campaigns abroad, got used to having no colonies. The economic foundations of the colonial empire crumbled. Sugar made from European sugar beets competed ever more successfully with the colonial product made from West Indian cane. In addition, the planters suffered from a serious manpower problem, as the decline of the slave trade deprived the sugar grow-

ers of imported labor and slavery finally disappeared.

Abolitionism, however, never became a popular movement in France capable of evoking the same interest in colonial affairs as in Britain. The French antislavery movement was led mainly by secular-minded intellectuals; one of its principal advocates was the Abbé Grégoire, a former petrê constitutionel, but his name held no appeal for the Catholic masses. Abolitionist enthusiasm was strong among French Protestants, and they produced a number of outstanding missionary statesmen who generally took an Anglophile line, but Protestantism remained numerically weak. Some of the outstanding Protestant pioneers of the Gospel, such as Francois Coillard, employed their energies in British spheres of influence; Protestantism did not make any great impact on public opinion at home, and the "nonconformist conscience" hardly affected decision making in the colonies.

Otherwise French governments were subject to many of the same pressures that affected the British. There were the exigencies of a "turbulent frontier" in Senegal; there were demands for expansion from local traders such as Victor Régis, a well-connected Marseilles merchant on the African West Coast. Local governors sometimes managed to impose their views on Paris. French governments in general would try to satisfy Catholic missions and strategically placed trading interests, but France as yet lacked any broad currents of public opinion with an interest in tropical Africa. When high policy demanded that sectional interests should be overridden, this was done without qualms. An important commercial treaty with Britain in 1860 thus abolished duties on most imported raw materials. This ended many long-established commercial privileges affecting commodities such as Senegalese gum, a merchandise important in the local West African setting but of small account for French trade as a whole.

French governments were, however, influenced more than the British by their citizenry's supposed thirst for martial glory.

47

Napoleon I's successors wrongly imagined that they were still expected to win victories on the battlefield. They failed to realize that the Napoleonic legend was now a weapon for the domestic opposition rather than a desire for warlike successes. Charles X thus meant to gain popularity for his dynasty by seizing Algeria in 1830; he succeeded only in giving employment to the army by embroiling French troops in endless guerrilla wars. In the eyes of British contemporaries, Algeria became a symbol of imperial folly. Louis Philippe sought prestige in protecting French missions in the Far East; Napoleon III sent soldiers to the Crimea, Italy, Mexico, China, and Cochinchina but never gained his fundamental objective of consolidating power at home; in the end he endangered the very basis of his monarchy.

The Germans showed even less interest in colonial affairs than the French, although missionary enthusiasm did strike a chord in the hearts of the pious. German sailing ships became a common sight around the world; in Zanzibar, for instance, the Sultan concluded a trade agreement with the Hanseatic cities of Northern Germany in 1859. Emigrants left the Fatherland for the Americas. However, concern with colonies as such, remained negligible. Germany remained divided. Austria and Prussia, the two great Germanic powers, were concerned only with Continental problems. The duel between Hohenzollern and Hapsburg, the struggle for unification, and constitutional and social conflicts at home absorbed all Germany's energies.

Throughout Western Europe interest in colonial affairs thus remained confined to a limited number of specialists. The most powerful lobbies perhaps were missionary societies, whose middle- and lower-middle-class supporters provided funds for mission stations and avidly read evangelical publications. Some missionaries and humanitarian merchants dreamed of opening Africa to the Gospel and to Christian commercial enterprise, arguing quite correctly that only legitimate traffic in tropical produce like palm oil and cotton would do away with the ravages of the slave trade and give Africans alternative export goods.

Geographers, often associated with missionary enterprises, represented another intellectual pressure group. Organizations such as the African Association, formed in Britain in 1788 with the special object of exploring the interior, the Société de Géographie de France, or the German Centralverein für Handelsgeographie, founded in 1863, all justified their activities by pointing to the practical utility of their work.

* * *

Other special-interest groups played their part. The French army had a vested interest in the expansion of Africa's military frontier and was sometimes able to shape policy with scant reference to its political superiors in Paris. A number of British, German, and French mercantile groups, interested in tropical goods like cocoa and palm oil, had a natural concern with colonial questions. However, the great majority of Europeans stood aloof. Except for geographers and specialists in tropical medicine, European scholars displayed relatively little interest in empire matters, while social critics remained primarily concerned with domestic affairs. Even Karl Marx, who knew a great deal about British colonial history, had little to say on the imperial questions of his time. He linked the earlier stages of "primitive capital accumulation" with colonial expansion, which, with all its attendant cruelties, had helped to usher in the rosy dawn of capitalism, and castigated Wakefield's settlement scheme on the grounds that Wakefield wished to manufacture wageworkers. Marx's sympathies went to white settlers in the Antipodes, though not to Maori or Australian aborigines, for whom he found no word of sympathy.

In some respects Marx even defended the cause of colonialism in India. The British might be actuated by the vilest of self-interests in initiating a social revolution on the subcontinent, but whatever their crimes, they were a tool of history: "English interference . . . [in India], produced the greatest, and to speak the truth, the only social revolution ever heard of in Asia." They broke up traditional forms of society and smashed Indian domestic industry. They also began to regenerate a backward society by establishing for the first time a political unity, destined to be strengthened and perpetuated by the electric telegraph. The British built a modern "native army"; they introduced a free press and private property in land; they created an educated Indian class, endowed with the requirements for government and imbued with Western science; they provided India with railways; they initiated regular and rapid communications with Europe through steam vessels. Therefore they would be unable to prevent the growth of modern industry; factory work would in turn break down hereditary division of labor, the base of the Indian caste system, and thereby usher in a happier future for the subcontinent.

Marx believed that in such a case the bourgeoisie were unwitting agents of a great dialectical process whereby capitalism conquered the world and destroyed more backward forms of social organization, such as feudalism, before it perished in turn of its own inner contradictions and gave way to socialism. This view in one respect paralleled that of such humanitarian bourgeois reformers as David Livingstone, a great medical missionary and explorer, who looked to "commerce and Christianity," to steam transport, missionary propaganda, and permanent white settlement, to spread civilization in Africa and do away with the slave trade and depredations of petty warlords. Marx was, in fact, as convinced of Germany's cultural superiority over the Slavs as British colonial reformers were of their mission to Anglify backward races, white or black. Neither Marx nor Livingstone reproached Western capitalists for being too warlike, or too interventionist, or expansionist-minded. Livingstone felt ashamed that his country did not do more to put down Arab slave traders in East Africa and called down God's blessing on anyone

who would. Marx did not anticipate a new imperialist scramble, and far from scolding the Western bourgeoisie for being colonialists he reproached the British and French capitalists for their timid and pacifist policy concerning tsarist Russia.

In summary, few European thinkers of the day thought that Western colonization was wrong in itself; hardly any were afraid of making what it has become the fashion to call ethnocentric value judgments. None predicted a scramble for colonies or thought that overseas issues would ever dominate future policies. Publications on colonial questions remained limited in number, and colonization remained an affair for specialists, in which Europeans as a whole took little interest.

This state of affairs continued until about the beginning of the 1870s and later gave rise to a strange doctrine of discontinuity. Both Marxist and nationalist historians subsequently discovered a caesura in European development. From the 1870s on, Europe supposedly began to turn outward, embarking on a new career of conquest overseas which contrasted with the more pacific, laissez-faire, free-trading past. There was, in fact, no such chasm. British and French power during the period from 1815 to 1870 simply continued to expand as of old, and the doctrine of discontinuity fitted only Germany and Italy, two recently united nations. British politicians of the mid-Victorian era might fling the epithet "Little Englander" at their rivals but no responsible British statesman of the period seriously meant to break up the empire. Colonial reformers might proudly maintain their stand for imperial unity, but they usually exaggerated the differences between themselves and their opponents, who basically shared their assumptions.

Early Victorian Englishmen enjoyed an unparalleled naval and industrial superiority over their competitors; access to overseas markets were freer than ever before or since. British governments accordingly saw no reason to enlarge the bounds of formal empire and thereby incur more expenses if they could avoid it. Indirect influence and universal free trade remained the ideals, though the Redcoats often had to intervene in practice. "Native" governments might prove hostile to British trade, or they might not be able to protect person and property. British arms constantly had to be used on the turbulent frontiers of empire, either to protect existing commitments or to establish what soldiers regarded as a strategically more favorable boundary line. The search for a defensible frontier itself was likely to provoke trouble.

* * *

Although no European state deliberately aimed at massive expansion overseas, the number and extent of European acquisitions kept going up. The territories brought under white sway between 1815 and 1870, the supposedly preimperial era, fill an impressive list. Britain's Indian empire continued to grow; Assam, the Punjab, Lower Burma, Jansi, Nagpur, and Oudh all succumbed to the British raj. Pioneers pushed their way deeper into Canada and Australia, while settlers and Redcoats fought the Maori in New Zealand. The British acquired a chain of bases for their fleet, including Singapore, Aden, and Hong Kong. In Africa the British held on to the Cape in the post-Napoleonic peace settlement. They annexed Natal in 1843, turned the Gold Coast into a crown colony in the same year, and seized Lagos Island in 1861. British soldiers in Africa fought as far afield as the eastern Cape and Abyssinia.

The French conducted a long and bitter war in Algeria, which ended only with the surrender of Abd-el-Kader in 1847; General Louis Léon César Faidherbe vastly extended French power in Senegal during his governorship in 1854 to 1865. Even the Portuguese tightened their grip on some outlying possessions in Africa, and the Spaniards fought a war with Morocco and seized Tetuán in 1860. This expansion did not, however, make a very profound impression on the consciousness of Europe. Systematizers have been unable to find a common historical pattern for a movement composed of so many different facets. Hong Kong was acquired as a trading base with a specifically economic function; Queensland was born of Australian internal settlement; acquisitions such as the Punjab in India or Basutoland in South Africa stood out as evidence that an existing empire would always tend to expand its boundary against more backward communities until it met with some immovable political or geographical obstacle. Social theorists usually had only a limited interest in these matters; they preferred to think about such vital questions nearer home as German or Italian unity, the progress of industrialization in Europe, or the future distribution of power between the social classes. Europe therefore remained inward-looking, and the great change in its intellectual climate had to await the last quarter of the nineteenth century.

II. *The New Imperialism: 1874-1919*

For nearly one hundred years of the liberal era, the acquisition of colonies had been officially condemned in Europe as economically wasteful and politically reprehensible. Suddenly, in the last quarter of the nineteenth century an almost hysterical competition broke out among all the western powers for the annexation of hitherto obscure areas of Africa, Asia, and the South Seas. This new overseas expansion represents less of a departure from immediately previous developments than is suggested by much of the drama with which it was surrounded. Nevertheless, the accelerated pace of formal colonization and the self-conscious tone of both vindication and denunciation that accompanied the entire process, must be treated as a distinct and significant phase in the history of imperialism.

The new tone emerged initially from the writings of relatively respectable scholars such as the French economic geographer Leroy-Beaulieu (1), the British historian Seeley (2) and the American naval historian Mahan (3). None of these men really urged the acquisition of new colonies—particularly the paternalist dependencies which emerged from late nineteenth-century imperialism—but they all directed the attention of their many readers to the importance and value of colonial empires.

The new colonial conquests took place mainly in areas distinguished less for their economic attractiveness than for their critical role in a complex and often remote system of nationalistic and strategic interests. In part it was the intrusion of latecomers, who identified national self-realization with the possession of colonies, which forced Britain, France, and even Portugal to take a more active interest in their informal spheres of overseas control. Among the earliest, most aggressive, and possibly shrewdest of these new imperialists was Leopold II of the Belgians (4). In the abandonment of mutual imperialist self-restraint among the great powers, however, a more decisive role was played by Germany, where the aspirations of such spokesmen as Carl Peters (5) finally received qualified support from Bismarck. Like Peters, the British archconquistador of this period, Cecil Rhodes (6), was given license to form a chartered company for the acquisition of new territories. Like Bismarck, Lord Salisbury, the contemporary British Prime Minister, wanted to achieve limited aims of colonial policy with a minimum of governmental expenditure.

Militarism also played its role in the new expansion. Professional officers such as the French Captain Marchand (7) sought colonial prizes with an ideological zeal which could not always maintain the support of state policy. Once the opportunity for movement was given, however, nonindustrial peoples found it difficult to offer effective resistance to the power of European armaments (8).

Responsible European statesmen, while necessarily involved in maneuvers for colonial annexation throughout this period, came relatively late and often unsuccessfully to any enthusiastic advocacy of such policies. Jules Ferry (9), while Prime Minister of France, had consistently weakened his domestic political position by the somewhat underhanded way in which he promoted expansion in Tunisia, West Africa, Indochina, and Madagascar. It was only after his second fall from power that he offered any systematic defense of these measures. The new imperialism was already well under way when Joseph Chamberlain (10) became British Colonial Secretary. Again, a delayed voter reaction against Chamberlain's aggressive South African policies as well as his unpopular scheme for an imperial tariff union helped to drive him and his party from office. Bülow (11), the only German Chancellor ever to win the close trust of Kaiser Wilhelm II, did so by playing up to a grandiose notion of *Weltpolitik*, which included colonialism. But here too, the issue was a second wave of annexations rather than the initiation of the process, and the diplomatic costs proved far in excess of the territorial gains. During America's first overseas imperialist venture, the 1898 war with Spain, Theodore Roosevelt (12) was still a relatively uninfluential figure, but his vigorous approval of this event was later translated with very great success into the imposition of informal United States hegemony upon the Caribbean.

The spectacular manner in which so many new territories were annexed in this period produced not only colonial enthusiasts, but also a highly effective rhetoric of anti-imperialism. On the very morrow of the Spanish American War, the Democratic party nominee for the United States Presidency, William Jennings Bryan (13), chose anti-imperialism as one of his major campaign issues. Ironically, what has come to be known as the "Marxist" interpretation of imperialism, i.e., that new colonies were founded as an outlet for an overaccumulation of finance capital, was given its widest circulation after the Anglo-Boer War by the non-Marxist British economist and publicist J. A. Hobson (14). Continental Marxist theorists, however, had independently arrived at similar conclusions, and during World War I Lenin (15) combined their studies with the simpler analysis of Hobson to produce what has become the official communist canon on the subject. Immediately after the war, Joseph Schumpeter (16), an Austrian economist and sociologist, developed the classic capitalist attack upon imperialism by identifying it with militarist groups that were unable to find a role in industrial society.

More recent scholars, whose work has been synthesized by Fieldhouse (17), tend to stress the continuity between the imperialism of the mid-nineteenth century and that of the late nineteenth century, thus rejecting the Hobson-Lenin thesis outright and playing down the sharp contrast between liberalism and imperialism posited by such writers as Bryan and Schumpeter.

THE IDEOLOGUES

Paul Leroy-Beaulieu

1. MODERN COLONIALISM

As professor of political and liberal sciences at the prestigious College de France, Paul Leroy-Beaulieu (1843-1916) was in a position, even at the relatively young age when he wrote the work cited here, to exercise considerable influence among French thinkers. While his book mainly discusses particular aspects of colonialism in extensive detail and provides only very ambivalent prescriptions, Leroy-Beaulieu did succeed in lending a new respectability to the entire subject by showing its compatibility with concurrent ideas of liberal economics and evolutionary sociology.

It is said that colonization began at the same time as the world; from a certain point of view, this may be true. The first man can, in certain respects, be considered as a colonist: emigration followed closely upon the formation of the first human family; the earth was populated only by stages, from one area to the next, by grace of that expansive force found in every society, no matter how small and how primitive it may be; also, thanks to that natural instinct, highly developed in certain individuals, which urges man towards adventure and the unknown. But emigration, the taking into possession of new soil and virgin country, does not suffice to constitute, in the true sense of the word, *colonization*. The latter is something greater and includes a different element. Emigration is a matter of instinct which belongs to all ages of societies; colonization is a matter of reflection, subject to rules, which can arise from only very advanced societies. Savages and barbarians sometimes, even often, emigrate; the successive invasion of the islands of Oceania by the Malaysian race is one among many proofs of this: only civilized peoples colonize.

While emigration and taking possession of new soil remain, generally, in the category of individual matters, colonization belongs incontestably to the category of social matters: it is one of the most elevated functions of societies which have arrived at an advanced state of civilization; it plays in the social order the same role which, in the order of the family, is played not only by procreation, but also by education. A society colonizes when, having itself arrived at a high degree of maturity and strength, there emanates from its womb a new society to which it gives birth, protection, and proper conditions for development and the attainment of virility. Colonization is one of the most complex and delicate phenomena of social physiology.

The comparison has often been made between a colony and a branch which is detached from a plant when its sap is rising and which is planted in newer, less exhausted, more fertile soil. The parallel here is ingenious, but cannot pass the test of closer investigation. While no real relation persists between the cutting and the plant from which it was detached, each one separately pursuing its development as marked out by

Paul Leroy-Beaulieu, *De la colonisation chez les peuples modernes* (Paris, Guilaumin, 1874).

the invariable laws of nature, there is between the society in a state of infancy and growth and the adult society which gave it birth a permanent exchange of influences, a reciprocity of services, a continuity of correspondences, in a word, a mutual dependence, which constitutes precisely that which it is convenient to call *colonization*.

* * *

With colonization, as with education itself, the principles have varied and have been transformed with the times; the conception of the relationship between the mother country and the colony were quite different in other periods from what they are today. In the early stages of modern colonization, the metropoles principally kept their own interests in mind and put the interests of their dependencies in second place; there was a sort of exploitation of the colony by the mother country, analogous to the exploitation of a child by its father in those societies which are not yet far advanced along the path of civilization, justice, and liberty. The colony remained in a perpetual minority; it belonged unconditionally to the metropole; it owed obedience and service in return for the protection which it received: a situation truly analogous to that of the son in the old Roman family law. Under the influence of progress in moral and political ideas, and also by a more just conception of the interests of the two parties, the principles have been modified: we have arrived at notions conforming more closely to natural right, which insists that all societies are equal to one another and none of them, no matter how small and how young, should be sacrificed to one which is older and greater.

* * *

CHAPTER III. COLONIAL TRADE AND ITS
UTILITY FOR THE METROPOLE

The great utility of colonies, as has been proven in the previous chapters, is not to serve as a dam for the overflow of the population of the metropole but is to give a major impulse to its commerce, to activate and encourage its industry, and to furnish the inhabitants of the mother country, industrialists, workers, and consumers, with an increase in profits, salaries, or goods. But, in accordance with the natural order of things, these advantages rising from the creation and prosperity of colonies are not limited to the metropoles alone, but extend to all the countries of the Old World, and it can thus be said that there is not a nation which does not draw benefits from this augmentation of the field of human productivity. Adam Smith believed also that it was necessary to distinguish between the general advantages which Europe, considered as a single vast country, drew from the colonies and the special advantages which each mother country drew from its particular colonies.

* * *

We have arrived at the end of this long study; we have no intention of closing it with a dithyramb. The facts are too evident to the eyes of any man of sense for it to be necessary to formulate them in resonant periods. Colonization is the expansive force of a people; it is their power of reproduction, it is their enlargement and multiplication through space, it is the submission of the universe, or of a large part, to their language, customs, ideas, and laws. A people which colonizes is a people which stretches forth the arch of their greatness and supremacy into the future. All the vital forces of a colonizing nation are increased by this overflow of their exuberant activity. From a material viewpoint, the number of individuals who constitute the race is augmented in unlimited proportions; there is an immeasurable growth in the quantity of new resources, new products, and equivalents in exchange, unknown up to now, which prove a stimulus to metropolitan industry; the field of employ for the capital of the metropole and the domain of exploitation opened up to the activity of its citizens are infinite. From the moral and intellectual viewpoint, this growth in the number and strength of human intellects, these diverse conditions where all intellects and all forces find places will multiply and diversify intellectual productivity. Who can deny that the literature, the arts, and the sciences of a race thus amplified acquire a resource which is not found among peoples of a more passive and sedentary nature? In the intellectual domain a phenomenon analogous to that which we have noted in the domain of industry is produced. . . . Is not Boston already a center of culture which rivals Paris, London, Edinburgh, or Berlin? From whatever viewpoint we look, be it restricted to the consideration of material prosperity and power, to political authority and influence, or, if we raise ourselves to the contemplation of intellectual grandeur, we arrive at one word of indisputable truth: the people who colonizes the most is the first among peoples; if it is not so today, it will be tomorrow.

Sir John Robert Seeley

2. THE EXPANSION OF ENGLAND

Like Leroy-Beaulieu, Sir John Robert Seeley (1834—1895) set forth his imperialist ideas from a particularly advantageous platform, the Cambridge University Regius Professorship of Modern History. The most immediate effect of the lectures, which became the following highly popular book, was to encourage an ultimately unsuccessful movement for closer unity among the white dominions of the British Empire. More generally, however, Seeley articulates an anxiety shared by many Englishmen of his time that only by renewed attention to formal empire could they preserve the great power status of their nation. The selection below is from Seeley's concluding lecture.

Thus I admitted very much of what is urged by the pessimists against the bombastic school. I endeavoured to judge the Empire by its own intrinsic merits, and to see it as it is, not concealing the inconveniences which may attend such a vast expansion, or the dangers to which it may expose us, nor finding any compensation for these in the notion that there is something intrinsically glorious in an Empire "upon which the sun never sets," or, to use another equally brilliant expression, an Empire "whose morning drum-beat, following the sun and keeping company with the hours, encircles the globe with an unbroken chain of martial airs." But though there is little that is glorious in most of the great Empires mentioned in history, since they have usually been created by force and have remained at a low level of political life, we observed that Greater Britain is not in the ordinary sense an Empire at all. Looking at the colonial part of it alone, we see a natural growth, a mere normal extension of the English race into other lands, which for the most part were so thinly peopled that our settlers took possession of them without conquest. If there is nothing highly glorious in such an expansion, there is at the same time nothing forced or unnatural about it. It creates not properly an Empire, but only a very large state. So far as the expansion itself is concerned, no one does or can regard it but with pleasure. For a nation to have an

The Expansion of England (London, 1883), 343-346, 349-350, 353-356.

outlet for its superfluous population is one of the greatest blessings. Population unfortunately does not adapt itself to space; on the contrary, the larger it is the larger is its yearly increment. Now that Great Britain is already full it becomes fuller with increased speed; it gains a million every three years. Probably emigration ought to proceed at a far greater rate than it does, and assuredly the greatest evils would arise if it were checked. But should there be an expansion of the State as well as of the nation? "No," say the pessimists, "or only till the colony is grown-up and ready for independence." When a metaphor comes to be regarded as an argument, what an irresistible argument it always seems! I have suggested that in the modern world distance has very much lost its effect, and that there are signs of a time when states will be vaster than they have hitherto been. In ancient times emigrants from Greece to Sicily took up their independence at once, and in those parts there were almost as many states as cities. In the eighteenth century Burke thought a federation quite impossible across the Atlantic Ocean. In such times the metaphor of the grown-up son might well harden into a convincing demonstration. But since Burke's time the Atlantic Ocean has shrunk till it seems scarcely broader than the sea between Greece and Sicily. Why then do we not drop the metaphor? I have urged that we are unconsciously influenced by a historic parallel which when examined turns out to be inapplicable. As indeed it is true generally that one urgent reason why politicians should study history is that they may guard themselves against the false historical analogies which continually mislead those who do not study history! These views are founded on the American Revolution, and yet the American Revolution arose out of circumstances and out of a condition of the world which has long since passed away. England was then an agricultural country by no means thickly peopled; America was full of religious refugees animated by ideas which in England had lately passed out of

fashion; there was scarcely any flux and reflux of population between the two countries, and the ocean divided them with a gulf which seemed as unbridgeable as that moral gulf which separates an Englishman from a Frenchman. Even then the separation was not effected without a great wrench. It is true that both countries have prospered since, nevertheless they have had a second war and may have a third, and it is wholly an illusion to suppose that their prosperity has been caused or promoted by their separation. At any rate all the conditions of the world are altered now. The great causes of division, oceans and religious disabilities, have ceased to operate. Vast uniting forces have begun to work, trade and emigration. Meanwhile the natural ties which unite Englishmen resume their influence as soon as the counteracting pressure is removed—I mean the ties of nationality, language, and religion. The mother-country having once for all ceased to be a stepmother, and to make unjust claims and impose annoying restrictions, and since she wants her colonies as an outlet both for population and trade, and since on the other hand the colonies must feel that there is risk, not to say also intellectual impoverishment, in independence,—since finally intercourse is ever increasing and no alienating force is at work to counteract it, but the discords created by the old system pass more and more into oblivion,—it seems possible that our colonial Empire so-called may more and more deserve to be called Greater Britain, and that the tie may become stronger and stronger. Then the seas which divide us might be forgotten, and that ancient preconception, which leads us always to think of ourselves as belonging to a single island, might be rooted out of our minds. If in this way we moved sensibly nearer in our thoughts and feelings to the colonies, and accustomed ourselves to think of emigrants as not in any way lost to England by settling in the colonies, the result might be, first that emigration on a vast scale might become our remedy for pauperism, and secondly that some organisation might gradually be arrived at which might make the whole force of the Empire available in time of war.

* * *

Lastly, let us observe that the question, whether large states or small states are best, is not one which can be answered or ought to be discussed absolutely. We often hear abstract panegyrics upon the happiness of small states. But observe that a small state among small states is one thing, and a small state among large states quite another. Nothing is more delightful than to read of the bright days of Athens and Florence, but those bright days lasted only so long as the states with which Athens and Florence had to do were states on a similar scale of magnitude. Both states sank at once as soon as large countrystates of consolidated strength grew up in their neighbourhood. The lustre of Athens grew pale as soon as Macedonia rose, and Charles V speedily brought to an end the great days of Florence. Now if it be true that a larger type of state than any hitherto known is springing up in the world, is not this a serious consideration for those states which rise only to the old level of magnitude? Russia already presses somewhat heavily on Central Europe; what will she do when with her vast territory and population she equals Germany in intelligence and organisation, when all her railways are made, her people educated, and her government settled on a solid basis?— and let us remember that if we allow her half a century to make so much progress her population will at the end of that time be not eighty but nearly a hundred and sixty millions. At that time which many here present may live to see, Russia and the United States will surpass in power the states now called great as much as the great country-states of the sixteenth century surpassed Florence. Is not this a serious consideration, and is it not especially so for a state like England, which has at the present moment the choice in its hands between two courses of action, the one of which may set it in that future age on a level with the greatest of these great states of the future, while the other will reduce it to the level of a purely European Power looking back, as Spain does now, to the great days when she pretended to be a world-state.

But what I have been saying does not apply to India. If England and her colonies taken together make, properly speaking, not an Empire but only a very large state, this is because the population is English throughout and the institutions are of the same kind. In India the population is wholly foreign, and the institutions wholly unlike our own. India is really an Empire and an Oriental Empire.

* * *

And thus we founded our [Indian] Empire, partly it may be out of an empty ambition of conquest and partly out of a philanthropic desire to put an end to enormous evils. But, whatever our motives might be, we incurred vast responsibilities, which were compensated by no advantages. We have now acquired a great Indian trade, but even this we purchase at the expense of a perpetual dread of Russia, and of all movements in the Mussulman world, and of all changes in Egypt. Thus a review of the history of British India leaves on the mind an impression quite different from that which our Colonial Empire produces. The latter has grown up naturally, out of the operation of the plainest causes; the former seems to have sprung from a romantic adventure; it is highly interesting, striking, and curious, but difficult to understand or to form an opinion about. We may hope that it will lead to good, but hitherto we have not ourselves reaped directly much good from it.

I have shown you however that, though it may be called an Oriental Empire, it is much less dangerous to us than that description might seem to imply. It is not an Empire attached to England in the same way as the Roman Empire was attached to Rome; it will not drag us down, or infect us at home with Oriental notions or methods of government.

Nor is it an Empire which costs us money or hampers our finances. It is self-supporting, and is held at arm's length in such a way that our destiny is not very closely entangled with its own.

Next I have led you to consider what may be the effect of our Indian Empire upon India itself. We perhaps have not gained much from it; but has India gained? On this question I have desired to speak with great diffidence. I have asserted confidently only thus much, that no greater experiment has ever been tried on the globe, and that the effects of it will be comparable to the effect of the Roman Empire upon the nations of Europe—nay, probably they will be much greater.

* * *

Another thing almost all observers see, and that is that the experiment must go forward, and that we cannot leave it unfinished if we would. For here too the great uniting forces of the age are at work; England and India are drawn every year for good or for evil more closely together. Not indeed that disuniting forces might not easily spring up, not that our rule itself may not possibly be calling out forces which may ultimately tend to disruption, nor yet that the Empire is altogether free from the danger of a sudden catastrophe. But for the present we are driven both by necessity and duty to a closer union. Already we should ourselves suffer greatly from disruption, and the longer the union lasts the more important it will become to us. Meanwhile the same is true in an infinitely greater degree of India itself. The transformation we are making there may cause us some misgivings, but though we may be led conceivably to wish that it had never been begun, nothing could ever convince us that it ought to be broken off in the middle.

Alfred Thayer Mahan

3. COLONIES AND SEA POWER

Captain (later Admiral) Alfred Thayer Mahan (1840-1914) was an obscure instructor in the United States Naval War College when he wrote his now world-famous study of naval history in the seventeenth and eighteenth centuries. Although this book appeared too late to be held responsible for the first stages of the new European imperialism, which took place in the 1880s, Mahan's advocacy of colonies as a corollary maritime strategy had an immediate and acknowledged effect on the second generation of imperialists in America, Germany, and Britain.

The needs of commerce, however, were not all provided for when safety had been secured at the far end of the road. The voyages were long and dangerous, the seas often beset with enemies. In the most active days of colonizing there prevailed on the sea a lawlessness the very memory of which is now almost lost, and the days of settled peace between maritime nations were few and far between. Thus arose the demand for stations along the road, like the Cape of Good Hope, St. Helena, and Mauritius, not primarily for trade, but for defence and war; the demand for the possession of posts like Gibraltar, Malta, Louisburg, at the entrance of the Gulf of St. Lawrence,—posts whose value was chiefly strategic, though not necessarily wholly so. Colonies and colonial

The Influence of Sea Power upon History (1890), 27—28, 55—57.

posts were sometimes commercial, sometimes military in their character; and it was exceptional that the same position was equally important in both points of view, as New York was.

In these three things — production, with the necessity of exchanging products, shipping, whereby the exchange is carried on, and colonies, which facilitate and enlarge the operations of shipping and tend to project it by multiplying points of safety — is to be found the key to much of the history, as well as of the policy, of nations bordering upon the sea. The policy has varied both with the spirit of the age and with the character and clear-sightedness of the rulers; but the history of the seaboard nations has been less determined by the shrewdness and foresight of governments than by conditions of position, extent, configuration, number and character of their people, — by what are called, in a word, natural conditions. It must however be admitted, and will be seen, that the wise or unwise action of individual men has at certain periods had a great modifying influence upon the growth of sea power in the broad sense, which includes not only the military strength afloat, that rules the sea or any part of it by force of arms, but also the peaceful commerce and shipping from which alone a military fleet naturally and healthfully springs, and on which it securely rests.

* * *

In yet another way does the national genius affect the growth of sea power in its broadest sense; and that is in so far as it possesses the capacity for planting healthy colonies. Of colonization, as of all other growths, it is true that it is most healthy when it is most natural. Therefore colonies that spring from the felt wants and natural impulses of a whole people will have the most solid foundations; and their subsequent growth will be surest when they are least trammelled from home, if the people have the genius for independent action. Men of the past three centuries have keenly felt the value to the mother-country of colonies as outlets for the home products and as a nursery for commerce and shipping; but efforts at colonization have not had the same general origin, nor have different systems all had the same success. The efforts of statesmen, however far-seeing and careful, have not been able to supply the lack of strong natural impulse; nor can the most minute regulation from home produce as good results as a happier neglect, when the germ of self-development is found in the national character. There has been no greater display of wisdom in the national administration of successful colonies than in that of unsuccessful. Perhaps there has been even less. If elaborate system and supervision, careful adaptation of means to ends, diligent nursing, could avail for colonial growth, the genius of England has less of this systematizing faculty than the genius of France; but England, not France, has been the great colonizer of the world. Successful colonization, with its consequent effect upon commerce and sea power, depends essentially upon national character; because colonies grow best when they grow of themselves, naturally. The character of the colonist, not the care of the home government, is the principle of the colony's growth.

This truth stands out the clearer because the general attitude of all the home governments toward their colonies was entirely selfish. However founded, as soon as it was recognized to be of consequence, the colony became to the home country a cow to be milked; to be cared for, of course, but chiefly as a piece of property valued for the returns it gave. Legislation was directed toward a monopoly of its external trade; the places in its government afforded posts of value for occupants from the mother-country; and the colony was looked upon, as the sea still so often is, as a fit place for those who were ungovernable or useless at home. The military administration, however, so long as it remains a colony, is the proper and necessary attribute of the home government.

The fact of England's unique and wonderful success as a great colonizing nation is

59

too evident to be dwelt upon; and the reason for it appears to lie chiefly in two traits of the national character. The English colonist naturally and readily settles down in his new country, identifies his interest with it, and though keeping an affectionate remembrance of the home from which he came, has no restless eagerness to return. In the second place, the Englishman at once and instinctively seeks to develop the resources of the new country in the broadest sense. In the former particular he differs from the French, who were ever longingly looking back to the delights of their pleasant land; in the latter, from the Spaniards, whose range of interest and ambition was too narrow for the full evolution of the possibilities of a new country.

THE CONQUISTADORS

Leopold II

4. EXTERIOR DOMAINS

The peculiar role of Leopold II of the Belgians (born 1835, reigned 1865-1909) as King of a strictly limited constitutional monarchy allowed him neither to complete the study of modern colonialism so brilliantly outlined here in a letter to an aide nor to execute his ideas upon the open stage of history. Instead, Leopold became the archrepresentative of hypocritical and underhanded imperialist scheming. By playing off the naïveté and mutual jealousies of Britain, France, Germany, Portugal, and the United States, he succeeded during the 1880's in carving out a central African "exterior domain" that belonged to and was financed by himself rather than the Belgian state. In 1908, however, Belgium finally had to take over Leopold's Congo when it was revealed that, in order to maintain profitable operations, the King had allowed his agents to establish a regime of shockingly ruthless and brutal exploitation.

LEOPOLD TO COLONEL BRIALMONT
July 26, 1863

No country has attained historical greatness without colonies. Look at the annals of England, of France, of Russia, of Spain, of Holland. Consider the history of Venice, of Rome, of ancient Greece. No nation is complete without overseas activity and possessions.

In 1863 it is no more possible for maritime people to restrict themselves to Europe than it is possible for an individual to read and take interest in only what occurs exclusively in this part of the world. The steamship and electricity have obliterated distances.

There are three kinds of colonies:
1. Slave colonies—Cuba.
2. Colonies containing a populous native race which has been reduced to dependency by some European state—Java, the Philippines, Cochin China, India.
3. Colonies founded by the emigration of the white race—America, Australia, Natal (temperate climates).

No one thinks any more of founding slave

Léon le Febve de Vivy, *Documents d'histoire précoloniale belge* (Brussels, Institut Royal des Sciences Coloniales, 1955), 18 – 21.

colonies, so it will suffice for us to consider the two other methods of exploiting distant provinces.

SECOND CATEGORY

Natives subjugated by a European people: Such countries are not true colonies; these are exterior domains, very productive when they are well chosen. Java is immensely profitable and your documents prove that over the centuries the benefits can be calculated to have surpassed the expenses.

In Java there is a form of forced labor, *the only means of civilizing and moralizing these indolent and corrupt peoples of the Far East. Some day it will be possible to abolish this labor without endangering public safety and without loss to the metropole.* The cultivators, enriched by this *corvée* (see the documentation of Major Goffinet) will be able one day to buy their freedom from the state and become property owners. Taxation will replace labor.

The Far East is very backward: to treat it as one treats Europe *would be to push it back towards barbarism and to proclaim the liberty of every kind of laziness, of disorder, and of crime.*

Everyone knows what advantages Holland draws from Java. It can be said that this property represents a very good investment of funds for the Netherlands without beginning to compute the political advantages and the advantages of *investing* and *employing* their *activities* which more than 30,000 Dutchmen have found here for centuries.

The Army of the Indies, the Navy of the Indies, the Administration of the Indies, three immense careers open to the activity of young Netherlanders *do not weigh at all upon the budget of the mother country*, or, better said, pay for themselves by an annual *profit* of 75 millions.

For those peoples whose working class does not emigrate but whose middle class lacks employment, such domains are precious.

* * *

[British] India and Java are inexhaustible mines. The question thus amounts to this: is it profitable to possess gold mines?

* * *

Armed with the lessons of history and relying on statistics and documents, we will try to demonstrate:

1. That everywhere since the foundation of states in the world, overseas provinces have been sought and found useful to the mother country.
2. That everywhere, even in America and Australia, the State has had to intervene in the foundation of colonies and their protection. . . .
3. That overseas provinces are astoundingly profitable for the mother country, well beyond what they have cost and that such domains are very good investments for states. . . .
4. That, despite Free Trade and the opening of all colonies of various people for commerce, the full possession of overseas domains remains advantageous. We will be happy to see Belgium trade with and exploit colonies in general but we feel that, in the interest of the country, it should have its own outside possessions. . . .

Belgium is not an exploiter of the world: this is a taste which must be developed here. Since it is necessary to preach on the subject, we prefer that our compatriots work for the profit of the nation; in this sense, that they become the owners of distant proportion over which our flag flies in preference to seeing them scatter themselves over the United States and elsewhere and to see them consume without profit to *Belgian society*. The Germans emigrate in great numbers but lose themselves among the Americans, and Germany remains without a fleet and without influence outside Europe.

All of these facts having been demonstrated and understood, we shall propose that the legislature decree the *extension of the nation* along honorable and legal paths, worthy of our century and in a fashion which will advance civilization by our new establishments rather than halting its progress by the execution of ambitious projects at the expense of our neighbors.

We propose that these extensions, a luxury complimenting our beloved independence, be realized in the following manner:

A certain as yet undetermined sum will be allocated from the surpluses of state revenues. This sum will be placed in a fund called "Overseas Affairs." This fund will also receive gifts and legacies. When a certain number of millions have been amassed, the exploitation of some worthwhile country will be undertaken according to the best available examples.

This Belgian domain will have a separate account and budget. The beginnings will be moderate and, whether in Japan, Borneo, Central America, or on the coast of Africa, the only funds involved will be those of the overseas fund. . . .

Carl Peters

5. A MANIFESTO FOR GERMAN COLONIZATION

The colonial movement in Germany lacked any historical foundations or leadership other than the frustrations that a dynamic bourgeoisie suffered in a state dominated by a military aristocracy. German colonialism, therefore, tended to take on more hysterical forms than was the case in Britain, France, or Belgium. Carl Peters (1856−1918) was both a leading colonial agitator at home and the founder of German East Africa, today Tanzania. Characteristically Peters suffered throughout his life from a fixation upon England. Within half a year after issuing the following appeal for support, Peters succeeded in staking out a claim to an East African protectorate which was to provide Germany with no benefits beyond the opportunity for exercising paternalistic rule over a particularly impoverished region. For such efforts Peters himself proved to be totally unsuited, whether as head of a short-lived chartered company regime or as a paid official of direct imperial administration. Under indictment for brutality, he finished his career in obscure exile.

MANIFESTO OF
THE SOCIETY FOR GERMAN COLONIZATION
April 1884

In the partition of the earth, as it has proceeded from the beginning of the fifteenth century up to our times, the German nation received nothing. All the remaining European culture-bearing peoples possess areas outside our continent where their languages and customs can take firm root and flourish. The moment that the German emigrant leaves the borders of the Reich behind him, he is a stranger sojourning on foreign soil. The German Reich, great in size and strength through its bloodily achieved unity, stands in the leading position among the continental European powers: her sons abroad must adapt themselves to nations which look upon us with either indifference or even hostility. For centuries the great stream of German emigration has been plunging down into foreign races where it is lost sight of. Germandom outside Europe

---

Carl Peters, *Die Gründung von Deutsch-Ostafrika* (Berlin, Schwetschke, 1906), 43−45.

has been undergoing a perpetual national decline.

This fact, so painful to national pride, also represents a great economic disadvantage for our *Volk*. Every year our Fatherland loses the capacity of approximately 200,000 Germans. The greatest amount of this capacity flows directly into the camp of our economic competitors and increases the strength of our rivals. Germany's imports of products from tropical zones originate in foreign settlements whereby many millions of German capital are lost every year to alien nations. German exports are dependent upon the discretion of foreign tariff policies. Our industry lacks an absolutely safe market for its goods because our *Volk* lacks colonies of its own.

The alleviation of this national grievance requires taking practical steps and strong action.

In recognition of this point of view, a society has been organized in Berlin with the goal of mobilizing itself for such steps and such action. The Society for German Colonization aims to undertake on its own, in a resolute and sweeping manner, carefully chosen colonization projects and thereby supplement the ranks of organizations with similar tendencies.

Its particular tasks will be:

1. to provide necessary sums of capital for colonization;
2. to seek out and lay claim to suitable districts for colonization;
3. to direct German emigrants to these regions.

Imbued as we are with the conviction that it is no longer permissible to hesitate in energetically mobilizing ourselves for this great national task, we venture to come before the German *Volk* with a plea for active support of the endeavors of our Society! The German nation has proven time and again its willingness to make sacrifices for general patriotic undertakings: may she also bring her full energies to play in the solution of this great historical task.

Every German whose heart beats for the greatness and the honor of our nation is entreated to come to the side of our Society. What is at stake is compensation for centuries of deprivation: to prove to the world that, along with the splendor of the Reich, the German *Volk* has inherited the old German national spirit of its forefathers!

6. BRITISH SOUTH AFRICA AND BEYOND

Cecil John Rhodes (1853–1902) went as a young man from England to South Africa, where he quickly made a fortune in diamond mining. Originally he was a believer in Boer-British unity and a minimum of interference by the London government in local colonial affairs. The fiasco of the 1895 Jameson Raid against the independent Boer government of the Transvaal, however, destroyed his political position in what is today the Republic of South Africa. As indicated in the following documents Rhodes' British South Africa Company still succeeded in conquering and exploiting the territories which today constitute Rhodesia and Zambia, although, again, Rhodes failed to create a continuous line of British territorial control from that area to Egypt.

1

When I look back at the past and see what has been accomplished, I feel that we must congratulate ourselves on our present condition in so far as the success of the charter is concerned. It is nearly three years ago that my friend Mr. Maguire went into the unknown regions of Lobengula, sat down with that naked savage, and obtained from him the concession for us and others. That concession was I think, really obtained not from the purely speculative point of view. It was a conception that the North would have to be taken with the hinterland of the country, and would have to be developed, and the basis for obtaining that was to get a concession. I will not weary you with the various negotiations that subsequently occurred, but we had the satisfaction afterwards of obtaining a charter from Her Majesty's Government. The work, however, had only then begun, because, although we had a charter, we had not got the country, which was occupied by savages; and although the

chief of the country had given us a concession, he was not at all pleased that we should derive any benefit therefrom—that was, that we should occupy the country. After a careful study of the map, it was seen that the proper course to pursue was to try and occupy the territory to the east, at that time occupied by Mashonas, who were yearly raided by him. We formed a force which marched through that territory, and I agree with the chairman that the highest tribute is to be paid to those young men who marched for a thousand miles, four hundred of which were through a dense forest, and who had to cut their way day by day through it until they finally reached "the promised land." One thing which that expedition taught me is the audacity of our race, and in connection with our race I would mention the colonists of South Africa, both Dutch and English, because that force was composed of Englishmen from home, Englishmen in South Africa, and Dutch colonists resident there also. This

Address at second annual meeting of B.S.A.C. stockholders, 29 Nov. 1892. Address to B.S.A.C. stockholders, 18 Jan. 1895. Vindex (F. Verschoyle) *Cecil Rhodes: His Political Life & Speeches* (London, 1900), 198−301, 312−314, 416−419.

combination brought about the occupation of "the promised land," and then the usual thing occurred—they found that "the promised land" was beautiful, but it was an open waste. Everything had to be done; there was nothing before them and nothing to take. In fact, I came to the conclusion that it was easier to conquer an old country than to occupy a new one—because, in the one case, however terrific the contest might be, there was the wealth of the land and of the citizens, the wealth of the country, as perhaps the reward. In their case, however, after unheard-of difficulties, they simply had an open country, which had been lately devoted only to barbarism. They made an occupation, they founded a Government, and so far as the first occupants went, there was the natural reaction. They found that they could not pick up gold like gooseberries, and that to acquire it necessitated work, toil, and patience, and the result was that depression ensued after the first sanguine hopes as to the nature of "the promised land." Then the rains fell, and they found themselves shut up in the country, and there were all sorts of miserable reports; but I am glad to say that the majority of the people bore without complaint the hardships they had to endure.

That lasted for about six months. Then the river fell, and a further number of emigrants was able to enter the country, as well as certain expeditions from home. Meantime we had formed an organised Government, and had begun the first groundwork of making a country. It is needless for me to refer to the various expeditions from home. They also thought that a fortune was to be made in about a week or a month; but they too found a bare country, whose future must depend upon the energy of its first occupants, and that a race out from home and a race back would not in any part of the world give one a quarter of a million of money. Then, undoubtedly, came a true period of depression. The condemnation of the home papers could only be compared to their previous undue sanguineness. They condemned the country as everything that was bad. Subse-quently, we were removed from the criticism of the English papers, as they thought the country too bad to say anything about it. Those on the spot, however—about fifteen hundred strong—remained doggedly and determinedly in the country. They went to work to find their reefs, but they were removed seventeen hundred miles from the coast, and their food cost them £70 a ton. Shortly after that, my friend Dr. Jameson agreed to assume the charge of the country. Dr. Jameson had been up in the country before, having just got back from a seven hundred mile walking tour—across the country of Gungunhana, a chief from whom he had obtained the whole of the coast region as a concession. Dr. Jameson was suffering from a very bad malarial fever, but when I asked him to go back he agreed to do so without a word. He was fortunate enough to fall upon a trek of dissatisfied Transvaal agitators, who were determined to take the northern country from this Company. By the measures he took and his good management, Dr. Jameson dispersed the trekkers, and many of them have since taken land under the Company's flag.

* * *

I have now fairly sketched out our position, and I think that such a record for two years is a very fair record for any company. I would now resume my seat, only I have been allowed to put something personal to the shareholders. The question I am about to submit to you has no connection whatever with the charter; it is no liability of the charter. I may say that when the charter was commenced I always had the idea of an overland telegraph to Egypt, and the other day, when I was returning home, I hastened my journey when I saw that there was a certain section of the English people desirous of abandoning Uganda. I proposed to Her Majesty's Government to build a telegraph to Uganda. I found that this would cost about £140,000 to £150,000—that was to reach Uganda, and subsequently it would go on to Egypt. This was no wild scheme. We are earning upon the telegraph up to the

Zambesi four per cent on the capital expended. From the Zambesi to Uganda there were no difficult tribes to deal with. The distance is fourteen hundred miles, and the line would cost about £150,000. If I extend the telegraph to Uganda we shall certainly not hear any more about the abandonment of that place. You might ask me what commercial results I expect from such a telegraph. From a commercial point of view I feel perfectly clear that when I get to Uganda I shall get through to Wady Halfa. I do not propose to fight the Mahdi, but to "deal" with him. I have never met any one in my life whom it was not as easy to deal with as to fight. I am perfectly clear that if I get the money to make the line to Uganda I shall get the money with which to extend the line to Egypt. I agree that it will take from five to ten years, but in such matters we have to go slowly. The line to Egypt provided the Mahdi is "squared," will cost £300,000 to £400,000, and we have lying to the east and west of the coast cables which have cost £3,000,000. We are now charged 9s. 6d. a word for our communications, but when we can get to Egypt by the telegraph I am referring to we shall be able to do it for 1s. 7d. from Egypt to England or in all about 2s. 6d. against 9s. 6d. a word as at present. There is the commercial aspect as well as the imaginative, and I feel no doubt about the success of the undertaking.

There are fourteen thousand shareholders in the various companies I represent, and if they like to send me, not a charitable contribution, but about £10 each, there would be my line to Uganda, and I maintain that it will give an excellent return.

* * *

The contributions I have spoken of—not charitable contributions—can be sent to the secretary of the company at St. Swithin's Lane. There may be in various towns in England people who take an interest in Africa, and in the suppression of the slave-trade. If this telegraph is made, there will be an end to the slave-trade, and it will also give us the keys to the continent.

2

Mr. Chairman and Gentlemen, I have to thank you for the reception which you have accorded to me, but I think that you naturally desire that we should deal with the practical part of the Company's development in Matabeleland and Mashonaland, because you must remember that the English are a very practical people. They like expansion, but they like it in connection with practical business. I will not refer to the causes that led to our late war, but I may tell you very frankly that we either had to have that war or to leave the country. I do not blame the Matabele. Their system was a military system; once a year they raided the surrounding people, and such a system was impossible for our development. Conclusions were tried, and they came to a successful issue so far as we were concerned. I might make one remark with respect to that war; that to refer to the men who took part in it as political adventurers was a mistake. You can quite understand that, however bad times were, you would not risk your life unless there was something other than profit from the possible chance of obtaining a farm at the end of the war of the value now of about £50. Really, why the people volunteered so readily was that they had adopted this new country as their home, and they saw very clearly that unless they tried issues with the Matabele they would have to leave the country. I think that is the best reply to the charge that the men who took a part in that war did it for the sake of loot and profit.

Now, in looking at this question we have to consider what we possess, and I can tell you that we possess a very large piece of the world. If you will look at the map, let us consider what we have north of the Zambesi. We have now taken over the administration of the land north of the Zambesi save and except the Nyassaland Protectorate. We have also received sanction for all our Concessions there; that is, the land and minerals north of the Zambesi belong to the Chartered Company—with one exception, the small piece termed the Nyassaland Protectorate. Even in that, however, we have considerable rights as to the minerals and land, in return for the property we took over from a Scotch company called The Lakes Company. We have, however, been relieved from the cost of administration of the Nyassaland Protectorate. Her Majesty's Government and the British people have at last felt it their duty to pay for the administration of one of their own provinces, and I think we have a very fair reply to the Little Englanders, who are always charging us with increasing the responsibilities of Her Majes-ty's Government, and stating that the "Charters," when in difficulty, always appeal to the mother-country. Our reply must be that the boot is on the other leg. For four years we have found the cost of administration of one of your own provinces, and we are proud to think that we have yearly paid into Her Majesty's Treasury a sum for the administration of one of our own provinces because Governments were unable to face the House of Commons to ask them to contribute to their obligations.

7. CAPTAIN MARCHAND RACES TO FASHODA

The French equivalent to Rhodes' dream of a "Cape to Cairo" British African axis was a belt of influence following the basin of the Mediterranean, from West to East. Britain's occupation of Egypt in 1882 forced the French to seek compensation south of the Sahara, and in 1896 Captain Jean Baptiste Marchand (1863– 1934) was despatched from Gabon on the West African coast to establish French claims on the upper Nile valley. Soon after writing the letter cited here, Marchand reached his goal, the river village of Fashoda, only to be confronted with an entire British army which had just completed the conquest of the Sudan. France and Britain came to the brink of war over their conflicting claims to Fashoda, but, in the face of superior force, the French finally backed down, to be compensated several years later by British recognition of their control over Morocco.

MARCHAND TO PAUL BOURDAIRE
Bahr-el-Ghazal, March 1898

Fortunately, we are supported here by two motives more elevated than the honor of material reward: love of our nation, for which we still cherish an old-fashioned prejudice despite everything and more that is done to demonstrate its inanity to us; hatred of Albion [England] in the face of which we have the honor and pride to stand here, one against a thousand . . . an admiring and respectful hatred, to be sure, such as one feels before a rival possessing all the qualities and splendid faults which characterize strong nations, prouder and stronger in direct proportion to their age.

The risk to my own head resulting from such an involvement seems a small thing in the light of the outcome, remote but possible, which could be so fine for our country —ultimately even more for the moral support and sense of strength which it would give us than the material territorial benefits which would accrue later.

At least do not go and think that I believe myself to be carrying a whole universe on my shoulders and that I exaggerate the importance of the role we are playing here. Certainly not. That would be ridiculous. I simply think, but I think in the depth of my bones, that an example, no matter how humble its source, is always an example, that its effect depends far more on the thea-

From Jacques Delebecque, *La Vie du Général Marchand* (Paris, 1936), pp. 115–116. Reprinted by permission of Librairie Hachette.

tre in which it is played than on the value of him who presents it, and that it is always to be respected when his motive is to render to his own nation that sense of its true strength, of its mission in the world, begun a good five centuries ago and which we all have the obligation to uphold under the penalty of national cowardice.

A la Grace de Dieu! That's what you say when you play your whole bankroll on one final card. I am about to play mine in the firm belief that if it is a bit of a blind chance, at least it is without hesitation, as a Frenchman of the Old France. And my bankroll consists of these valiant men, white and black, who surround me and thanks to whom I have come this far.

8. WINSTON CHURCHILL WITNESSES THE BATTLE OF OMDURMAN

An early twentieth-century epigram on British imperialism applies particularly well to the Battle of Omdurman (Sept. 2, 1898):

The difference is that we have got

The Maxim gun and they have not.

At Omdurman, British-led Anglo-Egyptian forces finally destroyed the "Dervish" armies of the Mahdi, Mohammed Ahmed, self-proclaimed prophet of an Islamic revival movement in the Sudan. Formerly a province of Egypt, the Sudan had been made an independent theocracy by the Mahdi in 1885. In 1899, following an agreement with France (see selection 7 above), the Sudan effectively became a British colony and regained its independence as the Sudan Republic in 1956. Churchill went on from youthful participation in this and similar imperialist adventures to play his well known role as a British and world statesman. These early experiences sufficiently marked him, however, so that, even after World War II, he risked political office rather than agree "to preside over the dissolution of the British Empire."

The attack developed. The left, nearly 20,000 strong, toiled across the plain and approached the Egyptian squadrons. The leading masses of the centre deployed facing the *zeriba* and marched forthwith to the direct assault. As the whole Dervish army continued to advance, the division with the white flags, which had until now been écheloned in rear of their right, moved up into the general line and began to climb the southern slopes of Surgham Hill. Meanwhile yet another body of the enemy, comparatively insignificant in numbers, who had been drawn up behind the "White Flags," were moving slowly towards the Nile, écheloned still further behind their right, and not far from the suburbs of Omdurman. These men had evidently been posted to prevent the Dervish army being cut off from the city and to secure their line of retreat; and with them the 21st Lancers were destined to have a much closer acquaintance about two hours later.

The Dervish centre had come within range. But it was not the British and Egyptian army that began the battle. If there was one arm in which the Arabs were beyond all comparison inferior to their adversaries, it

From Winston Churchill, *The River War* (London, 1899), pp. 272–275. Reprinted by permission of Eyre & Spottiswoode Ltd., London, and The Hamlyn Publishing Group Limited.

was in guns. Yet it was with this arm that they opened their attack. In the middle of the Dervish line now marching in frontal assault were two puffs of smoke. About fifty yards short of the thorn fence two red clouds of sand and dust sprang up, where the projectiles had struck. It looked like a challenge. It was immediately answered. Great clouds of smoke appeared all along the front of the British and Soudanese brigades. One after another four batteries opened on the enemy at a range of about 3,000 yards. The sound of the cannonade rolled up to us on the ridge, and was re-echoed by the hills. Above the heads of the moving masses shells began to burst, dotting the air with smoke-balls and the ground with bodies. But a nearer tragedy impended. The "White Flags" were nearly over the crest. In another minute they would become visible to the batteries. Did they realise what would come to meet them? They were in a dense mass, 2,800 yards from the 32nd Field Battery and the gunboats. The ranges were known. It was a matter of machinery. The more distant slaughter passed unnoticed, as the mind was fascinated by the approaching horror. In a few seconds swift destruction would rush on these brave men. They topped the crest and drew out into full view of the whole army. Their white banners made them conspicuous above all. As they saw the camp of their enemies, they discharged their rifles with a great roar of musketry and quickened their pace. For a moment the white flags advanced in regular order, and the whole division crossed the crest and were exposed. Forthwith the gunboats, the 32nd British Field Battery, and other guns from the zeriba opened on them. About twenty shells struck them in the first minute. Some burst high in the air, others exactly in their faces. Others, again, plunged into the sand and, exploding, dashed clouds of red dust, splinters, and bullets amid their ranks. The white banners toppled over in all directions. Yet they rose again immediately, as other men pressed forward to die for the Mahdi's sacred cause and in the defence of the successor of the True Prophet. It was a terrible sight, for as yet they had not hurt us at all, and it seemed an unfair advantage to strike thus cruelly when they could not reply. Under the influence of the shells the mass of the "White Flags" dissolved into thin lines of spearmen and skirmishers, and came on in altered formation and diminished numbers, but with unabated enthusiasm. And now, the whole attack being thoroughly exposed, it became the duty of the cavalry to clear the front as quickly as possible, and leave the further conduct of the debate to the infantry and the Maxim guns. All the patrols trotted or cantered back to their squadrons, and the regiment retired swiftly into the zeriba, while the shells from the gunboats screamed overhead and the whole length of the position began to burst into flame and smoke. Nor was it long before the tremendous banging of the artillery was swollen by the roar of musketry.

Taking advantage of the shelter of the river-bank, the cavalry dismounted; we watered our horses, waited, and wondered what was happening. And every moment the tumult grew louder and more intense, until even the flickering stutter of the Maxims could scarcely be heard above the continuous din. Eighty yards away, and perhaps twenty feet above us, the 32nd Field Battery was in action. The nimble figures of the gunners darted about as they busied themselves in their complicated process of destruction. The officers, some standing on biscuit-boxes, peered through their glasses and studied the effect. Of this I had one glimpse. Eight hundred yards away a ragged line of men were coming on desperately, struggling forward in the face of the pitiless fire — white banners tossing and collapsing; white figures subsiding in dozens to the ground; little white puffs from their rifles, larger white puffs spreading in a row all along their front from the bursting shrapnel.

The infantry fired steadily and stolidly, without hurry or excitement, for the enemy were far away and the officers careful. Besides, the soldiers were interested in the work and took great pains. But presently the mere physical act became tedious. The tiny figures seen over the slide of the back-sight seemed a little larger, but also fewer at each successive volley. The rifles grew hot—so hot that they had to be changed for those of the reserve companies. The Maxim guns exhausted all the water in their jackets, and several had to be refreshed from the water-bottles of the Cameron Highlanders before they could go on with their deadly work. The empty cartridge-cases, tinkling to the ground, formed a small but growing heap beside each man. And all the time out on the plain on the other side bullets were shearing through flesh, smashing and splintering bone; blood spouted from terrible wounds; valiant men were struggling on through a hell of whistling metal, exploding shells, and spurting dust—suffering, despairing, dying. Such was the first phase of the battle of Omdurman.

The Khalifa's [successor to the Mahdi] plan of attack appears to have been complex and ingenious. It was, however, based on an extraordinary miscalculation of the power of modern weapons; with the exception of this cardinal error, it is not necessary to criticise it.

THE STATESMEN

9. JULES FERRY DEFENDS COLONIAL EXPANSIONISM

Jules Ferry (1832–1893) began his political career as a champion of the middle-class French Third Republic, distinguishing himself mainly for his fervor in secularizing the national school system. Ferry's later responsibility for French expansion in Africa and Asia twice cost him the office of Prime Minister. While he was actually involved in acquiring colonies, it is unlikely that Ferry held anything like the clear ideas which he expresses in the following speech, delivered on the occasion of his final fall from power. Nevertheless Ferry's themes here—the abandonment of liberal economics, the insistence on a "civilizing mission," and the defense of Republican patriotism—remained significant elements in the sentiments which supported French imperialism.

SPEECH, JULY 28, 1883, BEFORE THE
FRENCH NATIONAL ASSEMBLY

M. Jules Ferry: Gentlemen, it embarrasses me to make such a prolonged demand upon the gracious attention of the Chamber, but I believe that the duty I am fulfilling upon this platform is not a useless one. It is as strenuous for me as for you, but I believe that there is some benefit in summarizing and condensing, in the form of arguments, the principles, the motives, and the various interests by which a policy of colonial expansion may be justified; it goes without saying that I will try to remain reasonable, moderate, and never lose sight of the major continental interests which are the primary concern of this country. What I wish to say, to support this proposition, is that in fact, just as in word, the policy of colonial expansion is a political and economic system; I wish to say that one can relate this system to three orders of ideas: economic ideas, ideas of civilization in its highest sense, and ideas of politics and patriotism.

In the area of economics, I will allow my-

Speech before the French National Assembly, July 28, 1883 in *Discours et opinions*, ed. P. Robiquet (Paris, 1897), Vol. V, 199-220.

self to place before you, with the support of some figures, the considerations which justify a policy of colonial expansion from the point of view of that need, felt more and more strongly by the industrial populations of Europe and particularly those of our own rich and hard working country: the need for export markets. Is this some kind of chimera? Is this a view of the future or is it not rather a pressing need, and, we could say, the cry of our industrial population? I will formulate only in a general way what each of you, in the different parts of France, is in a position to confirm. Yes, what is lacking for our great industry, drawn irrevocably on to the path of exportation by the [free trade] treaties of 1860, what it lacks more and more is export markets. Why? Because next door to us Germany is surrounded by barriers, because beyond the ocean, the United States of America has become protectionist, protectionist in the most extreme sense, because not only have these great markets, I will not say closed but shrunk, and thus become more difficult of access for our industrial products, but also these great states are beginning to pour products not seen heretofore onto our own markets. . . . It is not necessary to pursue this demonstration any farther. Yes, gentlemen, I am speaking to the economists, whose convictions and past services no one appreciates more than I do; I am speaking to the honorable M. Passy, whom I see here and who is one of the most authoritative representatives among us of the old school of economics [smiles]; I know very well what they will reply to me, what is at the bottom of their thoughts . . . the old school, the great school, gentlemen; one, M. Passey, which your name has embellished, which was led in France by Jean-Baptiste Say and by Adam Smith in England. I do not mean to treat you with any irony, M. Passy, believe me.

I say that I know very well the thoughts of the economists, whom I can call doctrinaires without offending M. Passy. They say to us, "The true export markets are the commercial treaties which furnish and assure them." Gentlemen, I do not look down upon

commercial treaties: if we could return to the situation which existed after 1860, if the world had not been subjected to that economic revolution which is the product of the development of science and the speeding up of communications, if this great revolution had not intervened, I would gladly take up the situation which existed after 1860. It is quite true that in that epoch the competition of grain from Odessa did not ruin French agriculture, that the grain of America and of India did not yet offer us any competition; at that moment we were living under the regime of commercial treaties, not only with England, but with the other great powers, with Germany, which had not yet become an industrial power. I do not look down upon them, these treaties; I had the honor of negotiating some of less importance than those of 1860; but gentlemen, in order to make treaties, it is necessary to have two parties: one does not make treaties with the United States; this is the conviction which has grown among those who have attempted to open some sort of negotiations in this quarter, whether officially or officiously.

* * *

Gentlemen, there is a second point, a second order of ideas to which I have to give equal attention, but as quickly as possible, believe me; it is the humanitarian and civilizing side of the question. On this point the honorable M. Camille Pellatan has jeered in his own refined and clever manner; he jeers, he condemns, and he says "What is this civilization which you impose with cannonballs? What is it but another form of barbarism? Don't these populations, these inferior races, have the same rights as you? Aren't they masters of their own houses? Have they called upon you? You come to them against their will, you offer them violence, but not civilization." There, gentlemen, is the thesis; I do not hesitate to say that this is not politics, nor is it history: it is political metaphysics. ["Ah, Ah" on far left].
. . . Gentlemen, I must speak from a higher and more truthful plane. It must be

stated openly that, in effect, superior races have rights over inferior races. [*Movement on many benches on the far left.*]

M. JULES MAIGNE: Oh! You dare to say this in the country which has proclaimed the rights of man!

M. DE GUILLOUTET: This is a justification of slavery and the slave trade!

M. JULES FERRY: If M. Maigne is right, if the declaration of the rights of man was written for the blacks of equatorial Africa, then by what right do you impose regular commerce upon them? They have not called upon you.

M. RAOUL DUVAL: We do not want to impose anything upon them. It is you who wish to do so!

M. JULES MAIGNE: To propose and to impose are two different things!

M. GEORGES PERIN: In any case, you cannot bring about commerce by force.

M. JULES FERRY: I repeat that superior races have a right, because they have a duty. They have the duty to civilize inferior races. . . . [*Approbation from the left. New interruptions from the extreme left and from the right*]

* * *

That is what I have to answer M. Pelletan in regard to the second point upon which he touched.

He then touched upon a third, more delicate, more serious, and upon which I ask your permission to express myself quite frankly. It is the political side of the question. The honorable M. Pelletan, who is a distinguished writer, always comes up with remarkably precise formulations. I will borrow from him the one which he applied the other day to this aspect of colonial policy.

"It is a system," he says, "which consists of seeking out compensations in the Orient with a circumspect and peaceful seclusion which is actually imposed upon us in Europe."

I would like to explain myself in regard to this. I do not like this word, "compensation," and, in effect, not here but elsewhere it has often been used in a treacherous way. If what is being said or insinuated is that any government in this country, any Re-

publican minister could possibly believe that there are in any part of the world compensations for the disasters which we have experienced, an injury is being inflicted . . . and an injury undeserved by that government. [*Applause at the center and left.*] I will ward off this injury with all the force of my patriotism! [*New applause and bravos from the same benches.*]

* * *

Gentlemen, there are certain considerations which merit the attention of all patriots. The conditions of naval warfare have been profoundly altered. ["Very true! Very true!"]

At this time, as you know, a warship cannot carry more than fourteen days' worth of coal, no matter how perfectly it is organized, and a ship which is out of coal is a derelict on the surface of the sea, abandoned to the first person who comes along. Thence the necessity of having on the oceans provision stations, shelters, ports for defense and revictualling. [*Applause at the center and left. Various interruptions.*] And it is for this that we needed Tunisia, for this that we needed Saigon and the Mekong Delta, for this that we need Madagascar, that we are at Diégo-Suarez and Vohemar [two Madagascar ports] and will never leave them! [*Applause from a great number of benches.*] Gentlemen, in Europe as it is today, in this competition of so many rivals which we see growing around us, some by perfecting their military or maritime forces, others by the prodigious development of an ever growing population; in a Europe, or rather in a universe of this sort, a policy of peaceful seclusion or abstention is simply the highway to decadence! Nations are great in our times only by means of the activities which they develop; it is not simply "by the peaceful shining forth of institutions" [*Interruptions on the extreme left and right*] that they are great at this hour.

* * *

As for me, I am astounded to find the monarchist parties becoming indignant over the fact that the Republic of France is following a policy which does not confine itself to that ideal of modesty, of reserve, and, if you will allow me the expression, of bread and butter [*Interruptions and laughter on the left*] which the representatives of fallen monarchies wish to impose upon France. [*Applause at the center.*]

. . . [The Republican Party] has shown that it is quite aware that one cannot impose upon France a political ideal conforming to that of nations like independent Belgium and the Swiss Republic; that something else is needed for France: that she cannot be merely a free country, that she must also be a great country, exercizing all of her rightful influence over the destiny of Europe, that she ought to propagate this influence throughout the world and carry everywhere that she can her language, her customs, her flag, her arms, and her genius. [*Applause at center and left.*]

Joseph Chamberlain

10. BRITAIN'S UNDEVELOPED ESTATES

Originally a left-wing Liberal mainly concerned with domestic social reform, Joseph Chamberlain (1836-1914) abandoned his party chief, Gladstone, in 1886 in protest against the latter's commitment to home rule for Ireland. In subsequent coalition with the Conservatives of Lord Salisbury, Chamberlain deliberately chose the post of Colonial Secretary for himself and proceeded to direct large amounts of both political and financial capital into building up the Empire. His position grew even stronger with Britain's victory in the 1899-1902 Boer War in South Africa. Chamberlain's insistence on risking higher domestic food prices for an imperial tariff union, however, helped bring about his party's cataclysmic electoral defeat in 1906.

My right hon. Friend who opened this Debate in the first instance suggested some change in the arrangement of the Colonial and Foreign Offices, and some redistribution of duty. I have only just entered on the administration and control of probably one of the largest dominions, and although I am credited with some personal ambition, at the present moment I do not desire any new world to conquer. My right hon. Friend spoke of the extension of railways in West Africa, and he asked whether I could give the Committee any information as to the policy we have adopted in that matter. The first question he asked was whether these railways were to be made by Imperial assistance, or by the colonies, or by private speculators. Of course, I do not know what the deputation which is to wait upon me tomorrow will have to say on the subject, but I can say at once that the Government are of opinion that, wherever it is possible, it is better that railways in these circumstances should be made either by the colony or by the Imperial Government, rather than handed over to private speculators. In these cases there is more probability of an economical progress of the work if it is taken up by the Government instead of by private speculators. ["Hear, hear!"] Then there arises the important question as to whether communications are to be made or assisted by the Imperial Government. My hon. Friend has explained that in the present in-

Great Britain, *Hansard Parliamentary Debates*, 4th ser., XXXVI (August 22, 1895): 640-644.

stance there is no claim for Imperial assistance; it has not been asked for, and the conditions of those colonies are not such as to make it necessary. Nothing is more extraordinary to my mind during my short experience at the Colonial Office than the extraordinary growth of trade in those West African colonies. A few years ago they were thought of as almost worthless possessions, but I believe at the present time the trade with those colonies alone is as much as that with some considerable European countries. [*Cheers.*] Not only so; the trade is rapidly increasing, because we are rapidly getting into communication with the interior. No trade is possible as long as native disturbances are taking place, and when hon. Members, animated no doubt by philanthropic intentions, protest against expeditions, punitive or otherwise, which are now the only way we can establish peace between contending savage tribes in Africa, they are protesting against the only system of civilising and practically of developing the trade of Africa. These internecine contests with the native tribes are brought about, not by the general will of the people, but by the arbitrary action of the chiefs; and it has often happened in the past that those persons who have hitherto held authority are taught by a sharp lesson that they cannot be allowed to continue to conduct those operations, and peace is thereby secured, and immediately there will be a large development of trade. In the case of those colonies, as far as I know, there is absolutely no necessity for Imperial intervention; but, if my right hon. Friend wishes from me a further declaration of policy, I am not sorry that an opportunity has been given to me to make it. I regard many of our colonies as being in the condition of undeveloped estates, and estates which can never be developed without Imperial assistance. [*Cheers.*] It appears to me to be absurd to apply to savage countries the same rules which we apply to civilised portions of the United Kingdom. Cases have already come to my knowledge of colonies which have been British colonies, perhaps, for more than 100

years, in which up to the present time British rule has done absolutely nothing; and if we left them to-day we should leave them in the same condition as that in which we found them. How can we expect, therefore, either with advantage to them or to ourselves that trade with such places can be developed? I shall be prepared to consider very carefully myself, and then, if I am satisfied, to confidently submit to the House, any case which may occur in which, by the judicious investment of British money, those estates which belong to the British Crown may be developed for the benefit of their population and for the benefit of the greater population which is outside. [*Cheers.*] My right hon. Friend seems to be afraid that these railways may lead to an extension of slavery. I think those fears have been removed, seeing that the railways will be carried out by the Government of the colonies under the Imperial advice and control. I entirely agree with my hon. Friend behind me, that the provision of railways will be the greatest security you can have for the ultimate extirpation of slavery. Reference has also been made to the introduction of spirituous liquors. It seems to be thought that it may be increased. Let me explain that I am as extremely anxious to prevent the introduction of these liquors into uncivilised countries as anyone can be. I agree, in the first place, that they inevitably bring about the deterioration and probably, ultimately, the extinction of the native population, so that we should kill the goose that lays the golden eggs — the people we want to be our best customers. Therefore, in our own interest, putting aside altogether questions of philanthropy, it should be our object, and it will be our object, to prevent the extension of this traffic. Let me say that my information is that the liquor is not so bad as is said, and I am assured by the Europeans that it is very tolerable drink. The real difficulty lies, as my hon. Friend said, in the acts of other countries. My right hon. Friend spoke yesterday of the promise we made to Europe and had not kept. What happened at the Berlin Congress? The British Government proposed a uniform duty of 10s. per gallon on spirits all round. It was voted down by France and Germany, and the figure fixed upon was 6s. 6d. a gallon. There is no doubt that in our endeavours to limit the evils consequent on this trade we are very much hampered. It must not be supposed that the question is confined to the amount of trade in strong drink. What unfortunately happens is this—that if the liquor is prohibited in the British protectorate the natives get it in a neighbouring protectorate. They will go almost any distance to get the coveted luxury, and where they get the liquor they make their other purchases, so that our traders not only lose the liquor traffic but cotton goods as well. That is not a reason for doing nothing, but it is a reason for proceeding with some caution, and before I can say anything more positive with regard to my intentions I must have time and opportunity, which I intend to take immediately, to communicate with the governors, and see whether any suggestions I may be able to make will enable them to deal with the matter. In the meantime I can assure my right hon. Friend that every effort will be made to reduce the trade to a considerable extent. Another point brought before the Committee is the proposed annexation of Bechuanaland to the Cape.* This is one of those cases, of which there are a great number in the Colonial Office, in which any person occupying my position has not really a free hand to deal with them; he is trammelled by the action of his predecessors for many years past. He finds that pledges have been given, promises or quasi-promises have been made, by which his hands are practically tied. What is the history of Bechuanaland? It was coveted by the Boers of the Transvaal. When I was a Member of Mr. Gladstone's Government the Boers were credited with the desire to set up a number of petty republics, which, no doubt, in a short time would have drifted to the larger republic, and so Bechuanaland would practically have become part of the Transvaal. That was

thought to be undesirable, and it would have been in direct violation of conventions with the Boers. Although the Transvaal would not *eo nomine* enter upon that course, yet it was a result that might have ensued. In order to prevent further mischief an expedition was sent out under Sir Charles Warren, and the country was taken possession of in the name of Great Britain. The expedition cost a million and a half. I should say it was not in any way to be debited to Bechuanaland proper; it was part of the general outlay of this Government in South Africa. After the expedition a positive offer was made to the Cape to take up the annexation; but the matter was not carried through, because the Cape Government was not prepared at that time to accede to the terms and conditions we proposed to make for the protection of the natives. The matter has been more or less under negotiation ever since. Without entering into detail, it appears to me we were practically committed when the Cape, by the unanimous resolution of its Parliament, expressed a desire for complete annexation. Since I read the papers the Bill has been received. Practically, the conditions which I think it my duty to enforce for the protection of the natives have been conceded entirely by the Cape Government. Let me, however, say that, although my argument has hitherto gone to this extent, that practically the policy of annexation was imperative upon us, it has not gone upon the merits. Yet on the merits there is a good deal to be said. One of the objections of the hon. Member for Holderness is handing over vast territories of this kind before they have been developed. I am sorry to say, unless the policy of this country is, as I hope it will be, considerably changed, they never will be developed under British rule, because, by our practice of leaving these possessions absolutely to themselves at a time when they possess no attraction for colonists, they never will be developed until, at all events, proper communications are made.

*Cape Colony, then the only self-governing British dependency in South Africa.

75

Count Bernhard von Bülow

11. GERMANY'S PLACE IN THE SUN

After the initial annexation of its four African colonies under Bismarck, Germany entered a period of conciliatory colonial policy. A second advance under Kaiser Wilhelm II and his favorite Chancellor, Count (later Prince) Bernhard von Bülow (1849–1929), was accompanied by a highly aggressive naval construction policy. (The Kaiser and the German Naval Minister, von Tirpitz, were heavily influenced by Mahan.) The main direction of annexation thus shifted to China and the South Seas, although highly controversial designs were still entertained against Portuguese Africa, Morocco, and the Congo. The following speech, von Bülow's maiden address in the Reichstag, was a prelude to Germany's virtual acquisition of Kiachow, on the Shantung peninsula, through a ninety-nine year lease from the Chinese Empire.

HERR VON BÜLOW (Foreign Secretary): The honorable member, Dr. Schoenlauf, seems to fear that in the Orient we want to throw ourselves into some kind of adventure. Gentlemen, you need have no fear! The honorable Imperial Chancellor and his coworkers are hardly the sort of people to seek out any unnecessary business. We do not at all feel compelled to stick our fingers in every pot. But at the same time we are of the opinion that it is not incumbent upon Germany to exclude herself beforehand from competing with other peoples for promising territories. ["Bravo!"]

The time has passed when Germany could abandon the land to one of its neighbors, the sea to another, and reserve for herself the heavens, where pure doctrine is king. [*Laughter.* "Bravo!"]

These times are passed. We consider it one of our most solemn duties to forward and to nourish the interests of our shipping, our trade, and our industry, particularly in the Orient.

The sending of a German cruiser squadron to the Bay of Kiachow and the occupation of this Bay are designed, on the one hand, to gain full retribution for the murder of German and Catholic missionaries and, on the other hand, to attain greater security in the future against the recurrence of such events. Discussions of the interests involved in both these questions are at an undecisive stage, and the nature of diplomatic negotiations and procedures forces me to guard my words. Nevertheless, I can say the following: our intentions toward China are entirely benevolent and friendly. [*Laughter on the left.*]

* * *

We have to guarantee that the German missionary and the German entrepreneur and German goods and the German flag and

Stenographische Berichte über die Reichstagsverhandlungen, Period 9, Session 5, December 6, 1897.

German ships receive the same respect in China as those of other powers. [*Lively "Bravo."*]

We are, of course, quite prepared to pay heed to the interests of other major powers in the Orient with the clear expectation that our own interests will likewise be valued according to their merits. ["Bravo!"]

In a word: we do not want to put anyone else into the shade, but we also demand our place in the sun. ["Bravo!"]

In the Orient, as in the West Indies, we will remain faithful to the traditions of German policy by defending our rights and our interests with neither unnecessary aggressiveness nor any show of weakness. [*Enthusiastic applause.*]

12. THEODORE ROOSEVELT WAVES AMERICA'S BIG STICK

The United States acquired its main formal overseas possessions — the Philippines, Hawaii, and Puerto Rico — in the burst of expansionist enthusiasm that surrounded the War of 1898 with Spain. A more sustained form of imperialism, however, developed during the 1901-1909 presidential term of Theodore Roosevelt (1858-1919), an early disciple of Mahan and a rabid supporter of the Spanish-American War. Roosevelt added to the possessions of the United States the zone in Central America through which the Panama Canal was then built. He extended the longstanding Monroe Doctrine, by which European colonialism was excluded from Latin America, to include United States hegemony in the Caribbean and the rights of the United States to "police action" against Latin American states who threatened the interests of foreign investors.

1

The Monroe Doctrine is not international law, and though I think one day it may become such, this is not necessary as long as it remains a cardinal feature of our foreign policy and as long as we possess both the will and the strength to make it effective. This last point, my fellow-citizens, is all important, and is one which as a people we can never afford to forget. I believe in the Monroe Doctrine with all my heart and soul; I am convinced that the immense majority of our fellow-countrymen so believe in it; but I would infinitely prefer to see us abandon it than to see us put it forward and bluster about it, and yet fail to build up the efficient fighting strength which in the last resort can alone make it respected by any strong foreign power whose interest it may ever happen to be to violate it.

Boasting and blustering are as objectionable among nations as among individuals, and the public men of a great nation owe it to their sense of national self-respect to speak courteously of foreign powers, just as a brave and self-respecting man treats all around him courteously. But though to boast is bad, and causelessly to insult another, worse; yet worse than all is it to be guilty of boasting, even without insult, and when called to the proof to be unable to make such boasting good. There is a homely old adage which runs: "Speak softly and carry a big stick; you will go far." If the

1. Speech delivered in Chicago, April 2, 1903, in *Addresses and Presidential Messages of Theodore Roosevelt, 1902-1904* (N.Y. 1904) pp. 121-122.
2. From Theodore Roosevelt to Cecil Spring Rice, July 24, 1905, in *Letters and Friendships of Cecil Spring Rice*, ed. Stephan Gwynn, Vol. I (London, 1929), p. 480.
Reprinted by permission of Constable & Co. Ltd. and Houghton Mifflin Company.

American nation will speak softly, and yet build, and keep at a pitch of the highest training, a thoroughly efficient navy, the Monroe Doctrine will go far. I ask you to think over this. If you do, you will come to the conclusion that it is mere plain common-sense, so obviously sound that only the blind can fail to see its truth and only the weakest and most irresolute can fail to desire to put it into force.

2

I am having my hands full also in endeavouring to make our people act on a rational interpretation of the Monroe Doctrine. No such policy as that of the Monroe Doctrine can remain fossilized while the nation grows. Either it must be abandoned or it must be modified to meet the changing needs of national life. I believe with all my heart in the Monroe Doctrine and have, for instance, formally notified Germany to that effect. But I also believe that we must make it evident on the one hand that we do not intend to use the Monroe Doctrine as a pretence for self-aggrandisement at the expense of the Latin-American republics, and on the other hand that we do not intend it to be used as a warrant for letting any of these republics remain as small bandit-nests of a wicked and inefficient type. . . .

THE OPPOSITION

William Jennings Bryan

13. THE IMPERIALIST THREAT TO DEMOCRACY

In the spring of 1898 the American public all but unanimously supported United States entry into a war with Spain for the ostensible purpose of freeing Cuba from colonial oppression. Immediately after the easy American victory, however, serious dissension arose over the disposal of two other captured Spanish possessions, Puerto Rico and the Philippines. Even when the decision had been taken to annex both, prolonged Filipino resistance to American rule kept alive the issue of anti-imperialism. Thus in 1900 William Jennings Bryan (1860-1925) could include a denunciation of imperialism in the following speech, with which he accepted the nomination of the Democratic Party for the Presidency. Bryan lost the ensuing election, but the widespread attitude he represented influenced both the rapid steps taken by later American governments towards granting Philippine independence and a general opposition to formal imperialism in American foreign policy.

If it is right for the United States to hold the Philippine Islands permanently and imitate European empires in the government of colonies, the Republican party ought to state its position and defend it, but it must expect the subject races to protest against such a policy and to resist to the extent of their ability.

The Filipinos do not need any encouragement from Americans now living. Our

Speech delivered at Indianapolis, Aug. 8, 1900, in *Speeches of William Jennings Bryan* (N.Y., Funk and Wagnalls, 1909).

whole history has been an encouragement, not only to the Filipinos, but to all who are denied a voice in their own government. If the Republicans are prepared to censure all who have used language calculated to make the Filipinos hate foreign domination, let them condemn the speech of Patrick Henry. When he uttered that passionate appeal, "Give me liberty or give me death," he expressed a sentiment which still echoes in the hearts of men.

Let them censure Jefferson; of all the statesmen of history none have used words so offensive to those who would hold their fellows in political bondage. Let them censure Washington, who declared that the colonists must choose between liberty and slavery. Or, if the statute of limitations has run against the sins of Henry and Jefferson and Washington, let them censure Lincoln, whose Gettysburg speech will be quoted in defense of popular government when the present advocates of force and conquest are forgotten.

Some one has said that a truth once spoken can never be recalled. It goes on and on, and no one can set a limit to its ever-widening influence. But if it were possible to obliterate every word written or spoken in defense of the principles set forth in the Declaration of Independence, a war of conquest would still leave its legacy of perpetual hatred, for it was God himself who placed in every human heart the love of liberty. He never made a race of people so low in the scale of civilization or intelligence that it would welcome a foreign master.

Those who would have this Nation enter upon a career of empire must consider, not only the effect of imperialism on the Filipinos, but they must also calculate its effects upon our own nation. We cannot repudiate the principle of self-government in the Philippines without weakening that principle here.

Lincoln said that the safety of this Nation was not in its fleets, its armies, or its forts, but in the spirit which prizes liberty as the heritage of all men, in all lands, everywhere, and he warned his countrymen that they could not destroy this spirit without planting the seeds of despotism at their own doors.

Even now we are beginning to see the paralyzing influence of imperialism. Heretofore this Nation has been prompt to express its sympathy with those who were fighting for civil liberty. While our sphere of activity has been limited to the Western Hemisphere, our sympathies have not been bounded by the seas. We have felt it due to ourselves and to the world, as well as to those who were struggling for the right to govern themselves, to proclaim the interest which our people have, from the date of their own independence, felt in every contest between human rights and arbitrary power.

Three-quarters of a century ago, when our nation was small, the struggles of Greece aroused our people, and Webster and Clay gave eloquent expression to the universal desire for Grecian independence. In 1898 all parties manifested a lively interest in the success of the Cubans, but now when a war is in progress in South Africa, which must result in the extension of the monarchical idea, or in the triumph of a republic, the advocates of imperialism in this country dare not say a word in behalf of the Boers.

* * *

The forcible annexation of territory to be governed by arbitrary power differs as much from the acquisition of territory to be built up into States as a monarchy differs from a democracy. The Democratic party does not oppose expansion when expansion enlarges the area of the Republic and incorporates land which can be settled by American citizens, or adds to our population people who are willing to become citizens and are capable of discharging their duties as such.

The acquisition of the Louisiana territory, Florida, Texas and other tracts which have been secured from time to time enlarged the Republic and the Constitution followed the flag into the new territory. It is now proposed to seize upon distant territory already more densely populated than our own country and to force upon the people a government for which there is no warrant in our Constitution or our laws.

Even the argument that this earth belongs to those who desire to cultivate it and who have the physical power to acquire it cannot be invoked to justify the appropriation of the Philippine Islands by the United States. If the islands were uninhabited American citizens would not be willing to go there and till the soil. The white race will not live so near the equator. Other nations have tried to colonize in the same latitude. The Netherlands have controlled Java for three hundred years and yet today there are less than sixty thousand people of European birth scattered among the twenty-five million natives.

After a century and a half of English domination in India, less than one-twentieth of one per cent of the people of India are of English birth, and it requires an army of seventy thousand British soldiers to take care of the tax collectors. Spain had asserted title to the Philippine Islands for three centuries and yet when our fleet entered Manila bay there were less than ten thousand Spaniards residing in the Philippines.

A colonial policy means that we shall send to the Philippine Islands a few traders, a few taskmasters and a few office-holders and an army large enough to support the authority of a small fraction of the people while they rule the natives.

If we have an imperial policy we must have a great standing army as its natural and necessary complement. The spirit which will justify the forcible annexation of the Philippine Islands will justify the seizure of other islands and the domination of other people, and with wars of conquest we can expect a certain, if not rapid, growth of our military establishment.

That a large permanent increase in our regular army is intended by Republican leaders is not a matter of conjecture, but a matter of fact. In his message of December 5, 1898, the President asked for authority to increase the standing army to 100,000. In 1896 the army contained about 25,000. Within two years the President asked for four times that many, and a Republican House of Representatives complied with the request after the Spanish treaty had been signed, and when no country was at war with the United States.

If such an army is demanded when an imperial policy is contemplated, but not openly avowed, what may be expected if the people encourage the Republican party by indorsing its policy at the polls?

A large standing army is not only a pecuniary burden to the people and, if accompanied by compulsory service, a constant source of irritation, but it is ever a menace to a republican form of government.

The army is the personification of force and militarism will inevitably change the ideals of the people and turn the thoughts of our young men from the arts of peace to the science of war. The government which relies for its defense upon its citizens is more likely to be just than one which has at call a large body of professional soldiers.

A small standing army and a well-equipped and well-disciplined State militia are sufficient at ordinary times, and in an emergency the nation should in the future as in the past place its dependence upon the volunteers who come from all occupations at their country's call and return to productive labor when their services are no longer required—men who fight when the country needs fighters and work when the country needs workers.

John A. Hobson

14. THE ECONOMIC BASIS OF IMPERIALISM

John A. Hobson (1858–1940) wrote his famous study of imperialism as a direct response to the Anglo-Boer War, in which large capitalists such as Cecil Rhodes had played a major role. However much it may have been invalidated by later investigations of the actual flow of European foreign investments during this period, Hobson's analysis did help to rally British radical opinion against the entire spirit of imperialism.

. . . it appears that the period of energetic Imperialism coincided with a remarkable growth in the income for foreign investments.

These figures, however, only give the foreign income which can be identified as such. The closer estimates made by Sir R. Giffen and others warrant the belief that the actual income derived from foreign and colonial investments amounted to not less than £100,000,000, the capital value of the same reaching a sum of about £2,000,000,000.

Income tax returns and other statistics descriptive of the growth of these investments indicate that the total amount of British investments abroad at the end of the nineteenth century cannot be set down at a lower figure than this. Considering that Sir R. Giffen regarded as "moderate" the estimate of £1,700,000,000 in 1892, the figure here named is probably below the truth.

Now, without placing any undue reliance upon these estimates, we cannot fail to recognise that in dealing with these foreign investments we are facing the most important factor in the economics of Imperialism. Whatever figures we take, two facts are evident. First, that the income derived as interest upon foreign investments enormously exceeded that derived as profits upon ordinary export and import trade. Secondly, that while our foreign and colonial trade, and presumably the income from it, were growing but slowly, the share of our import values representing income from foreign investments was growing very rapidly.

In a former chapter I pointed out how small a proportion of our national income appeared to be derived as profits from external trade. It seemed unintelligible that the enormous costs and risks of the new Imperialism should be undertaken for such small results in the shape of increase to external trade, especially when the size and character of the new markets acquired were taken into consideration. The statistics of foreign investments, however, shed clear light upon the economic forces which dominate our policy. While the manufacturing and trading classes make little out of their new markets, paying, if they knew it, much more in taxation than they get out of them in trade, it is quite otherwise with the investor.

It is not too much to say that the modern foreign policy of Great Britain has been primarily a struggle for profitable markets

From John A. Hobson, *Imperialism: A Study* (London, 1902), pp. 52–55, 81. Reprinted by permission of George Allen & Unwin Ltd.

of investment. To a larger extent every year Great Britain has been becoming a nation living upon tribute from abroad, and the classes who enjoy this tribute have had an ever-increasing incentive to employ the public policy, the public purse, and the public force to extend the field of their private investments, and to safeguard and improve their existing investments. This is, perhaps, the most important fact in modern politics, and the obscurity in which it is wrapped has constituted the gravest danger to our State.

What was true of Great Britain was true likewise of France, Germany, the United States, and of all countries in which modern capitalism had placed large surplus savings in the hands of a plutocracy or of a thrifty middle class. A well-recognised distinction is drawn between creditor and debtor countries. Great Britain had been for some time by far the largest creditor country, and the policy by which the investing class used the instrument of the State for private business purposes is most richly illustrated in the history of her wars and annexations. But France, Germany, and the United States were advancing fast along the same path. The nature of these imperialist operations is thus set forth by the Italian economist Loria:

"When a country which has contracted a debt is unable, on account of the slenderness of its income, to offer sufficient guarantee for the punctual payment of interest, what happens? Sometimes an out-and-out conquest of the debtor country follows. Thus France's attempted conquest of Mexico during the second empire was undertaken solely with the view of guaranteeing the interest of French citizens holding Mexican securities. But more frequently the insufficient guarantee of an international loan gives rise to the appointment of a financial commission by the creditor countries in order to protect their rights and guard the fate of their invested capital. The appointment of such a commission literally amounts in the end, however, to a veritable conquest. We have examples of this in Egypt, which has to all practical purposes become a British province, and in Tunis, which has in like manner become a dependency of France, who supplied the greater part of the loan. The Egyptian revolt against the foreign domination issuing from the debt came to nothing, as it met with invariable opposition from capitalistic combinations, and Tel-el-Kebir's success bought with money, was the most brilliant victory wealth has ever obtained on the field of battle."

But, though useful to explain certain economic facts, the terms "creditor" and "debtor," as applied to countries, obscure the most significant feature of this Imperialism. For though, as appears from the analysis given above, much, if not most, of the debts were "public," the credit was nearly always private, though sometimes, as in the case of Egypt, its owners succeeded in getting their Government to enter a most unprofitable partnership, guaranteeing the payment of the interest, but not sharing in it.

Aggressive Imperialism, which costs the taxpayer so dear, which is of so little value to the manufacturer and trader, which is fraught with such grave incalculable peril to the citizen, is a source of great gain to the investor who cannot find at home the profitable use he seeks for his capital, and insists that his Government should help him to profitable and secure investments abroad.

If, contemplating the enormous expenditure on armaments, the ruinous wars, the diplomatic audacity or knavery by which modern Governments seek to extend their territorial power, we put the plain, practical question, *Cui bono?* the first and most obvious answer is, the investor.

* * *

The process, we may be told, is inevitable, and so it seems upon a superficial inspection. Everywhere appear excessive powers of production, excessive capital in search of investment. It is admitted by all business men that the growth of the powers of production in their country exceeds the growth in consumption, that more goods can be produced than can be sold at a profit, and that more capital exists than can find remunerative investment.

It is this economic condition of affairs that forms the taproot of Imperialism. If the consuming public in this country raised its standard of consumption to keep pace with every rise of productive powers, there could be no excess of goods or capital clamorous to use Imperialism in order to find markets: foreign trade would indeed exist, but there would be no difficulty in exchanging a small surplus of our manufacturers for the food and raw material we annually absorbed, and all the savings that we made could find employment, if we chose, in home industries.

V. I. Lenin

15. IMPERIALISM AS THE HIGHEST STAGE OF CAPITALISM

V. I. Lenin (Vladimir Ilyich Ulyanov, 1870-1924) wrote this essay-pamphlet on imperialism during World War I, very shortly before his successful leadership of the Russian Bolshevik Revolution. Without claiming any real originality of ideas, Lenin here not only links capitalism with imperialism but also joins the cause of the European industrial proletariat to that of non-European colonized populations.

We must now try to sum up and put together what has been said above on the subject of imperialism. Imperialism emerged as the development and direct continuation of the fundamental attributes of capitalism in general. But capitalism only became capitalist imperialism at a definite and very high stage of its development, when certain of its fundamental attributes began to be transformed into their opposites, when the features of the period of transition from capitalism to a higher social and economic system began to take shape and reveal themselves all along the line. The fundamental economic factor in this process is the substitution of capitalist monopolies for capitalist free competition. Free competition is the fundamental attribute of capitalism and of commodity production generally. Monopoly is exactly the opposite of free competition; but we have seen the latter being transformed into monopoly before our very eyes, creating large-scale industry and eliminating small industry, replacing large-scale industry by still larger-scale industry, finally leading to such a concentration of production and capital that monopoly has been and is the result: cartels, syndicates and trusts, and merging with them, the capital of a dozen or so banks manipulating thousands of millions. At the same time monopoly, which has grown out of free competition, does not abolish the latter, but exists alongside it and hovers over it, as it were, and, as a result, gives rise to a number of very acute antagonisms, friction and conflicts. Monopoly is a transition from capitalism to a higher system.

If it were necessary to give the briefest possible definition of imperialism we should have to say that imperialism is the monopoly stage of capitalism. Such a definition would include what is most important,

From V. I. Lenin, *Imperialism: The Highest Stage of Capitalism* (New York, 1939), pp. 88–90. Reprinted by permission of International Publishers Co. Inc. Copyright © 1939.

for, on the one hand, finance capital is the bank capital of the few big monopolist banks, merged with the capital of the monopolist combines of manufacturers; and, on the other hand, the division of the world is the transition from a colonial policy which has extended without hindrance to territories unoccupied by any capitalist power, to a colonial policy of the monopolistic possession of the territories of the world which have been completely divided up.

But very brief definitions, although convenient, for they sum up the main points, are nevertheless inadequate, because very important features of the phenomenon that has to be defined have to be especially deduced. And so, without forgetting the conditional and relative value of all definitions, which can never include all the concatenations of a phenomenon in its complete development, we must give a definition of imperialism that will embrace the following five essential features:

1) The concentration of production and capital developed to such a stage that it creates monopolies which play a decisive role in economic life.

2) The merging of bank capital with industrial capital, and the creation, on the basis of "finance capital," of a financial oligarchy.

3) The export of capital, which has become extremely important, as distinguished from the export of commodities.

4) The formation of international capitalist monopolies which share the world among themselves.

5) The territorial division of the whole world among the greatest capitalist powers is completed.

Imperialism is capitalism in that stage of development in which the domination of monopolies and finance capital has established itself; in which the export of capital has acquired pronounced importance; in which the division of the world among the international trusts has begun; in which the partition of all the territories of the globe among the great capitalist powers has been completed.

We shall see later that imperialism can and must be defined differently if consideration is to be given, not only to the basic, purely economic factors — to which the above definition is limited — but also to the historical place of this stage of capitalism in relation to capitalism in general, or to the relations between imperialism and the two main tendencies in the working class movement. The point to be noted just now is that imperialism, as interpreted above, undoubtedly represents a special stage in the development of capitalism. In order to enable the reader to obtain as well grounded an idea of imperialism as possible, we deliberately quoted largely from *bourgeois* economists who are obliged to admit the particularly indisputable facts regarding modern capitalist economy. With the same object in view, we have produced detailed statistics which reveal the extent to which bank capital, etc., has developed, showing how the transformation of quantity into quality, of developed capitalism into imperialism, has expressed itself. Needless to say, all the boundaries in nature and in society are conditional and changeable, and, consequently, it would be absurd to discuss the exact year or the decade in which imperialism "definitely" became established.

Joseph Schumpeter

16. IMPERIALISM AS A SOCIAL ATAVISM

As professor of economics, first in his native Austria and then in Germany and the United States, Joseph Schumpeter (1883–1950) was mainly concerned with the study of trade cycles, entrepreneurship, and innovation in capitalist economic development. His explanation of imperialism was essentially sociological in nature. At its initial publication in 1919, his book attracted little attention. Since then, however, it has become a standard tool in the refutation of the Hobson-Lenin thesis.

Our analysis of the historical evidence has shown, first, the unquestionable fact that "objectless" tendencies toward forcible expansion, without definite, utilitarian limits—that is, non-rational and irrational, purely instinctual inclinations toward war and conquest—play a very large role in the history of mankind. It may sound paradoxical, but numberless wars—perhaps the majority of all wars—have been waged without adequate "reason"—not so much from the moral viewpoint as from that of reasoned and reasonable interest. The most herculean efforts of the nations, in other words, have faded into the empty air. Our analysis, in the second place, provides an explanation for this drive to action, this will to war—a theory by no means exhausted by mere references to an "urge" or an "instinct." The explanation lies, instead, in the vital needs of situations that molded peoples and classes into warriors—if they wanted to avoid extinction—and in the fact that psychological dispositions and social structures acquired in the dim past in such situations, once firmly established, tend to maintain themselves and to continue in effect long

after they have lost their meaning and their life-preserving function. Our analysis, in the third place, has shown the existence of subsidiary factors that facilitate the survival of such dispositions and structures—factors that may be divided into two groups. The orientation toward war is mainly fostered by the domestic interests of ruling classes, but also by the influence of all those who stand to gain individually from a war policy, whether economically or socially. Both groups of factors are generally overgrown by elements of an altogether different character, not only in terms of political phraseology, but also of psychological motivation. Imperialisms differ greatly in detail, but they all have at least these traits in common, turning them into a single phenomenon in the field of sociology, as we noted in the introduction.

Imperialism thus is atavistic in character. It falls into that large group of surviving features from earlier ages that play such an important part in every concrete social situation. In other words, it is an element that stems from the living conditions, not of the present, but of the past—or, put in terms of

Reprinted by permission of the owners from Joseph A. Schumpeter, *Imperialism and the Social Classes*, New York: Augustus M. Kelley, pp. 83-86, 128-130 Copyright 1951, by Elizabeth B. Schumpeter. Translated by Heinz M. Norden.

the economic interpretation of history, from past rather than present relations of production. It is an atavism in the social structure, in individual, psychological habits of emotional reaction. Since the vital needs that created it have passed away for good, it too must gradually disappear, even though every warlike involvement, no matter how non-imperialist in character, tends to revive it. It tends to disappear as a structural element because the structure that brought it to the fore goes into a decline, giving way, in the course of social development, to other structures that have no room for it and eliminate the power factors that supported it. It tends to disappear as an element of habitual emotional reaction, because of the progressive rationalization of life and mind, a process in which old functional needs are absorbed by new tasks, in which heretofore military energies are functionally modified. If our theory is correct, cases of imperialism should decline in intensity the later they occur in the history of a people and of a culture. Our most recent examples of unmistakable, clear-cut imperialism are the absolute monarchies of the eighteenth century. They are unmistakably "more civilized" than their predecessors.

It is from absolute autocracy that the present age has taken over what imperialist tendencies it displays. And the imperialism of absolute autocracy flourished before the Industrial Revolution that created the modern world, or rather, before the consequences of that revolution began to be felt in all their aspects. These two statements are primarily meant in a historical sense, and as such they are no more than self-evident. We shall nevertheless try, within the framework of our theory, to define the significance of capitalism for our phenomenon and to examine the relationship between present-day imperialist tendencies and the autocratic imperialism of the eighteenth century.

* * *

Here we find that we have penetrated to the historical as well as the sociological sources of modern imperialism. It does not

coincide with nationalism and militarism, though it *fuses* with them by supporting them as it is supported by them. It too is — not only historically, but also sociologically — a heritage of the autocratic state, of its structural elements, organizational forms, interest alignments, and human attitudes, the outcome of precapitalist forces which the autocratic state has reorganized, in part by the methods of early capitalism. It would never have been evolved by the "inner logic" of capitalism itself. This is true even of mere export monopolism. It too has its sources in absolutist policy and the action habits of an essentially precapitalist environment. That it was able to develop to its present dimensions is owing to the momentum of a situation once created, which continued to engender ever new "artificial" economic structures, that is, those which maintain themselves by political power alone. In most of the countries addicted to export monopolism it is also owing to the fact that the old autocratic state and the old attitude of the bourgeoisie toward it were so vigorously maintained. But export monopolism, to go a step further, is not yet imperialism. And even if it had been able to arise without protective tariffs, it would never have developed into imperialism in the hands of an unwarlike bourgeoisie. If this did happen, it was only because the heritage included the war machine, together with its socio-psychological aura and aggressive bent, and because a class oriented toward war maintained itself in a ruling position. This class clung to its domestic interest in war, and the pro-military interests among the bourgeoisie were able to ally themselves with it. This alliance kept alive war instincts and ideas of overlordship, male supremacy, and triumphant glory — ideas that would have otherwise long since died. It led to social conditions that, while they ultimately stem from the conditions of production, cannot be explained from capitalist production methods alone. And it often impresses its mark on present-day politics, threatening Europe with the constant danger of war.

This diagnosis also bears the prognosis of imperialism. The precapitalist elements in our social life may still have great vitality; special circumstances in national life may revive them from time to time; but in the end the climate of the modern world must destroy them. This is all the more certain since their props in the modern capitalist world are not of the most durable material. Whatever opinion is held concerning the vitality of capitalism itself, whatever the life span predicted for it, it is bound to withstand the onslaughts of its enemies and its own irrationality much longer than essentially untenable export monopolism — untenable even from the capitalist point of view. Export monopolism may perish in revolution, or it may be peacefully relinquished; this may happen soon, or it may take some time and require desperate struggle; but one thing is certain — it *will* happen. This will immediately dispose of neither warlike instincts nor structural elements and organizational forms oriented toward war — and it is to their dispositions and domestic interests that, in my opinion, much more weight must be given in every concrete case of imperialism than to export monopolist interest, which furnish the financial "outpost skirmishes" — a most appropriate term — in many wars. But such factors will be politically overcome in time, no matter what they do to maintain among the people a sense of constant danger of war, with the war machine forever primed for action. And with them, imperialisms will wither and die.

It is not within the scope of this study to offer an ethical, esthetic, cultural, or political evaluation of this process. Whether it heals sores or extinguishes suns is a matter of utter indifference from the viewpoint of this study. It is not the concern of science to judge that. The only point at issue here was to demonstrate, by means of an important example, the ancient truth that the dead always rule the living.

A MODERN VIEW

D. K. Fieldhouse

17. INTERPRETATIONS OF IMPERIALIST PARTITION

The following evaluation of late nineteenth-century imperialism comes from the first general work to make use of recent research and perspectives on the entire phenomenon of modern overseas expansion. D. K. Fieldhouse is Beit Lecturer in the History of the Commonwealth and a Fellow of Nuffield College at Oxford University.

Three features distinguish the thirty years between 1883 and the outbreak of the First World War. The rate of imperial expansion increased considerably: more colonial territory was acquired than during the previous three-quarters of a century. Annexation was no longer usually or necessarily the outcome of strong pressures from the circumference on reluctant European governments. The number of European powers concerned was multiplied by the revival of Spanish and Portuguese interest and by the intervention of states with no previous colonial tradition —Germany, Italy, the United States and King Leopold II of the Belgians. These facts were of sufficient importance to distinguish the period of partition from that of expansion: yet by no means all was new. There was no break in the continuity of European expansion, and the forces already making for imperial growth continued. The fundamental question after 1883 is why selective acquisition by a few states as a response to problems on the periphery became headlong partition of the world among so many.

Four basic interpretations have been provided: two assign one overriding cause for the new imperialism. The first alleges that partition was due to economic necessity.

The industrialization of continental Europe and the revived protectionism of the last quarter of the century made tropical colonies necessary as never before to provide markets for manufactures, fields for the investment of surplus capital, and an assured source of raw materials. Colonies were deliberately acquired to fill these needs, and were circumscribed by tariffs and monopolies to ensure the advantage of the metropolis. This economic approach was given a specialized form by liberal-socialist writers like J. A. Hobson and by Marxists such as V. I. Lenin. Lenin emphasized the need of industrial capitalism in Europe to invest overseas, on the principle that the growth of "finance capital" and monopoly within Europe resulted in ever-declining profit margins for new investment. Thus tropical colonization was a means of staving off the eventual sterility of European capitalism and the coming of the socialist revolution.

Another single-cause explanation regards imperialism as an expression of European nationalism. By the 1870's the unification of Germany and Italy, the defeat of France in 1870–71, and the growth of jingoism in all countries generated a degree of international rivalry unknown since 1815. Colonies

Reprinted from *The Colonial Empires: A Comparative Study from the Eighteenth Century*, by D. K. Fieldhouse, Delacorte World History, 207, 212, 221-22. Copyright © 1965 Fisher Bucherei K. G. Frankfurt am Main. Copyright © 1966 by Dell Publishing Co., Inc. and George Weidenfeld & Nicolson Ltd. Used by permission of the publisher, Delacorte Press.

became sources of national power and symbols of prestige. Pressure of the uneducated mass vote in this first phase of European democracy forced aristocratic statesmen to acquire colonies; competition produced partition.

The weak points of these explanations cannot be examined in detail. Basically, both fall down on chronology. The phenomena on which they concentrate existed at one time or another, but developed too late to have been critical in the vital period before 1900. The great age of "finance capital," international cartels, banking trusts, etc., was after 1900 and still more after 1920. Britain, Russia, Germany, Italy, Spain, Portugal, and France were not seriously affected by them during the period of partition. Jingoistic imperialism also came late, reaching its peak in the 1920's: certainly there is little evidence that European statesmen were acting under such pressures in the 1880's and 1890's; more usually they had to stimulate public enthusiasm for acquisitions they had already made. In short, the colonial partition cannot be explained as the result of any one novel phenomenon within Europe.

A third approach assumes that partition was no more than a continuation of trends evident in the past half-century. Europe still did not hunger for new colonies; but the option was no longer open. Growing pressures on non-European societies now produced crises, similar to those in Tunisia or Fiji, in which indigenous governments cracked up or local nationalism reacted against "informal" alien interference. Thereafter "informal" control was no longer feasible: annexation became the alternative to evacuation. General partition was necessary both because older imperialisms had reached points of collision in West Africa, the Pacific and South-East Asia; and because more European states now had commercial or other interests in the colonial world which had to be accommodated. There are elements of truth in this theory: it rightly stresses that many new acquisitions can be explained in terms equally applicable to the previous half-century and were the

result of pre-existing situations. Yet it is not a full explanation of the partition. It is satisfactory only in certain cases. It cannot explain the new speed or extent of European expansion, for there were no irresistible local stimuli to European action in many places made colonies in the twenty years after 1882.

The fourth interpretation denies that Europe needed tropical colonies for economic reasons or that there was a great public demand for them. It recognizes that previous trends were accelerating, and were likely to generate full occupation and partition of certain regions. But it maintains that the suddenness and speed with which Africa and the Pacific were divided after 1882 were not fully explicable in these terms, and looks for new influences. It sees the answer in new diplomatic patterns within Europe, and pinpoints Bismarck's sudden claim for German colonies in 1884–5 as the genesis of the new situation. Bismarck treated colonies as undifferentiated diplomatic pawns which any great power could claim and use as bargaining counters. By staking large claims in Africa and the Pacific, and by bringing colonial disputes in West Africa to an international conference table, he created a stock-market in colonial properties which none could thereafter ignore. Any power which failed to make its own claims, however unsubstantiated, was liable to find itself ultimately barred from further expansion. Thus the essence of the partition was that a central-European statesman imposed continental methods of procedure on maritime powers who had hitherto treated colonies as their special preserve. Only along these lines is it possible to explain the sudden partition of Africa and the Pacific, or contemporary events in South-East Asia after 1882.

* * *

The eight years after 1883 were the most important in the second expansion of Europe. By 1890 the greater part of Africa and the Pacific had been claimed by one power or another as spheres of influence or full possessions; the partition of South-East Asia was almost complete; and it was predictable that the rest of the independent world would soon come under European rule.

The crisis which led to partition had its roots in the Congo situation and Anglo-French disagreement over Egypt; but it was made explosive by Bismarck. Leopold's Congolese claims could have been dealt with as a local issue. French resentment at British occupation of Egypt in 1882 was likely to stimulate French activity wherever she already had points of contact with Britain—in West Africa, South-East Asia and the Pacific. But it takes more than friction between two powers, who had no intention of fighting over such marginal issues, to generate a partition of the world. Partition could have come only if other major European powers entered the field. The entry of Germany as a claimant for colonies in 1884-5 was the cause of the new phase of European expansion.

The motives which led Otto von Bismarck, the German Chancellor, to claim colonies remain a matter of debate. It seems unlikely that he was convinced by the propaganda of theoretical German imperialists, or by German commercial groups with interests in Africa and the Pacific, that Germany needed colonies for economic reasons. He recognized that Germans needed protection in these places, and suffered from the absence of German bases; but it seems unlikely that Bismarck ever thought colonies intrinsically worth while. He remained a central European: security against Russia and France was infinitely more important than the dubious commercial advantage of possessing colonies. On the other hand by claiming colonies he might achieve strictly tactical political objectives on two fronts. Probably the more immediately important of these was to win the support of the National Liberals in the 1884 Reichstag elections by contriving a demonstration of national power in the colonial field. Certainly this policy succeeded, leading first to National Liberal support in 1884

and then to their coalition with the Conservatives in 1887. But the new colonial policy can also be linked closely with Bismarck's international calculations. His specific aim in 1884-5 was to mollify France by supporting her over Egypt and in West Africa. At the same time he wished to demonstrate to Britain the desirability of her working with rather than against Germany. He could achieve both objects by claiming colonies in areas which would not outrage France but would inconvenience Britain; claims which would, in fact, constitute weapons like the existing "Egyptian baton" which he could wield to bring Britain into line. Probably Bismarck had no long-term plan for using such colonies as diplomatic counters, though his successors in fact later did so. Devious though such motives may appear, it remains likely that the entry of Germany into colonial politics was in part the result of domestic political needs, in part, as has been said "the accidental by-product of an abortive Franco-German entente."

Bismarck's action in 1884-5 blew up half a century of imperial arrangements like a land-mine. In May 1884 he declared a protectorate over Angra Pequena, in South-West Africa, where there was already a private German claim to land. By July the German explorer Gustav Nachtigal had obeyed Bismarck's instructions to declare protectorates over Togoland, west of Lagos, and the Cameroons. In December Bismarck imposed a protectorate over the northern coast of New Guinea, on the basis of treaties made by a new German plantation company. Earlier a German warship had forced King Malietoa of Samoa to sign a new treaty giving Germany predominance in the Samoan group. Finally, in February 1885 Bismarck accepted treaties made by the German explorer, Carl Peters, imposing German protection on part of the East African coast opposite Zanzibar.

Tentative though these claims were—none amounting to more than a protectorate which could later be denounced—they set the tone of European expansion for the next quarter-century. Bismarck had demonstrated that any power strong enough to support its claims with authority could acquire colonies without occupying them: a few ambiguous treaties with native chiefs were all that was required. Once such lines had been drawn on the map they had considerable importance, for they could be erased by rivals only if they made counter-concessions to Germany. This demonstration had two consequences. It induced other states to make counter-claims for fear of losing their chances for good, or having later to pay too high a price for territory reserved by someone else; and it freed them from the need actually to occupy their claims. The first partition was, therefore, only an exercise in cartography by the chancellories of Europe, who were often hard put to find in the gazetteers the more remote places they now possessed. Yet it had serious consequences. The first claims could be relatively uncontroversial; there was still much to choose from. Taste grew with indulgence: by the 1890's the instinct to partition was stronger, yet had to be satisfied from a much reduced supply. The growing international bellicosity of the later 1890s and 1900s was a product of the bloodless partition of the 1880s.

* * *

By about 1890 the first phase of the partition was over and the outlines of the modern colonial empires were visible. The second phase, which lasted until 1914, was an inevitable consequence. Whereas the paper partition had been easy, cheap, and relatively amicable, the sequel was difficult, expensive and generated much international heat.

The period had two main features. First it was necessary for all who had taken part in the preliminary scramble to occupy their provisional spheres of interest—on pain of seeing them claimed by someone else—and to impose effective European authority on indigenous peoples who had hitherto met only a few individuals touting treaties. Occupation meant fighting. These were "lit-tle wars." They were expensive in money and lives, and in their effects on native societies, but they were inevitable. Apart from international dangers, each colonial power felt the financial burden of its new possessions. As in India and Indonesia in the past, and more recently in West Africa, the need to raise local revenues made it necessary to impose full government. There was also the incentive to "pacify" states on the periphery of existing colonies. Given metropolitan readiness to pay, there was now no military difficulty in doing this. The Maxim gun was the symbol of the second phase of the partition as the diplomats' cartography had been of the first.

By 1914 most of the new colonies had been pacified and occupied. The French fought long and expensive wars against the embattled Islamic states of the Western Sudan and in Dahomey, Madagascar, and Indo-China. Morocco had to be conquered as Algeria had been in the past. The British fought major campaigns against Ashanti, and the Khalifate of the Egyptian Sudan, and smaller campaigns in the Niger region and in East Africa. Rhodes' company fought the Matabele in 1893, and the British the Transvaal and Orange Free State from 1899–1902. The Germans had to suppress the Hereros rising in South-West Africa in 1904–7 and the Maji-Maji rising in Tanganyika in 1905–6, gaining an unjustified reputation for exceptional cruelty. The Belgians carried out a systematic conquest of the Congo region. Only the Italians were unsuccessful in their claim to rule "backward" peoples: in 1896 they were routed at Adowa by the Abyssinians, and had to give up their protectorate.

The other feature of this period was a growing bellicosity between the great powers which had various roots. After about 1904 it was primarily a reflection of European tensions and had little to do with colonies. Such jingoism was extended to the colonial sphere partly by its relevance to international diplomacy, partly by the growing imperialist enthusiasm evident in most European states. Though generated too late to influence the constructive phase of partition, such imperialism undoubtedly exacerbated its later stages, and embittered conflicts for the few remaining colonial lots. The fact that little of the world remained to divide gave it affinities with the last phase of the distribution of church properties in England during the 1550s, of which it was later said that

Such who had mannerly expected till the king carved for them out of abbey-lands, scrambled for themselves out of chantry-revenues, as knowing this was the last dish of the last course, and after chantries, as after cheese, nothing to be expected.

III. *Empires in Retreat: 1833-1960*

The patterns of both free trade and partitionist expansion in the nineteenth century had created a colonial world whose ultimate dissolution was virtually written into the charter of its establishment. There were occasional echoes of mercantilism among the advocates of the new imperialism; few of the recently acquired paternalist dependencies, however, proved sufficiently valuable — indeed, most were economic liabilities — to warrant the type of close control which had characterized the old regime. Thus, while the Old Colonial System had to be wrenched apart by an unexpected series of wars and revolutions, the new one expired more gradually and, in part at least, more gracefully.

Self-abrogation was first and most obviously foreseen by the nineteenth century builders of the paradigm of all paternalist colonies, British India. Responsible officials as early as Macaulay (1) spoke openly of ultimate self-government for India. By the latter part of the century, the nucleus of a modern Indian nationalist movement, the Indian National Congress, had, with British encouragement, made its first modest appearance (2).

Although overseas expansion had little direct bearing upon the outbreak of World War I, the conclusion of this conflict, which witnessed the long-awaited collapse of the Ottoman Empire, brought European imperialism to its territorial peak. At the same time the elimination of authoritarian Germany from the ranks of colonial powers and the combination of democratic idealism and profound cultural self-doubt which marked the Allied victory helped to shift the motif of paternalist colonialism even more sharply from expansion to preparation for self-rule. The Versailles Peace Treaty of 1919 set an official seal on this change by giving at least nominal control over the newly partitioned Ottoman and German possessions to the League of Nations in terms which clearly implied eventual emancipation (3).

Among those Europeans most directly responsible for maintaining the structure of colonial rule, the period between the two world wars witnessed the emergence of a somewhat ambivalent philosophy concerning the extent to which traditional non-European societies ought to be converted to western industrial values. This compound of political conservatism and cultural relativism is seen most easily in the British colonial doctrine of "Indirect Rule," but, even among the supposedly "assimilationist" French, it had important representatives (4). Britain, however, remained the center for more systematic reflection on this sort of "native policy," as evidenced in the writings of both officials and scholars (5).

Ideas such as Indirect Rule evolved in response not only to contradictions and doubts within the colonial system, but also to increasing pressure from outside, as western Europe became ever less an independent center of historical change. The most radical challenge to imperialism came from the Soviet Union and its agency, the Third Communist International (6). The Fascist powers also contributed to the anticolonial atmosphere, as Mussolini's posturing and brutal conquest of Ethiopia lent imperialism an odor from which it never recovered (7), while Japan conquered European possessions in the name of Asian self-determination (8). Finally, as the key World War II ally of the western powers, the United States exerted its influence for eventual decolonization (9).

Although the international and especially the internal groundwork had been laid long before (10), the actual emancipation of European colonies took place in two rapid stages after the Second World War. Again India set the relatively peaceful pattern (11) which was to be followed by much of southeast Asia during the latter 1940s and by Africa during the late 1950s and early 1960s (12). The less frequent but highly significant experience of colonial peoples seeking their independence by guerrilla warfare has occurred in French Indochina and Algeria, Portuguese Southern Africa, and the former Dutch Indonesia (13). Not all such struggles have yet achieved success, which is among the reasons that Part IV of this book will deal with the contemporary world as defined by the heritage of imperialism.

THE DISTANT PROMISE

T. B. Macaulay

1. THE EMANCIPATION OF INDIA

In his still popular historical writings, Thomas Babington Macaulay (1800–1859) eloquently represents all that was most smug and philistine in early nineteenth century English liberalism. During his brief but important service on the Council of the Indian Governor General, Macaulay demonstrated both sides of such an attitude, on the one hand condemning the barbarism of traditional oriental culture and on the other defending, as he does here in a later speech as a Member of Parliament, the rights of Indians to all the liberties implicit in the acceptance of British values.

There is . . . one part of the Bill on which . . . I feel myself irresistibly impelled to say a few words. I allude to that wise, that benevolent, that noble clause, which enacts that no native of our Indian Empire shall, by reason of his colour, his descent, or his religion, be incapable of holding office. At the risk of being called by that nickname which is regarded as the most opprobrious of all nicknames, by men of selfish hearts and contracted minds — at the risk of being called a philosopher — I must say that, to the last day of my life, I shall be proud of having been one of those who assisted in the framing of the Bill which contains that clause. We are told that the time can never come when the natives of India can be admitted to high civil and military office. We are told that this is the condition on which we hold our power. We are told, that we are bound to confer on our subjects — every benefit which they are capable of enjoying? — no — which it is in our power to confer on them? — no — but which we can confer on them without hazard to our own domination. Against that proposition I solemnly protest as inconsistent alike with sound policy and sound morality.

I am far, very far, from wishing to proceed hastily in this most delicate matter. I feel that, for the good of India itself, the admission of natives to high office must be effected by slow degrees. But that, when the fulness of time is come, when the interest of India requires the change, we ought to refuse to make that change lest we should endanger our own power — this is a doctrine which I cannot think of without indignation. Governments, like men, may buy existence too dear. "Propter vitam vivendi perdere causas," is a despicable policy either in individuals or in states. In the present case, such a policy would be not only despicable, but absurd. The mere extent of empire is not necessarily an advantage. To many governments it has been cumbersome; to some it has been fatal. It will be allowed by every statesman of our time, that the prosperity of a community is made up of the prosperity of those who compose the community, and that it is the most childish ambition to covet dominion which adds to no man's comfort or security. To the great trading nation, to the great manufacturing nation, no progress which any portion of the human race can make in knowledge, in taste for the conven-

Speech in the House of Commons, July 10, 1833, in *The Concept of Empire*, ed. George Bennett (London, 1953), 70-73.

iences of life, or in the wealth by which those conveniences are produced, can be matter of indifference. It is scarcely possible to calculate the benefits which we might derive from the diffusion of European civilisation among the vast population of the East. It would be, on the most selfish view of the case, far better for us that the people of India were well governed and independent of us, than ill governed and subject to us—that they were ruled by their own kings, but wearing our broad cloth, and working with our cutlery, than that they were performing their salams to English collectors and English Magistrates, but were too ignorant to value, or too poor to buy, English manufactures. To trade with civilized men is infinitely more profitable than to govern savages. That would, indeed, be a doting wisdom, which, in order that India might remain a dependency, would make it an useless and costly dependency—which would keep a hundred millions of men from being our customers in order that they might continue to be our slaves.

It was, as Bernier tells us, the practice of the miserable tyrants whom he found in India, when they dreaded the capacity and spirit of some distinguished subject, and yet could not venture to murder him, to administer to him a daily dose of the pousta, a preparation of opium, the effect of which was in a few months to destroy all the bodily and mental powers of the wretch who was drugged with it, and to turn him into an helpless idiot. That detestable artifice, more horrible than assassination itself, was worthy of those who employed it. It is no model for the English nation. We shall never consent to administer the pousta to a whole community—to stupify and paralyse a great people whom God has committed to our charge for the wretched purpose of rendering them more amenable to our control. What is that power worth which is founded on vice, on ignorance, and on misery— which we can hold only by violating the most sacred duties which as governors we owe to the governed—which as a people blessed with far more than an ordinary

measure of political liberty and of intellectual light—we owe to a race debased by three thousand years of despotism and priestcraft? We are free, we are civilized, to little purpose, if we grudge to any portion of the human race an equal measure of freedom and civilization.

Are we to keep the people of India ignorant in order that we may keep them submissive? Or do we think that we can give them knowledge without awakening ambition? Or do we mean to awaken ambition and to provide it with no legitimate vent? Who will answer any of these questions in the affirmative? Yet one of them must be answered in the affirmative, by every person who maintains that we ought permanently to exclude the natives from high office. I have no fears. The path of duty is plain before us: and it is also the path of wisdom, of national prosperity, of national honour.

The destinies of our Indian empire are covered with thick darkness. It is difficult to form any conjecture as to the fate reserved for a state which resembles no other in history, and which forms by itself a separate class of political phenomena. The laws which regulate its growth and its decay are still unknown to us. It may be that the public mind of India may expand under our system until it has outgrown that system; that by good government we may educate our subjects into a capacity for better government, that, having become instructed in European knowledge, they may, in some future age, demand European institutions. Whether such a day will ever come I know not. But never will I attempt to avert or to retard it. Whenever it comes, it will be the proudest day in English history. To have found a great people sunk in the lowest depths of slavery and superstition, to have so ruled them as to have made them desirous and capable of all the privileges of citizens would indeed be a title to glory all our own. The sceptre may pass away from us. Unforeseen accidents may derange our most profound schemes of policy. Victory may be inconstant to our arms. But there are triumphs which are followed by no reverses. There is an empire exempt from all natural causes of decay. Those triumphs are the pacific triumphs of reason over barbarism; that empire is the imperishable empire of our arts and our morals, our literature and our laws.

A. O. Hume

2. THE BEGINNINGS OF THE INDIAN NATIONAL CONGRESS

The following speech by Allan Octavian Hume (1829–1912), a retired British colonial officer who virtually founded the Indian National Congress in 1885, indicates the very moderate, not to say conservative, orientation of this organization in its earliest stages. Whatever the professed limitations of its aims, however, Congress soon became the vehicle for highly explosive political grievances and ultimately the instrument of Indian independence as well as the postindependence ruling party.

THE AIMS AND OBJECTS OF CONGRESS
30 April 1888

. . . It is desirable at the outset to explain that the Congress movement is only one outcome, though at the moment the most prominent and tangible, of the labours of a body of cultured men, mostly born natives of India, who some years ago banded themselves together to labour silently for the good of India. To understand the Congress thoroughly it is necessary to understand, first, what were the basal principles laid down by that body (which has since merged into the National Party) for their own guidance, — principles out of which the Congress and many other social and, if I may so term them, more spiritual movements (of which more will be heard as the years roll by) had their origin.

What these fundamental principles were I will take the liberty of reading to you. It is desirable that, in a matter out of which such momentous issues are, though as yet little noticed, already springing, there should be no mistake on a point like this. Well then the objects — the fundamental objects of what we may term from the designation assumed by its originators, the National movement — were threefold:

"First: the fusion into one national whole of all the different and, till recently, discordant elements that constitute the population of India;

"Second: the gradual regeneration along all lines, mental, moral, social and political, of the nation thus evolved; and

"Third: the consolidation of the union between England and India, by securing the modification of such of its conditions as may be unjust or injurious to the latter country."

* * *

Bearing in mind the basal objects of the larger movement, we shall now find less difficulty in realizing the scope of the special Congress machinery, constructed primarily in view to the political regeneration of the country. Bear that in mind; although it was perfectly realized that indirectly it would subserve other purposes, that indirectly it would promote the social, mental and moral progress of the nation, it was primarily and

From *The Evolution of India and Pakistan 1858-1947* by C. H. Philips, published by Oxford University Press. Reprinted by permission.

directly as a political institution that the Congress was founded. I dwell upon this because people are found fatuous enough to urge it as a reproach that the Congress does not directly meddle with social questions.

* * *

The Congress by its constitution can only pass resolutions in regard to questions on which there is a practical unanimity between all who take part in it. It was realized from the outset that there might be questions in regard to which Bombay would differ from Bengal, Europeans from Natives, Hindus from Mahomedans, Sunis from Sheahs; but all such are excluded from the Congress by its fundamental rule that it shall only pass and press resolutions on those questions in regard to which there is practically unanimity amongst the representatives of all classes and creeds of all provinces. Other questions, in regard to which no such general agreement can be arrived at, are left to be dealt with, as they may deem fitting, by the several provincial, local and sectional associations. The Congress is National, and it deals only with those questions on which the entire nation is practically agreed. If all or practically all the representatives of any province or any community object, the Congress must drop the subject.

* * *

But what have been its methods? Firstly, quiet teachings and preachings throughout the greater part of the country of simple elementary political truths. The people are taught to recognize the many benefits that they owe to British rule, as also the fact that on the peaceful continuance of that rule depend all hopes for the peace and prosperity of the country. They are taught that the many hardships and disabilities of which they complain are after all, though real enough, small in comparison with the blessings they enjoy, but that all these grievances may be and will be redressed if they all join to press their views and wishes unanimously, but temperately, on the Government

here and on the Government and people of England. The sin of illegal or anarchical proceedings are brought home to them, and the conviction is engendered that by united, patient, constitutional agitation they are certain ultimately to obtain all they can reasonably or justly ask for, while by any recourse to hasty or violent action they must inevitably ruin their cause and entail endless misery on themselves; and these teachings have gone on so quietly and unostentatiously that they have never once attracted even serious attention, much less unfavourable comment.

Second, amongst our methods is the distribution of elementary tracts setting forth similar doctrines and embodying teachings conceived in a like spirit in regard to the rights and duties of subjects. Of two of these, *viz.*, Mr. Veraraghava Chariar's Congress Catechism and a Conversation between Moulvi furreeduddeen and one Rambuksh of Kambakhtpur, some 50,000 copies were circulated during the past year, and perhaps half a million will be so circulated during the present year; and so far as I know these are the only tracts yet sent out. Although they are to be met with in every one of the twelve languages of India, they are also published in English, and every one of you may judge them for himself. I submit that when read as they stand, there is not one of you who will not agree that they are loyal and kindly alike in spirit and in word.

Third, amongst our methods must be reckoned public meetings — public meetings in hundreds — or rather, if we take the 28 months that have elapsed since the first Congress was held, public meetings to the number of more than one thousand — so marvellously orderly as a whole in their character as to astound even those most appreciative of the peaceful and law-abiding character of our population.

* * *

Do you not realise that by getting hold of the great lower middle classes before the development of the reckless demagogues, to which the next quarter of a century must otherwise give birth, and carefully inoculating them with a mild and harmless form of the political fever, we are adopting the only certain precautionary method against the otherwise inevitable ravages of a violent and epidemic burst of the disorder? I know that both in these provinces and the Punjab there are many officials — good men and true though not far-seeing — who are publicly and privately doing their utmost to impede the progress and hinder the happy development of this great and beneficent movement; but, Gentlemen, as they are good men, acting, though ignorantly, in all good faith, they will be very sorry later for this, and they will regret that before opposing they did not first take the trouble of thoroughly understanding the movement. . . .

Speaking, however, in these provinces, there is one more point that I feel most unwillingly compelled to touch upon — unwillingly, because on the one side stands a lifelong friendship, on the other the sacred duty that is imposed upon every man to speak the truth without fear or favour when the interests of his country and countrymen are at stake. I refer of course to the unfortunate schism of a section of the Musulmans, which threatens to impair temporarily the harmony of our movement and retard the fruition of the aspirations of India's best friends for her welfare. In dealing with this question I carefully distinguish between the doctrines preached and those who preach them. Against those gentlemen who are, as I hope, in all singleness of purpose and in good faith, preaching however unwisely, however blindly, the doctrines to which I shall refer, I have not one word to say. Their own consciences must be their judges to acquit or to condemn them. But the doctrines that these are preaching I must denounce, with all the earnestness, with all the energy, I possess.

3. THE LEAGUE OF NATIONS CONVENANT ON MANDATES

Like much in the agreements which ended World War I, the mandates provisions of the League of Nations Covenant represent a mixture of idealism and cynicism. The idealistic element—very directly, in this case, the product of the President of the United States, Woodrow Wilson—made the administration and emancipation of colonies as much an international question as had been their initial acquisition. Realistically, the mandates system vindicated, as had the earlier Berlin and Brussels agreements, the seizure of new overseas territories, in this case the Turkish and German possession which fell to Britain, France, and Belgium, Japan, South Africa and Australia. The supervisory powers of the League Permanent Mandates Commission proved also to be extremely limited. Nevertheless, the Arabic-speaking former Turkish provinces did receive their independence during the interwar period. Moreover, after World War II, the more aggressive successor to the Mandates Commission, the United Nations Trusteeship Council, has helped bring about the independence of Germany's former central African possessions. Former German Southwest Africa, however, remains under the disputed control of the Republic of South Africa.

ARTICLE 22

1. To those colonies and territories which as a consequence of the late war have ceased to be under the sovereignty of the States which formerly governed them and which are inhabited by peoples not yet able to stand by themselves under the strenuous conditions of the modern world, there should be applied the principle that the well-being and development of such peoples form a sacred trust of civilisation and that securities for the performance of this trust should be embodied in this Covenant.

2. The best method of giving practical effect to this principle is that the tutelage of such peoples should be entrusted to advanced nations who by reason of their resources, their experience or their geographical position can best undertake this responsibility, and who are willing to accept it, and that this tutelage should be exer-

cised by them as Mandatories on behalf of the League.

3. The character of the mandate must differ according to the stage of the development of the people, the geographical situation of the territory, its economic conditions and other similar circumstances.

4. Certain communities formerly belonging to the Turkish Empire have reached a stage of development where their existence as independent nations can be provisionally recognised subject to the rendering of administrative advice and assistance by a Mandatory until such time as they are able to stand alone. The wishes of these communities must be a principal consideration in the selection of the Mandatory.

5. Other peoples, especially those of Central Africa, are at such a stage that the Mandatory must be responsible for the administration of the territory under conditions which will guarantee freedom of conscience

and religion, subject only to the maintenance of public order and morals, the prohibition of abuses such as the slave trade, the
arms traffic and the liquor traffic, and the
prevention of the establishment of fortifica-
tions or military and naval bases and of military training of the natives for other than
police purposes and the defence of territory,
and will also secure equal opportunities for
the trade and commerce of other Members
of the League.

6. There are territories, such as South-
West Africa and certain of the South Pacific
Islands, which, owing to the sparseness of
their population, or their small size, or their
remoteness from the centres of civilisation,
or their geographical contiguity to the territory of the Mandatory, and other circumstances, can be best administered under the
laws of the Mandatory as integral portions
of its territory, subject to the safeguards
above mentioned in the interests of the indigenous population.

7. In every case of mandate, the Mandatory shall render to the Council an annual
report in reference to the territory committed to its charge.

8. The degree of authority, control or
administration to be exercised by the Mandatory shall, if not previously agreed upon
by the Members of the League, be explicitly
defined in each case by the Council.

9. A permanent Commission shall be
constituted to receive and examine the annual reports of the Mandatories and to advise the Council on all matters relating to
the observance of the mandates.

APOLOGETIC PATERNALISM

Marshal Lyautey

4. THE PRACTICAL NEED FOR INDIRECT RULE

As both a soldier and an administrator Marshal Louis Gonzalve Hubert Lyautey
(1854–1934) played a major role in much of modern French imperial history, including the conquests of Indochina, Madagascar, and North Africa and the establishment of peaceful rule in Morocco. The last of these ventures taught Lyautey to
appreciate the paradoxical necessity for limiting French cultural influence in order to safeguard French political dominion. In the following memorandum to his
Moroccan staff, Lyautey explains the reasons and methods for directing indigenous political energies into traditional channels.

PROTECTORATE POLICY
18 November 1920

The moment has now arrived to strike a
decisive blow in regard to native policy and
the participation of the Muslim element in
public affairs.

We have to take a very direct look at the
world situation and especially the situation
of the Muslim world and not allow ourselves to be overtaken by events.

It is more than a mere coincidence that
formulas concerning the rights of people to
self-determination and ideas of emancipation and evolution in a revolutionary sense
have been set loose throughout the world.

From Pierre Lyautey, ed., *Lyautey l'Africain*, Vol. IV (Paris, Plon, 1957), 25-36, with omissions. Reprinted by permission of Librairie
Plon.

We must avoid the belief that the Moroccans are free, or will be free very long, from this general movement. If the xenophobia of the Maghrib and its jealous spirit of independence has maintained for centuries a watertight bulkhead between it and the rest of the world and has kept it frozen in a rigid theocratic form, these times are over now.

First of all, the very fact of our arrival in the country and the consequent increasing European immigration, our journals, our habits of open discussion, and our maintenance of an independent attitude in the face of all authority, all these have been enough to help the country profoundly and make it aware of a mass of things hitherto unknown here. Moreover, the [First World] War intervened to multiply the points of contact. Thousands of Moroccans have been to France, to Europe, and not only fought there side by side with our own troops but served there in industries, lived in cities, learned to read and understand French, and have returned to Morocco full of new ideas. Furthermore, the barriers on the east coast have been lowered, allowing a growing influx of Algerian and Tunisian natives, whose mentality is less and less archaic and is not generally sympathetic to our domination. They are becoming little by little the most important businessmen, are in the administration, and infiltrate everywhere. Then, all these influences are falling upon a people which is by far the most intelligent and responsive of all North Africa.

* * *

In this country, already heavily populated and tending to rapid overpopulation, European immigration is limited, in any case, by the lack of vacant lands and will never constitute more than a very small minority. The occupation forces here are fatally undergoing a gradual reduction; moreover, since the War, the European element here is but a weak minority, which is still being reduced, little by little, to specialists alone. Practically the only consolidated European military force remaining here is the Foreign Legion, whose precarious fidelity depends upon our strength.

Thus we have only a very fragile dike to oppose the rising tide. Nothing would be more dangerous than to let the European immigrants indulge in costly indiscretions, than to let the germs of discontent and ill feeling grow among this [native] people.

Having noted the above, where are we left?

Our establishment in this country is based on the Doctrine of the Protectorate. We proclaim it; the Government proclaims it at every opportunity. But is it anything more than a fiction? In this respect, are we, after eight years, progressing or are we standing still, even regressing in certain areas?

* * *

The conception of the Protectorate is that of a country which retains its institutions, governing and administering itself with its own organs, merely under the control of a European power that takes its place in external affairs, generally takes charge of the administration of its army and its finances, and directs it in its economic development. The dominating characteristic of this conception is the formula *Control* as opposed to the formula *Direct Administration*.

It should have as its result a minimum of general expenses.

How does the Moroccan Protectorate work in actual practice?

First of all, in relation to the Sultan.

Great care to safeguard his external prerogatives, to surround him with the dignities of protocol. But, beneath this appearance, what is the reality?

All administrative measures are taken in his name. He signs the dahirs [decrees]. But in practice he has no real power, he has contact with only the Sheriffian [dynastic] councillor, whom he sees daily; but that is all. His advice is, in fact, requested only for the sake of form. He is too isolated, closed up in his palace, too much removed from the movement of public affairs, never going to see things for himself despite his unquestionable desire to do so and the very real interest that he takes in things, although maintaining great reserve and waiting until someone offers the opportunity to him.

In the beginning, at the expressed desire of the Resident General, the principal department chiefs went in turn to the weekly Council of Viziers [ministers], where the Director of the Information Department was in regular attendance to report the current political and military situation. Little by little, this habit has dissolved. The Director of Information has passed it on to a subordinate officer.

The Grand Vizier and the Viziers do not take part in any deliberations concerning the important affairs handled exclusively, and removed from them, by the French Service. They are kept up to date only very summarily by the Sheriffian Advisor, who himself has only a limited knowledge and is not equipped to clarify technical matters.

There is almost no contact between the Service, nor of the affairs under the control of the Service heads, and the Viziers. The Maghzen [traditional government], which nothing can stir to action, is in danger of sinking gently into sleep.

Below the level of the Maghzen, the participation of the native element in public affairs is still too insecure. . . .

In point of fact, everything is tending more and more toward direct administration.

Apart from its formal contradiction of the spirit of the Protectorate, this situation represents a very serious danger. It would be totally illusory to believe that the Moroccans do not take note of the extent to which they are kept out of public life. They suffer from it and talk about it.

It is only a step from here to the coming of the day when they will be receptive to hostile inspirations and suggestions for the vindication of their rights. More and more they will become aware of their own worth and power. They are neither a barbaric nor an inert people. They are very curious about what goes on around them and are well informed. They are eager for education and very adaptable. They have formed within their midst a young generation which senses its own life and wants to take action, which has a taste for education and public life. For want of those openings which our administration makes so narrow for them and under such subordinate conditions, they seek their way elsewhere, as an example, among those European groups who are quite prepared to welcome them and use them for their own purposes of opposition or else among external Muslim groups, and, finally, they seek to form their own groups to formulate their demands, as has already happened during last June following the unfortunate speech of M. Guyot, President of the Chamber of Agriculture of Chaouia, in which he called for an independent press, educational reforms, etc., etc. . . . .

We can be sure that immediately around us, without our knowledge, there is growing up an entire movement of ideas, of secret meetings, of commentaries on world events and the conditions affecting Islam and that one day all of this will become incarnate and burst forth if we do not give it our attention and if we delay in taking direction of the movement.

I know very well what the practical difficulties are. There is some value in calling them to mind. First of all, we have direct administration in our blood, civil administrators coming from France, military officers coming from Algeria. We do not know Arabic. We have no patience. And, to establish contacts between the service and the natives, patience will be needed, both at the beginning and for a long time afterwards. It is an ungrateful, tiring task because of the difference in mentality, in work habits, the difficulty of compelling them to conduct public affairs with precision and speed. Nevertheless, the result will be attained far more easily with the Moroccans than with any other Muslim race, insofar as one can judge them by the energy and practical sense which they bring to commercial affairs, by their coöperation with Europeans, by their private affairs. Yet, as far as we are concerned, almost everything having to do with administration more or less surrenders to a tendency to regard the natives as an inferior race and a negligible quantity.

It is high time that someone cried out, "Halt!" We can be sure, I repeat, that contact with Europeans, Algerians, and Tunisians will encourage the rapid formation of an ambitious younger generation which considers itself underemployed, which educates itself, which learns French, and which, as soon as it becomes conscious of its qualities and its strength, will ask why it is denied a role in the management of public affairs.

It is thus necessary to enter resolutely and quickly onto a new path.

The following is, in general, how I view the matter:

First of all the *Sultan* and the *Maghzen.*

I would like the organ in charge of directing the dynasty to have a permanent "galvanizer" function, that it not be limited to serving as a mailbox and an organ of transmission but that it undertake the education of the Sultan, of the Viziers, and of all the personnel of the Maghzen; that, instead of serving as a screen, it should assure their contact with all the French Services, spontaneously offering to the Council of the Viziers and to the offices of the Maghzen access to all the Service heads, taking advantage of the opportunity of every new measure to establish regular circulation between the Benikas [local chiefs] of the areas directly controlled by the Maghzen and the local European officials; that it encourage the Sultan to summon such and such a director to bring him up to date on important current matters on public works, education, finances, etc. . . . That, finally, the dynastic advisor take the initiative in having the Sultan visit various establishments, the principal workshops, which would fascinate him and cause him to have our agents make all sorts of explanations to him on the spot. That ought to be his role, and, if he has not fulfilled it in this way up to now, he ought resolutely to do so in the future.

It is necessary also to give the most careful attention to the education of the young princes of the blood and especially to the eldest, who will apparently be called upon to succeed his father some day.

It would be inexcusable for us not to prepare these children of twelve and ten years for their roles in a Protectorate regime. They have already begun the study of French, but, without any model to emulate and despite being gifted, they have not made the same progress as others. At their age, nothing is easier than to awaken their minds and to direct their curiosity towards all the questions which concern the development of Morocco. We must find a formula which, without abuse and without excess, will open up more contacts for them and induce them little by little towards a general participation in modern life.

I think that from now on the directors ought to take the initiative in causing them to be summoned to the Council of Viziers in order to set forth their concerns. . . .

But above all it is the Grand Vizier whose acquired experience in European affairs ought to be utilized by having him associate more and more with the general administration. . . . It would even be of interest if, with the agreement of the Sultan, he should often attend the presentation of administrative reports and even the monthly Councils of the government. . . . His presence in our midst would be the first and best affirmation of the practice of the Protectorate.

From another perspective, a young governmental personnel has come into existence. In recent times, there are, among the families of the Maghzen and those around them, young people who speak French, who are intelligent, ambitious, and who can be utilized, unless we wish to see them drift elsewhere, which would be to our great detriment. There are too many unemployed forces in this quarter. I address all directors to ask them to seek out these forces, that they give them employment, that they create for them honorable paying positions, and that they make openings for them. I foresaw four years ago (1916) that trainees for the various services would develop from the upper courses of the Muslim secondary schools. This has remained practically a dead letter. I ask that you refer back to that text. The ideal of a Protectorate administration should be to create a team of auxiliaries qualified progressively to replace Frenchmen in many jobs, thus remedying the shortage of personnel. . . .

EDUCATION

It is by this means above all that the most fruitful and effective work can be accomplished, that one can most activate the spirit of Young Morocco.

Here is a whole job to be undertaken, which has been neglected too long.

It is through the schools that we will create an elite ready to join with us and form the living substance of the personnel of the Protectorate:

Through the Muslim secondary schools in which, it goes without saying, we ought to instill the most intensive life, with the most carefully selected staff, without alienating them from the principles of their institutions.

Through schools for the upper classes, which also have to be given much more attention and developed.

Finally, *especially* through the secular secondary schools, where I think that we can begin to introduce, even if in very small numbers, elective subjects as soon as the students have decided to enter European professions (and there are some such). It is better to take these in hand ourselves than to let them put themselves into the tow of some Frenchman or go and seek higher education in France, which would inevitably happen.

And also through our agricultural schools, where I would be happy to see some native trainees, sons of large landowners.

It is thus that a native elite prepared to collaborate with us will be created. The remarkable results already achieved at the Maknes student officers school proves what real possibilities lie on the path of adaptation.

For the mass of the population, there are primary schools and, above all, professional schools, which are still only in an embryonic stage and which require much development.

* * *

And then, after we have taught the elite to work with us, to lean on us, after we have made sure that their aspirations and legitimate ambitions will have outlets worthy of their history, traditions, and aptitudes, there will be much less reason to fear that they will evolve away from us and come under the influence of external influences and revolutionary suggestions. It will not be necessary to feel terror at the creation of some Arab newspapers and periodicals which are liberal but directed and controlled by us. Moreover, this is an inevitable development from which we will not escape and for which we must prepare the terrain.

* * *

But what we must believe is that a new period is dawning and threatening.

The success of the Bolshevists in the Crimea, their approach to Constantinople and the Levant, the counterblow which Islam has produced, the proclamations of independence in Egypt and Tripolitania, these are world events which are going to create a new situation tomorrow. We must not let ourselves be taken by surprise. Tunisia and Algeria are already deeply disturbed. It would be inexcusable to go to sleep in Morocco and imagine that we could long evade the counterblow of such events. The best palliative is to give the Moroccan elite the means of evolving on their own terms as quickly as possible, to give satisfaction to their inevitable aspirations in time, to fulfill at their sides in the fullest sense the role of a tutor, a benevolent older brother with whom they are interested in remaining linked, and thus to profit from dealing not with dust but with a nation whose emancipation will take place under our tutelege, under our direction, to our gain, and it would be a perilous illusion indeed to imag-ine that we could keep it in hand indefinitely with our tiny and fragile pellicle of occupation.

Margery Perham

5. THE IDEOLOGY OF INDIRECT RULE

As an Oxford don and frequent governmental advisor on African affairs, the recently retired Dame Margery Perham was able to view the colonial scene through the eyes of administrators, metropolitan intellectuals, and even budding anticolonial nationalists who were studying in England. Miss Perham was an especially close friend, and later the biographer, of Lord Lugard, who coined the term "Indirect Rule" to describe his administration of Nigeria between 1900 and 1919. Here, in a report on the application of Lugard's methods to the former German territory of Tanganyika (today Tanzania), she expresses the spirit in which Indirect Rule was accepted during its interwar heyday.

The object of my visit to Southern and Eastern Africa was to make a comparative study, but I intend in this paper to deal with Tanganyika. This is not because I over-estimate its importance or its singularity. Indirect rule in its general sense is not an invention of this age, and even in the special sense it has acquired during the last twenty years the classic example is in Nigeria. I know that you will all feel with me what a privilege it is for us to meet here at the invitation and in the presence of that administrator [Lord Lugard] whose career was first bound up with the acquisition of East Africa and then with the construction of the system of government in West Africa, the influence of which now reacts upon the East. Exactly what Tanganyika owes to Nigeria could only, perhaps, be learned by "listening in" at a conversation between Lord Lugard and Sir Donald Cameron [Governor of Tanganyika, 1925-1931] of a kind that we may suspect has been taking place during the last few weeks. I certainly do not know myself, though I hope to go out shortly to the West Coast in order to find out, if only in part.

Nor, though I shall concentrate upon that very constructive piece of work that has been carried through during the last six years by Sir Donald Cameron, do I forget that Sir Horace Byatt had ably laid the foundations during a very difficult period; nor do I think Sir Donald's work stands in need of being exalted by a depreciation of German methods that has already gone a good deal farther than the truth.

Whether or not it is successful, the government of Tanganyika is bound to be important. Its large area lies between the northern and southern British territories, and whatever develops there will react north and south with increasing force. Tanganyika has already figured in a South African election, while the Nyassaland government has made an official investigation of the system in force north of the border, before revising some of its own native institu-

From Dame Margery Perham, "The System of Native Administration in Tanganyika," *Africa*, Vol. V (1931), pp. 302-312. Reprinted by permission of the International African Institute and the author.

tions. Moreover, this advanced system of native local government is being developed in a country where there is white settlement.

The importance of the system of native administration in Tanganyika, however, lies mainly in its intrinsic qualities, and it is these that I want to bring out. I do not think it is necessary for me to spend very much time upon the legal framework of the system, which is made up of the ordinances providing for native courts, native authority, and the rest. Their composition does not vary greatly from that of laws in force in Uganda and elsewhere, and such differences as there are would not convey any impression of the special character of the Tanganyika system. Briefly, units of native administration are recognized by the Government and clothed with statutory powers. These units combine executive, judicial, legislative, and financial powers within the limits proper to local government; not many of the affairs of an African peasantry go outside those limits. The measure of control on the part of the political officers varies in accordance with the varying development of the tribes, but is mostly confined to advice and supervision, to the checking of court records, and to very careful co-operation in all the business connected with finance.

* * *

I find some difficulty in choosing my third illustration of what I have called the evolutionary character of the administration, because so many interesting examples crowd upon my memory. I think, however, that of the Lindi clans of the Wamakinde is worth selecting as a very helpful piece of administrative experience.

In South-Eastern Tanganyika, partly as a result of disintegrating influence from the coast and partly of the battering-ram of the Angoni invasions and the hiving-off of the Wayao and the Wamakua, restless elephant-hunters who have managed to string themselves out all the way from the Zambesi to the Rufiji, the peoples have very little tribal solidarity, and in many cases the small clans live scattered and independent. There was no sign of a chief here; no one who could be made into a chief, and the first opinion in the administration was that nothing could be built out of such fine grains of sand, and that here the people must be ruled directly, by agents, or *akidas,* as the Germans had ruled in these parts. But no one concerned liked the idea of having an exception to a good system, and the long, difficult, and laborious process was begun of putting these small cells under the microscope, of examining the claims of some hundreds of *wakalungwa* or clan-heads, deciding their boundaries, and of putting all decisions to the judgement of the people concerned. Upon this broad and true foundation a first story is being erected of associations of neighbouring *wakalungwa* in courts and councils, which can be carried farther as the people become ready for wider co-operation. I emphasize this process because the argument is put forward that Kenya cannot adopt the Tanganyika principle because of the absence of chiefs. This small-cell organization, however, is the basis even where there are chiefs, and it may even prove all the easier with time and patience to build up really vital and democratic institutions where we have not the temptations which the office of chief presents to us and to which I shall shortly refer. (I need hardly say I use the word democratic in its most general sense.) It would seem that if an attempt should be made in Kenya to shift the basis of native local government more nearly upon indigenous foundations, then the experience so hardly earned in Tanganyika should be drawn upon. It is possible, even, that Uganda might find that experience interesting, in view of the problem presented by her less coherent Nilotic and north-eastern Bantu people, which she is trying to solve by rather different methods.

I have so far offered you only appreciation of what is being done in Tanganyika, selecting what I consider the more valuable features of the system. My standard of judgement has been that provided by my study of actual administration in Southern and East-ern Africa. There is, however, another and ideal standard from which the best system yet achieved must fall very short, and I think it is neither inconsistent nor idle to turn from appreciation by one standard to criticism by another.

I have spoken of the voluminous reports upon tribal history and institutions pouring into head-quarters to form the basis for the dispositions of the government. Regarded as anthropological material, their quality is of course very variable. Few of the officers engaged in this work had received any training at all, least of all in anthropological technique, and though many of them were gifted with those qualities of mind and character that enabled them to train them-selves and to produce valuable results, yet the very conditions of their work provided a further obstacle, in the constant transfers, in the wide varieties between the tribes, in the almost universal ignorance of their lan-guages, and in the huge numbers and areas that make up most of the districts. We have, indeed, no standard by which to measure our own ignorance, or to guess at the pro-portion of the unknown to the known. Some sense of this is felt by experienced officers and is, in this work, the beginning of wis-dom. It is tragic to think how many of our expensive administrative officers, and still more, perhaps, of our technical officers, through no fault of their own, are at this moment merely fingering the surface of their material, and in some cases actually rubbing it the wrong way. I believe that it is possible in Africa for the reports upon a dis-trict and even a province to be perfectly sat-isfactory while in fact the administration is being carried on in no kind of partnership with the people, and that this would not be due to any disingenuousness on the part of the officers concerned.

There are difficulties of another kind which are inherent in the policy of indirect rule. Perhaps we cannot with the best will — and we generally have that — surmount these difficulties, but it is well to recognize them. Under natural conditions tribal insti-tutions were strong and supple, like the muscles of an athlete in training, because the hard necessities of war, of migration, and of self-preservation were using them to the utmost. We have come and have im-posed our power above the chief's power, our peace for their conflict and danger, our crystallization for the fluidity of tribal movement. The change in the tribal body has been immediate and deep-seated; the muscles have gone slack, some organs are all but atrophied, and it is of this changed and weakened frame that we are asking heavy and strange tasks.

Let us take as a more particular example the position of the chief. I am no anthropol-ogist and I speak with a deep sense of my own fallibility. It would seem, however, from a study of the ceremonies which at-tend the inauguration of a new chief, that his office was based upon a composite foun-dation made up of hereditary eligibility, re-ligious sanction, popular choice, and some-thing having the significance of a social contract, or a coronation oath between chief and people. Just at the moment when the effect of our civilization is to eat away the greater part of this foundation we are piling up on the institution a topheavy structure composed all too largely of executive func-tions of a new and often distasteful kind.

This refers not only to chiefs but also to our Lindi clan-heads. We saw that by ordi-nary standpoints the Tanganyika govern-ment has done great things here: judging by our ideal standard, we must have certain doubts. The position of the small clan-heads, or *wakalungwa*, depends upon their having obtained from the head of the clan from which they have hived off or from that of the head to whose lands they have come, the right of *mbepesi*, or of conducting the ceremony of the sacred flour. At times of need when prayer to God through the me-diation of ancestors is required, the *mka-lungwa* goes with his people to the graves, and there flour is poured between the hands to make a cone. Over this a basket or cook-ing-pot is placed for protection, which in the morning is removed and the omens are read according to the shape retained by the cone. In these days, not only are the occasions for such prayers and ceremonies less in number, but education and Christian teaching are draining away their significance. The second feature of the *mkalungwa* was his judicial authority over his clan, which would have led to such a multiplication of courts if government recognition had been given, that a group of *wakalungwa* were put together to form a court, which, they say, is not at all the same thing to them. The third important mark of the position of the *mkalungwa* was that his people must build and maintain his house, and this has gone the way of all forced labour. I do not say that these changes are not necessary; only that we should remember them all the time that we are asking our Lindi headman to use the relics of his authority for the collection of taxation and the enforcement of various provisions for sanitation, the cleaning of cotton plots, and the like. The development must be attempted; it may prove possible, but it will not be automatic, and will need all the sympathy and understanding that we can give.

The question may reasonably be asked as to whether this dwelling upon difficulties, some of which seem unsurmountable, can do more than daunt and weaken us in our work in Africa. There are moments, indeed, when I think that we are like a man who in striding through a wood puts his foot through a beautiful cobweb, and, turning in regret, tries to reconstruct it. The next moment I throw the metaphor indignantly aside, for the stuff with which we are dealing is not gossamer, and it is living, and living vigorously enough to stand a great deal of injury and misuse.

I think, then, that it is worth while to dwell upon difficulties because we are thus reminded that the need is for study, and always more study. It is true that this is recognized to-day as never before. I only once came across a political officer in Africa who said, "The less you know about these people, the better you can run them." Yet the view is sometimes expressed that there are

limits beyond which this study should not be pressed, and that those who do so press it may be regarded as sentimental and rather undignified, like grown-ups who have been caught on the floor playing bears with the children. It is, therefore, perhaps not unnecessary to repeat, not only that sympathetic study alone will break down the arrogance and complacency which cut free communication between ourselves and the African, but also that the realist and the practical man who takes up the other attitude is simply showing his own limitations in his own field, since he is willing to study all the materials he must use for the progress he advocates except that human material without which all the rest will, in the end, become mere dead things, unresponsive to the touch of his capitalizing energy. If practical results are asked, they can be seen in Tanganyika in the achievements, great and small, which are possible when the strong forces of tribal life are harnessed to a progressive social policy, and in the ease and peacefulness with which government is carried on from day to day in this vast and rather primitive country. I was deeply struck by a contrast in South Africa, where the strong tribal feeling of the Zulus, defeated, restrained, and neglected, made me think of some large power-machine pushed on its side, still working, its energy running to waste, a sad, if not a dangerous, sight.

I think it is true to say that the more African society is studied, the more there is found in it to admire, not as a result of the first false reaction from our own complex and urbanized civilization, but because it contains certain solid elements which Europe would be glad to-day not to have lost. Most African tribes are true, natural democracies; they are the equalitarian societies of small peasant farmers rooted to the soil, and they have a solidarity that is powerful in co-operative effort. They have, in fact, many of the qualities that a Rome-weary Tacitus admired in our own ancestors. Vast changes will and must come, but I do not think that we need form the fatalistic conclusion that the African must tread every step of the long road we have trodden away from tribal society, and sojourn as we have done in the wildernesses of feudalism, despotism, and individualism. Are we not to-day trying to create by political art some of the advantages we have lost by nature? Should this not qualify us to help the African to carry over into the twentieth century whatever was socially valuable of the first? It is no easy task; I think it is being attempted in some degree in Tanganyika, but it demands an increasing improvement of all branches of our African administration, and a far more intimate knowledge of the people whose future we are attempting to direct.

INTERNATIONAL PRESSURES

6. COMINTERN THESES ON COLONIALISM

While the various international socialist organizations of the period before World War I had mainly served as forums for debate between independent ideological and national factions, the Bolshevik Revolution in Russia provided a center of power from which at least part of the socialist movement would accept guidance in both its doctrine and its tactics. In keeping with the following theses, drafted by Lenin himself, the Russian-dominated Third Communist International (Comintern) undertook consistent (if often relaxed) criticism of colonialism and offered various forms of support to anticolonial nationalist leaders.

* * *

2. As the conscious expression of the proletarian class struggle to shake off the yoke of the bourgeoisie, the communist party, in accordance with its chief task—which is to fight bourgeois democracy and expose its falseness and hypocrisy—should not advance abstract and formal principles on the national question, but should undertake first of all a precise analysis of the given environment, historical and above all economic; secondly, it should specifically distinguish the interests of the oppressed classes, of the workers and the exploited, from the general concept of so-called national interests, which signify in fact the interests of the ruling class; thirdly, it should as precisely distinguish the oppressed, dependent nations, unequal in rights, from the oppressing, exploiting nations with full rights, to offset the bourgeois-democratic lies which conceal the colonial and financial enslavement of the vast majority of the world's population by a small minority of the wealthiest and most advanced capitalist countries that is characteristic of the epoch of finance-capital and imperialism.

3. The imperialist war of 1914 demonstrated with the greatest clarity to all enslaved nations and oppressed classes of the entire world the falseness of bourgeois-democratic phraseology. Both sides used phrases about national liberation and the right of national self-determination to make good their case, but the treaties of Brest-Litovsk and Bucharest on one side, and the treaties of Versailles and St. Germain on the other, showed that the victorious bourgeoisie quite ruthlessly determine "national" frontiers in accordance with their economic

From *The Communist International, 1919-1943: Documents*, pp. 140-144. Edited by Jane Degras, published by Oxford University Press for the Royal Institute of International Affairs. Reprinted by permission.

interests. Even "national" frontiers are objects of barter for the bourgeoisie. The so-called League of Nations is nothing but the insurance contract by which the victors in the war mutually guarantee each other's spoils. For the bourgeoisie, the desire to re-establish national unity, to "re-unite with the ceded parts of the country," is nothing but an attempt of the defeated to assemble forces for new wars. The reunification of nations artificially torn apart is also in accordance with the interests of the proletariat; but the proletariat can attain genuine national freedom and unity only by means of revolutionary struggle and after the downfall of the bourgeoisie. The League of Nations and the entire post-war policy of the imperialist States disclose this truth even more sharply and clearly, everywhere intensifying the revolutionary struggle of the proletariat of the advanced countries and of the labouring classes in the colonies and dependent countries, accelerating the destruction of petty-bourgeois national illusions about the possibility of peaceful coexistence and of the equality of nations under capitalism.

4. From these principles it follows that the entire policy of the Communist International on the national and colonial question must be based primarily on bringing together the proletariat and working classes of all nations and countries for the common revolutionary struggle for the overthrow of the landowners and the bourgeoisie. For only such united action will ensure victory over capitalism, without which it is impossible to abolish national oppression and inequality of rights.

5. The world political situation has now placed the proletarian dictatorship on the order of the day, and all events in world politics are necessarily concentrated on one central point, the struggle of the world bourgeoisie against the Russian Soviet Republic, which is rallying round itself both the soviet movements among the advanced workers in all countries, and all the national liberation movements in the colonies and among oppressed peoples, convinced by

bitter experience that there is no salvation for them except in union with the revolutionary proletariat and in the victory of the Soviet power over world imperialism.

6. At the present time, therefore, we should not restrict ourselves to a mere recognition or declaration of the need to bring the working people of various countries closer together; our policy must be to bring into being a close alliance of all national and colonial liberation movements with Soviet Russia; the forms taken by this alliance will be determined by the stage of development reached by the communist movement among the proletariat of each country or by the revolutionary liberation movement in the undeveloped countries and among the backward nationalities.

* * *

9. In regard to relations within States, the Communist International's national policy cannot confine itself to the bare and formal recognition of the equality of nations, expressed in words only and involving no practical obligations, to which bourgeois democracies — even if they call themselves "socialist" — restrict themselves.

Offences against the equality of nations and violations of the guaranteed rights of national minorities, repeatedly committed by all capitalist States despite their "democratic" constitution, must be inflexibly exposed in all the propaganda and agitation carried on by the communist parties, both inside and outside parliament. But that is not enough. It is also necessary: first, to make clear all the time that only the Soviet system is able to ensure real equality for the nations because it unites first the proletarians, and then all the masses of the working people, in the struggle against the bourgeoisie; secondly, communist parties must give direct support to the revolutionary movements among the dependent nations and those without equal rights (e.g. in Ireland, and among the American Negroes), and in the colonies.

Without this last particularly important

condition the struggle against the oppression of the dependent nations and colonies, and the recognition of their right to secede as separate States, remains a deceitful pretence, as it is in the parties of the Second International.

10. To acknowledge internationalism in words only, while in fact adulterating it in all propaganda, agitation, and practical work with petty-bourgeois nationalism and pacifism, is a common characteristic not only of the parties of the Second International, but also among those which have left the Second International. This phenomenon even occurs not infrequently among parties which now call themselves communist. The fight against this evil, against deeply rooted petty-bourgeois national prejudices which make their appearance in every possible form, such as race hatred, stirring up national antagonisms, anti-semitism, must be brought into the foreground the more vigorously, the more urgent it becomes to transform the dictatorship of the proletariat from a national dictatorship (i.e. a dictatorship existing in one country alone, and incapable of conducting an independent world policy) into an international dictatorship (i.e. a dictatorship of the proletariat in at least a few advanced countries, which is capable of exercising decisive influence in the political affairs of the entire world). Petty-bourgeois nationalism calls the mere recognition of the equality of nations internationalism, and (disregarding the purely verbal character of such recognition) considers national egoism inviolable. Proletarian internationalism on the other hand demands: 1. Subordination of the interests of the proletarian struggle in one country to the interests of the struggle on a world scale; 2. that the nation which achieves victory over the bourgeoisie shall display the capacity and readiness to make the greatest national sacrifices in order to overthrow international capitalism.

That is why, in the States where capitalism is fully developed and which have workers' parties which really are the vanguard of the proletariat, the struggle against opportunist and petty-bourgeois pacifist distortions of the idea and policy of internationalism is the primary and most important task.

11. In regard to the more backward States and nations, primarily feudal or patriarchal or patriarchal-peasant in character, the following considerations must be kept specially in mind:

a. All communist parties must support by action the revolutionary liberation movements in these countries. The form which this support shall take should be discussed with the communist party of the country in question, if there is one. This obligation refers in the first place to the active support of the workers in that country on which the backward nation is financially, or as a colony, dependent.

b. It is essential to struggle against the reactionary and medieval influence of the priesthood, the Christian missions, and similar elements.

c. It is necessary to struggle against the pan-Islamic and pan-Asiatic movements and similar tendencies, which are trying to combine the liberation struggle against European and American imperialism with the strengthening of the power of Turkish and Japanese imperialism and of the nobility, the large landlords, the priests, etc.

d. It is particularly important to support the peasant movement in the backward countries against the landlords and all forms and survivals of feudalism. Above all, efforts must be made to give the peasant movement as revolutionary a character as possible, organizing the peasants and all the exploited wherever possible in soviets, and thus establish as close a tie as possible between the west European communist proletariat and the revolutionary peasant movement in the East, in the colonies and backward countries.

e. A resolute struggle must be waged against the attempt to clothe the revolutionary liberation movements in the backward countries which are not genuinely communist in communist colours. The Communist International has the duty of supporting the revolutionary movement in the colonies and backward countries only with the object of rallying the constituent elements of the future proletarian parties — which will be truly communist and not only in name — in all the backward countries and educating them to a consciousness of their special task, namely, that of fighting against the bourgeois-democratic trend in their own nation. The Communist International should collaborate provisionally with the revolutionary movement of the colonies and backward countries, and even form an alliance with it, but it must not amalgamate with it; it must unconditionally maintain the independence of the proletarian movement, even if it is only in an embryonic stage.

f. It is essential constantly to expose and to explain to the widest masses of the working people everywhere, and particularly in the backward countries, the deception practised by the imperialist Powers with the help of the privileged classes in the oppressed countries in creating ostensibly politically independent States which are in reality completely dependent on them economically, financially, and militarily. A glaring example of the deception practised on the working classes of an oppressed nation by the combined efforts of Entente imperialism and the bourgeoisie of that same nation is offered by the Zionists' Palestine venture (and by Zionism as a whole, which, under the pretence of creating a Jewish State in Palestine in fact surrenders the Arab working people of Palestine, where the Jewish workers form only a small minority, to exploitation by England). In present international conditions there is no salvation for dependent and weak nations except as an alliance of Soviet republics.

12. The centuries-old enslavement of the colonial and weak peoples by the great imperialist Powers has left behind among the working masses of the enslaved countries not only feelings of bitterness but also feelings of distrust of the oppressing nations as a whole, including the proletariat of these nations. The despicable treachery to socialism committed by the majority of the official leaders of that proletariat in the years 1914-1919, when the social-patriots concealed behind the slogan of "defence of the fatherland" the defence of the "right" of "their" bourgeoisie to enslave the colonies and plunder the financially dependent countries — such treachery could only strengthen that quite natural distrust. Since this distrust and national prejudice can only be eradicated after the destruction of imperialism in the advanced countries and after the radical transformation of the entire foundations of economic life in the backward countries, the removal of these prejudices can proceed only very slowly. From this it follows that it is the duty of the class-conscious communist proletariat of all countries to be especially cautious and particularly attentive to the national feelings, in themselves out of date, in countries and peoples that have been long enslaved; it is also their duty to make concessions in order to remove this distrust and prejudice the more quickly. Unless the proletariat, and all the working masses of all countries and nations of the entire world, themselves strive towards alliance, and unite as one, the victory over capitalism cannot be pursued to a completely successful end.

Benito Mussolini

7. FASCIST IMPERIALISM VERSUS LIBERAL EUROPE

In the general European scramble for colonies before World War I, Italy had suffered at the hands of both France, which annexed the "natural" Italian dependency of Tunisia, and Ethiopia, which managed, at the 1896 battle of Adua, to defeat an Italian army of would-be conquerors. The successful campaign against Ethiopia by the armies of the interwar Italian dictator Benito Mussolini (1883-1945) wiped out this earlier disgrace, but at the cost of sanctions from the League of Nations, which forced Italy into total diplomatic dependence upon Hitler's Germany. This identification of Fascism and imperialism both in deed and in ideology left a lasting imprint upon western political attitudes, although it should be noted that Hitler, with a much sounder case for the return of Germany's prewar colonies, never gave major priority to overseas expansion.

SPEECH TO THE CHAMBER OF DEPUTIES
January 1936

Yesterday in the [British] House of Commons a speech was made which cannot but have an echo in this assembly.

Foreign Minister Hoare stated explicitly the degree of his Government's attachment to Fascist Italy.

We are convinced that the [British] Foreign Office wants a strong Italy, with a strong Government like the Fascist one, an Italy capable of holding with dignity a competitive position in the life of Europe and the world. For fourteen years we have worked for this.

Given Hoare's premises, we can legitimately look forward to the consequences which must follow. Italy cannot remain strong in Europe as Hoare desires, and as we wish, without resolving the problem of the secure integration of its East African

colonies; it cannot remain strong without expanding its territory, its population, and its civilization beyond the present restricted territories, as Hoare himself has clearly recognized in an earlier speech.

Foreign Minister Hoare, who has known Italy at war, has enjoyed the opportunity of appraising the quality and the vital necessities of the Italian people. Since then many years have passed during which—thanks to Victory and the Revolution—the growth of the political consciousness of the Italian people has accelerated extraordinarily.

The Italian people hear the words, but judge from the facts. Now the fact which has been announced for the twelfth of this month, that is, the oil embargo, is such as to prejudice gravely the development of the situation.

As I have told the Mothers and Widows of the Fallen, it is the moral side of the sanctions which has aroused the conscious dis-

Speech to the Chamber of Deputies, in *Le Direttive del Duce sui Problemi della Vita Nazionale: l'Espansione Coloniale*, ed. Paolo Orano (Rome, Casa Editrice Pinciana, 1937), 167-168.

dain of the Italian people, especially when another speech of the House of Commons pointed out that "the application of sanctions in some future case remains problematical."

Thus, the Penal Code of the League of Nations has no past, since in sixteen years it has not been applied in cases infinitely more grave and substantial than ours; nor does it have a future. The Penal Code of the League of Nations, drafted when the memory of the War was still burning, now has only a present: it acts today only against Italy, exclusively against Italy, at fault for striking the fetters from slaves in barbarous lands, an Italy on which treaties, moral laws, sacrifices of blood confer an indisputable and already recognized priority of fifty years.

The penalty of death by economic asphyxiation decreed by the humanitarians of Geneva was never arrogated before 1935; it will probably never be attempted again and comes today upon Italy only because of her "poverty of basic resources." What the punishment of the Geneva Code hides is this: the rich peoples are armed with their wealth and the greater weapons which wealth makes possible.

Those who have put into motion the most explosive apparatus of war in recorded history have been mistaken in their calculations.

When it is taken up on the other side of the Alps—on official desks—the greater or lesser vulnerability of the Italian economy is forgotten for the time in place of figures and schemes, taking account of such material reserves of all kinds which a great nation accumulates slowly, almost inadvertently, in the course of centuries; and above all no account is taken of the value of the spirit of Fascist Italy, a spirit which remains firm at whatever the material cost in order to draw from itself the elements necessary for resistance and recovery.

I have the impression that the error will begin to be recognized when—based on abstract principles, formally interpreted as a classical case of *summum jus, summum injuria* —it is blown up, until finally it assumes the character of a world crisis, one of those colonial crises which other countries, even after the War, even after the League of Nations, have resolved by the employment of force.

I intend to affirm in a more concise manner that the epilogue of this crisis can consist only in the full recognition of our rights and the safeguarding of our African interests.

Otherwise, the action goes on, in Italy and in Africa, where Infantry and Black Shirts, united in the will and in the faith of the Revolution, will bring a deserved and decisive victory to the Fatherland.

8. JAPAN UNDERMINES WESTERN COLONIAL PRESTIGE

Although Japanese imperialism both before and after World War I largely reflects Japan's general emulation of western Europe, the pose as liberator from white oppression expressed in the following document was not without its effect. In 1905 the Japanese drove the Russians from Korea and Manchuria; during World War II they overran British Malaysia and Burma, French Indochina, Dutch Indonesia and the American Philippines. Japan governed its resulting Greater East Asia Co-Prosperity Sphere with an exploitative ruthlessness far surpassing European rule. Nevertheless, the spectacle of a colored people overcoming Europeans struck a crucial blow at the racist mystique of colonialism while in Indonesia and Burma the Japanese set up puppet regimes which formed the nucleus of later nationalist governments.

JOINT DECLARATION OF THE ASSEMBLY OF
GREATER EAST ASIATIC NATIONS
Tokyo, 5 November 1943

It is the basic principle for the establishment of world peace that the nations of the world have each its proper place and enjoy prosperity in common through mutual aid and assistance. The U.S.A. and the British Empire have in seeking their own prosperity oppressed other nations and peoples. Especially in East Asia they indulged in insatiable aggression and exploitation and sought to satisfy their inordinate ambition of enslaving the entire region, and finally they came to menace seriously the stability of East Asia. Herein lies the cause of the present war.

The countries of Greater East Asia, with a view to contributing to the cause of world peace, undertake to co-operate towards prosecuting the War of Greater East Asia to a successful conclusion, liberating their region from the yoke of British-American domination and assuring their self-exis-

tence and self-defence and in constructing a Greater East Asia in accordance with the following principles:

I. The countries of Greater East Asia, through mutual co-operation will ensure the stability of their region and construct an order of common prosperity and well-being based upon justice.
II. The countries of Greater East Asia will ensure the fraternity of nations in their region, by respecting one another's sovereignty and independence and practising mutual assistance and amity.
III. The countries of Greater East Asia, by respecting one another's traditions and developing the creative faculties of each race, will enhance the culture and civilization of Greater East Asia.
IV. The countries of Greater East Asia will endeavour to accelerate their economic development through close co-operation upon a basis of reciprocity and to promote thereby the general reciprocity of their region.
V. The countries of Greater East Asia will

From *Japan's New Order in East Asia* by F. C. Jones, pp. 470-471, published by Oxford University Press for the Royal Institute of International Affairs. Reprinted by permission.

cultivate friendly relations with all the countries of the world and work for the abolition of racial discrimination, the promotion of cultural intercourse, and the opening of resources throughout the world and contribute thereby to the progress of mankind.

9. THE UNITED STATES URGES DECOLONIZATION

The highly idealistic war aims of the western allies in World War II led many colonized peoples as well as European and American liberals and radicals to expect that, along with the destruction of Fascism, victory would bring substantial progress toward the dissolution of colonial empires. During the course of the war, the United States Secretary of State, Cordell Hull (1871-1955), did in fact propose measures for hastening decolonization. As the following materials indicate, however, Hull's position represented only a limited step beyond the settlement which followed World War I.

MEMORANDUM FOR THE PRESIDENT

Herewith is attached amended draft relating to dependent peoples, dated March 9, 1943.

C[ORDELL] H[ULL]

[Attachment]

March 9, 1943

DECLARATION BY THE UNITED NATIONS
ON NATIONAL INDEPENDENCE

In the Declaration signed on January 1, 1942, the United Nations pledged themselves to a complete victory in this war for the preservation of liberty, independence, human rights and justice. They also proclaimed their resolve to attain, for themselves and for the human race as a whole, the objectives stated in the Joint Declaration of President Roosevelt and Prime Minister Churchill dated August 14, 1941, known — from the region in which it was formulated — as the Atlantic Charter. That Charter sets forth certain fundamental principles and purposes, applicable to all nations and to all peoples, among which are the following:

Respect for the rights of all peoples to choose the form of government under which they will live;

Restoration of sovereign rights and self-government to those who have been forcibly deprived of them; and

Establishment of a peace which will afford to all nations the means of dwelling in safety within their own boundaries, and which will afford assurance that all the men in all the lands may live out their lives in freedom from fear and want.

By their adoption of the Atlantic Charter as an integral part of the Declaration of January 1, 1942, the 31 United Nations have thus affirmed their determination that the independence of those nations which now possess independence shall be maintained; that the independence of those nations which have been forcibly deprived of independence shall be restored; that opportunity to achieve independence for those peoples who aspire to independence shall be preserved, respected, and made more effective; and that, in general, resolute efforts will be made to create a system of world security which will provide for all nations and all peoples greater assurance of stable

United States Post War Foreign Policy, 1939-1945 (Washington, Government Printer, 1949).
From *The Memoirs of Cordell Hull in Two Volumes* (New York: Macmillan Company, 1948), Copyright 1948 by Cordell Hull. Reprinted by permission of the Macmillan Company.

peace and greater facilities for material advancement.

The carrying out of these pledges imposes important responsibilities upon those peoples who possess or who are seeking to regain independence and upon all peoples who aspire to independent status. The particular pledge that peoples who aspire to independence shall be given an opportunity to acquire independent status is, therefore, in varying degrees, of concern to all of the United Nations and to all nations and peoples which now, or which may hereafter, cooperate in carrying forward and applying the provisions of the Atlantic Charter. The effectuation of that pledge requires that all such nations and peoples collaborate to that end with each other to the fullest practicable extent. Accordingly, the United Nations hereby make the following Declaration:

I

1. It is the duty and the purpose of those of the United Nations which have, owing to past events become charged with responsibilities for the future of colonial areas to cooperate fully with the peoples of such areas toward their becoming qualified for independent national status. While some colonial peoples are far advanced along this road, the development and resources of others are not yet such as to enable them to assume and discharge the responsibilities of government without danger to themselves and to others. It is, accordingly, the duty and the purpose of each nation having political ties with colonial peoples:

a. To give its colonial peoples protection, encouragement, moral support and material aid and to make continuous efforts toward their political, economic, social, and educational advancement;

b. To make available to qualified persons among the colonial peoples to the fullest possible extent positions in the various branches of the local governmental organization;

c. To grant progressively to the colonial peoples such measure of self-government as they are capable of maintaining in the light of the various stages of their development toward independence;

d. To fix, at the earliest practicable moments, dates upon which the colonial peoples shall be accorded the status of full independence within a system of general security; and

e. To pursue policies under which the natural resources of colonial territories shall be developed, organized and marketed in the interest of the peoples concerned and of the world as a whole.

2. It is incumbent upon all peoples that aspire to independence to exert themselves in every feasible way to prepare and equip themselves for independence — socially, economically, and politically — to the end that they may, as soon as possible, be able to create, conduct and maintain, for, by and of themselves, efficient structures of stable self-government based on sound principles of social and political morality. In the present moment of world emergency, the capacity and desire of such peoples for the enjoyment of freedom can best be demonstrated by their contribution now toward the defeat of the Axis foes of all freedom and independence.

3. The carrying out of the policies above declared will necessarily call for much and continuous consultation and collaboration between and among the nations which are directly responsible for the future of various colonial areas and other nations which have substantial interests in the regions in which such areas are located. In order to provide an effective medium for such consultation and collaboration, there shall be created in each region, by agreement of the nations thus concerned, a commission on which each of those nations shall be represented and in the work of which the various colonial peoples concerned shall have appropriate opportunity to participate and to have or to achieve representation.

II

1. As a result of the last war, peoples in several areas still unprepared for full independence were released from political ties

with nations formerly responsible for them. Other peoples in like status may be similarly released from their former political ties as a result of this war. It is the purpose of the United Nations to assume with respect to all such peoples a special responsibility, analogous to that of a trustee or fiduciary. The United Nations hereby recognize it as their duty to give the fullest cooperation to such peoples in their efforts to prepare themselves for independence through political, economic, social, and moral advancement — and eventually to arrange for their assumption of independent status. To this end, they recognize it as their duty to observe in the case of such peoples each of the policies, obligations and methods hereinbefore set forth for observance by independent countries toward their own colonial peoples.

2. In order to carry out effectively the purposes and functions described in the preceding paragraph, the United Nations propose to establish, as soon as circumstances permit, an International Trusteeship Administration composed of representatives of the United Nations and of all other nations which now, or which may hereafter, cooperate in carrying forward and applying the provisions of the Atlantic Charter. The Administration will operate through regional councils composed of representatives of the nations having major interests in the respective regions. The machinery of each council will be so designed as to give the peoples of the territories held in trust in its region full opportunity to be associated with its work.

DEPENDENT PEOPLES

Two days after the White House Conference on March 27, 1943, at which the President brought up the subject of dependent peoples, Eden said to me that he was much interested in our draft and asked whether he might in strict confidence show it to the Ministers of the British Dominions. I agreed, although emphasizing that this was not a final proposal but only a draft to which

thought and attention might be given at this stage, with the understanding that the President might have further views when the recommendations came to be drawn up.

Now at Quebec in August I raised the subject with Eden again. In fact, I brought it up three times during the Quebec discussions in an effort to get his reactions. On the third occasion the Foreign Secretary said that, to be perfectly frank, he had to say he did not like our draft very much. He said it was the word "independence" that troubled him. He had to think of the British Empire system, which was built on the basis of Dominion and colonial status.

He pointed out that under the British Empire system there were varying degrees of self-government, running from the Dominions through the colonial establishments which had in some cases, like Malta, complete self-government, to backward areas that were never likely to have their own government. He added that Australia and New Zealand also had colonial possessions that they would be unwilling to remove from their supervisory jurisdiction.

I remarked that my thought in dealing with this problem had been to give encouragement to the peoples in dependent areas. This was not with any view to their being given, tomorrow or next week, complete independence as separate entities, but to offer them, at some time when they could prove they were capable of independence, the possibility of so conducting their political development that they might be able to hope for this achievement. I cited the example of the Philippines in that we had always held out independence to them as a possibility if and when they were able to assume the responsibilities that went with such status.

At the end of the long discussion that followed, Eden's position remained unchanged. His irremovable objection was to the word "independence." He felt this term could never have a satisfactory meaning that would cover what various governments might have in mind by it.

I believed the subject was too important

for the long-range advancement of the world to let it drop. Digging my toes in for a lengthy struggle, I brought it up again and again with the British in the months that followed. Two months later I presented it for discussion at the Moscow Conference of Foreign Ministers in October. Eventually these discussions led to the establishment of a United Nations trusteeship system, a material improvement over the old mandates system of the League of Nations. The principles I set forth for the treatment of dependent peoples appear today in Chapter XI—"Declaration Regarding Non-Self-Governing Territories"—of the United Nations Charter. And the word "independence" appears in Chapter XII—"International Trusteeship System."

ANTICOLONIAL NATIONALISM TRIUMPHANT

John H. Kautsky

10. **NATIONALISM AS ANTICOLONIALISM**

While international pressures and the remoteness of paternalist colonies from vital European concerns created the atmosphere which made decolonization possible, it was the demand for independence among educated colonials with mass movement support which ultimately forced the colonizing powers to choose between departure or expensive repressive measures. In the following essay, John H. Kautsky, a political scientist at Washington University, St. Louis, assesses the forces which produced such nationalist movements.

In the absence of a common language, culture, religion, or race, what is it, then that provides the focus for the unity among politically conscious elements from all strata of the population that is as characteristic of nationalist movements in underdeveloped countries as of European nationalist movements? Speaking of underdeveloped countries in general, there would seem to be no positive factor at all, but rather the dislike of a common enemy, the colonial power. Since nationalism is based on opposition to the colonial government, it is quite understandable that each colony's nationalist movement should operate within the existing boundaries and should not aim at a change in these boundaries. Thus, Indonesian nationalism is directed at the acquisition of Western New Guinea, because it is ruled by the Netherlands, the former colonial power in Indonesia, but makes no active claims to British-ruled Northern Borneo and Sarawak or Portuguese Timor, even though these are geographically, ethnically, and culturally much closer to Indonesia than Western New Guinea is. That the boundaries of a colony may cut across language and cultural lines is irrelevant; what matters is that they define the very purpose of the movement, anti-colonialism, and a change in them would therefore undermine the power of the movement and its leaders. Hence the general ineffectiveness of unification movements among former colonies, and the opposition by nationalists to movements of secession (as in Indonesia and the Congo),

Introduction to *Political Change in Underdeveloped Countries: Nationalism and Communism* (New York, John H. Wiley & Sons, Inc., 1962), 39-40, 44-49.

which are regarded as anti-nationalist, i.e., inspired by the colonial power.

However, nationalist movements are not confined to territories that are or were until recently administered by foreign powers as colonies, like India and most of Africa. Quite similar movements have appeared in independent underdeveloped countries like Turkey, China, and Mexico and, more recently, Egypt, Iraq, and Cuba. Unless they are virtually inaccessible, underdeveloped countries almost by necessity stand economically in a colonial relationship to industrial countries, in which the former serve as suppliers of raw materials (often made available by cheap native labor) and sometimes as markets for the industries of the latter. Anti-colonialism, then, must here be understood as opposition not merely to colonialism narrowly defined but also to a colonial economic status.

It is opposition to colonialism so defined and to those natives who benefit from the colonial relationship that constitutes nationalism in underdeveloped countries. As such, nationalism can unite not only people of quite different language and cultural background, but also, interestingly, people of all the major economic and social classes, even though it is directed against certain economic policies. To be sure, in underdeveloped countries, as in Europe, many have been opposed and many indifferent to nationalism. Remarkable unity across social class lines has nevertheless been attained by nationalism. This is probably even more marked in underdeveloped countries than it was in Europe, where first the aristocracy and later important strata among the intellectuals and industrial labor proved to be anti-nationalist. The social tensions which modernization and industrialization produce everywhere and which in Europe were necessarily turned inward, resulting in conflicts dividing societies, are, in underdeveloped countries, largely turned outward. Instead of blaming each other for the difficulties growing out of modernization, the various social strata all blame the colonial power, the result being, not internal conflict,

but that internal unity of anti-colonialism which is the basis of nationalism in underdeveloped countries.

* * *

THE ROLE OF THE INTELLECTUALS

The third of the new groups produced by modernization are the intellectuals. The peculiar importance of this group in the nationalist movements of underdeveloped countries requires that somewhat more space be devoted to it than to the others. For our purposes, we do not include among the intellectuals the scholars trained along traditional, usually religious (such as Islamic or Confucian) lines in the old society, but, on the other hand, our definition is a much broader one than that usually applied in advanced countries. Like the latter, it embraces persons with advanced standing in the humanities, sciences, and social sciences. However, it also includes all those natives in underdeveloped countries, most likely to be found among the aristocracy and the businessmen, who have, through the contacts afforded by colonialism become aware of the world beyond their own culture area, and have obtained an advanced education appropriate to an industrial country, or who are at present students obtaining such an education.

In some underdeveloped countries, especially those where such an education qualified a native to serve in the administrative service of his government, whether independent, as in Latin America, or colonial, as in India, significant numbers of natives have, for some decades, studied in industrialized countries in Western Europe, and increasingly in the United States and the Soviet Union, and in institutions of higher learning conducted according to European-American standards in their own countries. In other underdeveloped countries, only a handful of natives have been involved. Thus, there were said to be only 16 native college graduates in the entire population of about 13 million in the Belgian Congo when it became independent in 1960.

121

For our purposes of generalization, an image of the intellectuals will be conveyed which is, no doubt, often far too monolithic. For the study of any particular country or situation, it is subject to revision and refinement. Thus, one might have to draw distinctions and even note conflicts between intellectuals educated at home and those who studied abroad, between civilian and military intellectuals, and between the successive generations of nationalist intellectuals.

The key role of the intellectuals in the politics of underdeveloped countries is largely due to their paradoxical position of being a product of modernization before modernization has reached or become widespread in their own country. In the universities, the intellectuals absorb the professional knowledge and skills needed by an industrial civilization; they become students of the humanities and social sciences qualified to teach in universities, and they become lawyers and doctors, administrators and journalists, and increasingly also scientists and engineers. When they return from the universities, whether abroad or not, the intellectuals find, all too often for their taste, that in their old societies their newly acquired skills and knowledge are out of place. Not only is there as yet little need—though it is often rapidly growing—for engineers and scientists where there is little industry, but professors will find few advanced students and lawyers will find few clients in a society still operating largely through simple face-to-face contacts. Although there is plenty of sickness, most patients might prefer the traditional herb-doctor or medicine man to the trained physician and, in any case, could not pay him. Few administrators are needed where the sphere of government activity is still very limited and fewer still where all higher posts are occupied by representatives of a colonial power. Where the bulk of the population is illiterate journalists are confined to writing for their few fellow intellectuals. As a result, intellectuals in underdeveloped countries are frequently unemployed or underemployed, especially since, for all their "industrial" education, they are likely to have retained the aristocratic attitude that manual labor is demeaning and hence will refuse to do other than intellectual work.

During their studies, the intellectuals are likely to acquire more than new knowledge. They also absorb the values of an industrial civilization, above all the notion that continuing material improvement of the life of the mass of the population through continuing technological progress and popular participation in government is both possible and desirable, and they become admirers of the political systems and ideologies embodying these values, whether they be American liberalism, Western European democratic socialism or Soviet Communism. On their return, they discover that these values, too, are inappropriate to the old society. Continuous and cumulative technological progress, which is so typical of an industrial system, is absent from purely agrarian economies. Until industrialization (and changes in agricultural techniques resulting from industrialization) are introduced, a belief in any substantial improvement in the standard of living of the mass of the population is, in fact, unrealistic. At the same time, advocacy, based on such a belief, of ideals of democracy, equality, and social justice, which arose out of an industrial environment, is subversive to the existing order of government by the native aristocracy and the foreign colonial power and is therefore not likely to endear the intellectuals to these powerful forces.

To the extent, then, that a native intellectual has substituted for the values of his traditional society those of an industrial one—a process which need by no means be complete in each case—he becomes an alien, a displaced person, in his own society. What could be more natural for him than to want to change that society to accord with his new needs and values, in short, to industrialize and modernize it? A number of motivations intermingle to produce the intellectuals' drive for rapid modernization. Most obviously, there is their desire for gainful and satisfying employment, for an opportunity to use the knowledge and to practice the skills they have acquired. But beyond this relatively narrow motive, there may be the more or less clear realization that only through industrialization can an eventual end be put to the poverty prevalent in underdeveloped countries, that only rapid industrialization can solve the problem posed by increasing populations, and that only industrialization can produce the "better" society at home which the intellectuals have come to admire abroad.

The peasant's typical response to overpopulation and his consequent hunger for land (if he is sufficiently politically conscious and organizable to respond effectively at all) is the demand for land reform. The intellectuals echo and support that demand, for one thing, because it is in accord with their new ideas of justice and equality. These ideas also make it desirable for them to become the leaders of a mass movement, of "the people." Since most of the people are peasants, they are inclined to seek peasant support, and advocacy of land reform is the most obvious way of mobilizing such support. Intellectuals may favor land reform also because a higher standard of living for the peasantry would create a better market for, and thus further the growth of, native industry. Finally, they press for land reform not because of anything it will do *for* the peasants, but because of what it will do *to* the aristocracy. The latter is the intellectuals' only powerful domestic enemy, and land reform strikes at the very root of its economic and social position.

However, where overpopulation is greatest, as in China, redistribution of land by itself is no longer an adequate solution to the problem, because there is simply not enough arable land to go around. Thus there is underemployment among the peasantry, which in turn tends to depress the wages of labor in the cities. Sooner or later only industrialization can satisfy the "rising expectations" in underdeveloped countries, which are, first and foremost, the expecta-

tions of the intellectuals, though they have spread them to the poorer strata accessible to them in the rural and especially in the urban areas. Only through industrialization can the intellectuals hope to realize their various dreams of democracy, equality, and social justice, of liberalism, socialism, or Communism in their own countries.

As the only ones in their societies who can even visualize a new, and, to them, a better order, the intellectuals naturally think of themselves as the leaders of the future society and of the transition to it. Thus a more narrowly political motivation is added to the others underlying their desire for modernization. Modernization serves to undermine and ultimately do away with the leadership of the old aristocratic ruling strata, and replace it with that of the intellectuals. Similarly, industrialization is the only road to the economic independence and military strength that can eventually provide freedom from colonial domination for their "country," that is, their government, which means more power for its new leaders, the intellectuals. Their anti-colonial nationalism thus makes the intellectuals desire industrialization.

It is equally true, however, that it is their desire to industrialize that makes the intellectuals nationalists. They see colonialism as opposed to industrialization, in part because the colonial power does not want industries in the colony to compete with its own industries for the colonial supply of raw materials or for the colonial market, and more generally because, as we have seen, modernization in the colony constitutes a threat to colonialism. Hence colonialism is regarded as an obstacle in the intellectuals' path to modernization as well as in their path to power. This helps explain the apparent paradox of intellectuals in underdeveloped countries who were trained in the West and came to admire it and yet turn against the West in their policies. They do so exactly because they admire it and at the same time see the West as denying them, through colonialism, the opportunity to make their own country more like the West.

To the intellectuals in underdeveloped countries nationalism and modernization have become inextricably intertwined as means and ends. Each has become an essential aspect of the other.

In Western Europe, during the process of industrialization, the intellectuals played an important role in developing the ideology of liberalism, but industrialization itself was accomplished by industrial capitalists. In underdeveloped countries, the intellectuals, in effect, play the roles of both groups. A native class of industrial capitalists is virtually or completely absent, and sufficient wealth for the development of industry is not available in private hands—or, if available in the hands of aristocrats, is (for reasons to be indicated later) not likely to be invested in industry. Under these circumstances, the government appears to be the only possible major domestic source of capital, and the intellectuals—if they want to industrialize their country—must wrest control of it from the native aristocracy and the colonial administrators who oppose industrialization. This need to control their government in order to industrialize pro-

vides another reason both for the intellectuals' anti-colonialist nationalism and for the appeal of various "socialist" ideas, whether Communist or not, to them. Thus, Nehru and U Nu, Nkrumah and Touré, Castro and many other nationalist intellectuals regard themselves as "socialists."

Through the dominance of the intellectuals in the nationalist movements, which we will have to analyze next, it is their peculiar form of nationalism, which looks at steel mills both as symbols of anti-colonialism and as its instruments, that has become characteristic of nationalism in underdeveloped countries. To borrow some phrases from Marx's prophecies about capitalism, nowhere are the "internal contradictions" of colonialism, its dual nature as a modernizing and a conservative force in the underdeveloped countries, clearer than in its relation to the intellectuals. It produces the intellectuals and yet by its very existence it frustrates them and hence arouses their opposition. In them, it has thus produced "its own gravediggers," it has sown "the seeds of its own destruction."

11.   INDIA AND PAKISTAN: INDEPENDENCE BY NEGOTIATION

Britain's voluntary emancipation of her huge Indian dependency again set the pace for a new stage of colonialism — in this case a dissolution which, once accepted, proved far less damaging to the position of the metropole than had been anticipated. India demonstrated also in a most dramatic and tragic manner the extent to which colonial problems would continue to burden the successor states; in the communal rioting which accompanied the partition of the subcontinental British raj into independent India and Pakistan, over half a million people were killed and many millions more made homeless. Reproduced here is the speech by Prime Minister Clement R. Attlee made on the occasion of presenting the Indian Independence Bill to the British House of Commons, July 10, 1947.

* * *

I beg to move, "That the Bill be now read a Second time."

. . . This Bill brings to an end one chapter in the long connection between Britain and India, but it opens another. British rule which has endured so long is now, at the instance of this country, coming to an end.

There have been many instances in history when States at the point of the sword have been forced to surrender government over another people. It is very rare for a people that have long enjoyed power over another nation to surrender it voluntarily. My mind recalls as the nearest parallel the action of the Liberal Government of Sir Henry Campbell Bannerman, in 1906, when he gave back to the Dutch in South Africa the freedom to manage their own affairs which they had lost in the South African war. That was a great act of faith, an act of faith which bore fruit both in 1914 and 1939. I have often heard that great South African statesman, General Smuts, describing it as marking the end of imperialism.

* * *

We can recall how, 90 years ago, the Government of the East India Company came to an end when Parliament assumed responsibility for Indian affairs. During those long years there has been a change in the spirit of British administration. In the earlier days we were concerned mainly with trade providing opportunities for making fortunes. In the eighteenth century British citizens returning from India had often made fortunes and were known as nabobs. But, as time went on, there was an increasing appreciation of the responsibility which fell to the government of the East India Company, a responsibility for the lives of many millions who sought justice and a quiet life. The British administrator in India became more and more deeply concerned with the well-being of the people of India, the well-being of that great congeries of people divided by race, by caste, language and religion in this sub-continent.

To this change of spirit the House of Commons, in many famous Debates from the time of Burke onwards, made a most notable contribution. Perhaps it is not always realised how early that change took

Great Britain, *Hansard Parliamentary Debates*, 439 (1947): ca. 2441-46.

place. It was long before the transfer of sovereignty to the Crown. In the early days of the nineteenth century, great men, such as Sir Thomas Munro in Madras, set the standards which have since been followed by so many who have served India. Looking back today over the years, we may well be proud of the work which our fellow citizens have done in India. There have, of course, been mistakes, there have been failures, but we can assert that our rule in India will stand comparison with that of any other nation which has been charged with the ruling of a people so different from themselves.

There has been a great succession of Viceroys who have made their particular contributions and sought to serve India faithfully. I think not least among them would be accounted the present Viceroy. There is a roll of names of eminent Governors of Provinces, high among which is that of the right hon. Gentleman the Member for Scottish Universities (Sir J. Anderson). There has been a multitude of administrators, soldiers, missionaries and others who have served India with great devotion and have loved the Indian people. In every part of India are the graves of those who died in her service. Not least among those who have served India are the men who in the difficult and exacting times of the last four decades, under the stress of two great wars with all their repercussions on Indian life, have worked in the changing conditions that have resulted from the rise of Indian nationalism and the development of self-government.

May I recall here a thing that is not always remembered, that just as India owes her unity and freedom from external aggression to the British, so the Indian National Congress itself was founded and inspired by men of our own race, and further, that any judgment passed on our rule in India by Indians is passed on the basis, not of what obtained in the past in India, but on the principles which we have ourselves instilled into them. I am well aware that many of those who have been closely associated with India are anxious about the future of the millions for whom we are now relinquishing responsibility. I can understand their anxiety. They fear that the work to which they have devoted themselves for so many years may be brought to nought. They are anxious for those who would suffer most from a breakdown of administration — the poorest sections of the community.

We must all be anxious, but I think everybody realises that the service of Britain to India must now take another form. The constitutional change, vital as it is, does not, of course, mean the disappearance of the civilian European community in India. Not a few of those of the British race who have been in the Services in India will, we confidently expect, be willing, at the invitation of the two new Governments, to continue in official service in India and Pakistan. The business community in India has still, I am confident, a role to play in maintaining, between the populations in India and this country, trade and commerce, to the great benefit of both. To all those men and women, who, although domiciled in the United Kingdom, are intending to remain in India after Partition I would say "You have a great task in front of you, namely, to cement the bonds of friendship between this country, India and Pakistan. You can accomplish at least as much in achieving this end as can the British Government."

Many years ago, when we began the association of Indians in the responsibility of Government and set ourselves to train them in the methods of democracy, it was obvious that the time would come, sooner or later, when Indians would seek to secure the entire management of their own affairs. This was clear many years ago to some of our wisest administrators, and I quote from a letter of Mountstuart Elphinstone as long ago as 1854:

> The moral is that we must not dream of perpetual possession, but must apply ourselves to bring the natives into a state that will admit of their governing themselves in a manner that may be beneficial to our interests as well as their own, and that of the rest of the world; and to take the glory of the achievement and the

sense of having done our duty for the chief reward of our exertions.

It has been the settled policy of all parties in this country for many years that Indians, in course of time, should manage their own affairs. The question has always been how and when? It would, I think, be unprofitable today to go back into the past and to question whether, if some particular action had been taken by a British Government earlier, or if a different line of conduct had been taken by the Indian political leaders on certain occasions, a more satisfactory solution might have been found than that which I am commending to the House today.

There are hon. Members of this House, such as the noble Lord the Member for Horsham (Earl Winterton) and the hon. Member for Aylesbury (Sir S. Reed), whose connection with the Indian problem goes back far beyond mine. Some 20 years ago, I was first brought into contact with it by being placed on the Simon Commission, and I think they would agree with me that the major difficulty that has faced all of us in considering the best way of achieving Indian self-government has been the absence of mutual trust and toleration between the communities. It has sometimes been said by our enemies that this was a difficulty created by ourselves in order to perpetuate our own rule. Nothing could be more untrue. This same difficulty, which faced Mr. Edwin Montagu and the Simon Commission, faced the President of the Board of Trade in his Mission and my three Cabinet colleagues in theirs, and it was still the outstanding difficulty of the present Viceroy when he took office. Everyone who has touched the Indian problem has been brought up against this stumbling-block. They have all wanted to maintain the unity of India, to give India complete self-government and to preserve the rights of minorities. Every one of them has hoped that a solution might be found without resorting to partition. I know that many Indians of all communities passionately desire this, but it has not been found to be practicable.

We and the Indian statesmen have had to accept the only alternative — partition. For myself, I earnestly hope that this severance may not endure, and that the two new Dominions which we now propose to set up may, in course of time, come together again to form one great member State of the British Commonwealth of Nations. But this is entirely a matter for the Indians themselves. The demand for self-government has been insistently pressed for many years by the leaders of political thought in India, and has been stimulated by the external situation, and particularly by those great waves of nationalist feeling that accompanied both the great wars. This demand is not peculiar to India, but has spread thoughout Asia. It is the natural result of contact by dwellers in other continents with European political thought. The chief question has been as to how this desire could be gratified. Delay in granting it has always led to more and more extreme demands.

There has been a tendency to consider that nothing short of complete and absolute severance would satisfy this urge. There is a desire by some to cut every tie which connects them with their former rulers. On the other hand, in the age in which we live, there are very strong reasons which militate against the complete isolation which some demand. Many countries that long enjoyed their freedom and independence have lost it either permanently or temporarily, and some form of association with others for security and greater prosperity is the desire of many peoples. The League of Nations and the United Nations organisation express this desire, but the one great practical example of how complete freedom and independence can be combined with inclusion in a greater whole is the British Commonwealth of Nations.

The British Commonwealth of Nations is so unique that its nature is still not fully comprehended, and even many of our American friends do not understand that the Dominions are as free as Great Britain. They do not appreciate that membership of the British Commonwealth, in the words of the Prime Minister of New Zealand is, "in-

127

dependence with something added, not independence with something taken away." In this Bill, we set up two independent Dominions, free and equal, of no less status than the United Kingdom or the Dominion of Canada, completely free in all respects from any control by this country, but united by a common allegiance to the Sovereign and by a community of ideas, receiving from their membership of the Commonwealth great advantages, but in no way suffering any restriction. The Title of this Bill expresses this fact that the independence which has been the goal for so long of many Indians can be, and I believe will be realised within the British Commonwealth of Nations. It is my hope that these two new Dominions may continue in this great association, giving and receiving benefits.

I saw with great regret in one paper, and I think in one paper only, that the action which we are now taking was described as abdication. It is not the abdication, but the fulfilment of Britain's mission in India. It is the culminating point in a long course of events. The Morley-Minto proposals, the Montagu-Chelmsford proposals, the Simon Commission Report, the Round Table Conferences, the Act of 1935, the Declaration at the time of the Cripps Mission, the visit of my right hon. Friends to India last year, are all steps in the road that led up eventually to the proposals that I announced to the House on 3rd June last. This Bill is designed to implement those proposals, which met, I think, with general acceptance in this House and in the country.

* * *

Kwame Nkrumah

12. **THE STEPS TOWARD AFRICAN INDEPENDENCE**

Just as India set the pace for emancipation in Asia and the colonial world generally, so British West Africa, and particularly the Gold Coast (now Ghana) set loose what became a virtual avalanche of African independence movements. In the following account, which covers events of the years 1949-1951, Kwame Nkrumah (1909-   ) describes his methods of agitating against British rule and the feelings with which he greeted the transition from prison to prime ministership. Six years after taking office under British tutelage Nkrumah led Ghana to full independence. Until his deposition by a military coup in 1966, he remained the leading figure in the movement for radical decolonization and continental unification throughout Africa.

It soon became apparent that the feeling of unrest was rife not only among the rank and file of the people, but also among the Government officials, the chiefs and the intelligentsia. Their discontent, however, was not born of suffering but of fear—fear of what they might have to suffer if something was not done to check this surging nationalism, this sudden political awakening of the youth and of the man in the street. The words "positive action" which I had used at the June rally in Accra spelt fear in the

From Kwame Nkrumah, *Ghana: The Autobiography of Kwame Nkrumah* (New York, 1957), pp. 110-112, 136-137. Reprinted by permission of Thomas Nelson & Sons Ltd.

minds of my opponents and as soon as it became generally known that I intended leading the Party in a campaign of "non-violent positive action," rumors reached me that plans were being made to deport me from Accra. In fact the local Gold Goast radio announced that I had already been banished from the capital. Shortly after this, I received a letter asking me to appear before the Ga State Council, the traditional local authority, in order to discuss "the unfortunate lawless elements in the country and any possible solution."

I went along with two of my supporters and was surprised to find that among those present were the ex-members of the Working Committee of the U.G.C.C.* The agenda that had been drawn up for the meeting was never referred to. All the speeches that were made were on one subject alone, and the whole idea of the meeting appeared to be to censure me for introducing the words "Positive Action" into the country and thereby threatening violence.

"What exactly do you *mean* by Positive Action?" I was asked.

I took my time and explained to them as fully as I could but, as I might have expected, it did not satisfy certain of my long-standing political opponents who were present. The Ga Manche, the paramount chief who was presiding, then suggested that I should convene a meeting of my followers and explain to them, in the same terms that I had just used to the meeting, the meaning of Positive Action and to report to the State Council when I had done so. I agreed to do this and immediately left.

It seemed to me that this was a matter that should go down on record as a considered statement. I therefore took a pencil and paper and, a few hours later, completed a pamphlet entitled *What I mean by Positive Action*. In it I explained that because the term Positive Action had been erroneously interpreted and publicized as being a threat of violence, the imperialists and their agents were perturbed. I had been called before the Ga State Council where I had explained to those present the true meaning of the term.

That meeting concluded with a recommendation that I should call a meeting of the people and make the same explanation. I denied that I was going to be deported and protested against a false report in the foreign press that the Chiefs had demanded an undertaking from me to cause no trouble when the Coussey Report was published. If I refused, the report had said, I would be deported to Nzima.

I went on to discuss the aims of self-government and affirmed that the next step was a question of strategy; that although the British Government and the British people (with the die-hard imperialists) acknowledged the legitimacy of our demand for self-government, it was only by our own exertions that we would succeed.

I pointed out that there were two ways of achieving self-government, one by armed revolution and the other by constitutional and legitimate non-violent methods. As an example I gave the repulsion by British armed might of two German attempts at invasion and the victory over British imperialism in India by moral pressure. We advocated the latter method. Freedom, however, had never been handed over to any colonial country on a silver platter; it had been won only after bitter and vigorous struggles. Because of the educational backwardness of the colonies, the majority of the people were illiterate and there was only one thing they could understand — action.

I described Positive Action as the adoption of all legitimate and constitutional means by which we could attack the forces of imperialism in the country. The weapons were legitimate political agitation, newspaper and educational campaigns and, as a last resort, the constitutional application of strikes, boycotts, and non-cooperation based on the principle of absolute non-violence, as used by Gandhi in India.

It would appear, the pamphlet continued, that the Government was not pleased with our warning, that they would have pre-

*United Gold Coast Convention, the moderate, elitist party from which Nkrumah broke to form his radical, mass based Convention People's Party (CPP).

ferred us to have sprung a surprise on them. But we preferred justice and fair play and to act aboveboard. We had nothing to hide and the members of the C.P.P., as members of a democratic organization, had every right to be prepared for any eventuality.

* * *

LEADER OF GOVERNMENT BUSINESS

The day after my release from prison I was invited by the Governor to meet him at nine o'clock that morning. When I walked into the courtyard of Christianborg Castle, the official residence of the Governor, I suddenly realized that this was the very first time I had set eyes on the place. The glaring white stone of the battlements, the impressive forecourt and the beauty of this imposing building with the roaring surf battering against its foundations, seemed to me like a new world. Although Sir Charles Arden-Clarke and I had been opposing each other for so many months past, I had no idea what he looked like, for we had never met. I wondered how I should be received. Had I known this man before, I should not have doubted the courtesy that would be shown to me.

A tall, broad-shouldered man, suntanned, with an expression of firmness and discipline but with a twinkle of kindness in his eyes came towards me with his hand outstretched; a hand that I noticed was large and capable looking. He welcomed me and asked me how I was. As we both sat down I sensed that he must be feeling as alert and suspicious of me as I was of him. We lost little time, however, in coming down to the business on hand. I did my best to make it clear to him that I would be prepared at all times to place my cards face upwards on the table because it was only through frankness that mutual trust and confidence could be established. He agreed with me wholeheartedly in this and I sensed immediately that he spoke with sincerity. He was, I thought, a man with a strong sense of justice and fair play, with whom I could easily be friends even though I looked upon him as a symbol of British imperialism in the country.

In spite of the fact that I was fresh from the prison cell and had probably every reason to harbor hatred in my heart, I had forced myself to forget the sufferings and degradation that I had endured at the hands of the colonial administration, for I knew that revenge was bitter and that it was foreign to my make-up. It was with truth and sincerity that I made the statement soon after my release from jail that "I came out of jail and into the Assembly without the slightest feeling of bitterness to Britain. I stand for no discrimination against any race or individual, but I am unalterably opposed to imperialism in any form."

I left the Castle with instructions from the Governor to form a government. As I walked down the steps it was as if the whole thing had been a dream, that I was stepping down from the clouds and that I would soon wake up and find myself squatting on the prison floor eating a bowl of maize porridge.

13. ANTICOLONIAL GUERILLA WARFARE

After World War II, Indonesia was one of several Southeast Asian colonies in which the returning European power, in this case Holland, found that the aftermath of the Japanese occupation was an armed indigenous nationalist movement. General Abdul Haris Nasution, later Indonesian Defense Minister and a major anticommunist political figure, here indicates the complex relations between tactics and ideology which have made guerilla warfare such an essential element in the entire movement of anticolonial nationalism.

* * *

Because of the fact that we were unable to raise a regular army equal to the Dutch, we were forced to rely on guerilla tactics exclusively. This was unlike the actions in China and Vietnam where in addition to guerilla attacks, attacks by regiments and divisions were used to capture cities and to drive the enemy as far away as possible. We used guerilla warfare not because we believed in its "ideology" but because we were forced into it and could not establish a modern, organized force equal to the Dutch. Our guerilla fight was still in a period of weakening the enemy and we could not yet destroy him even section by section.

That is probably the reason why the leaders of the country did not entrust the entire fight to the military, but always chose the political way to find an agreement with the enemy, while at the same time threatening the use of guerilla war, scorched earth and international political pressure.

The case of the Red movement in China and the war of the Vietminh in Indo-China was different. Here, without compromise, a war was fought to defeat the enemy and army divisions were organized phase by phase to drive the enemy away.

3. Guerilla warfare cannot, by itself, bring final victory; guerilla warfare can only hope to weaken the enemy by draining his resources. Final victory must be achieved by a regular army in a conventional war, because only such an army can stage an offensive of the nature that will subdue the enemy.

The principles of warfare clearly state that only by means of an offensive can the enemy be defeated because he can only be destroyed by being attacked. Napoleon said: "Do not go on the defensive, except when there is no other way. When you face this problem you must fully realize that you do this only to gain time to concentrate your reserve forces and to trick the enemy away from its base of operation, without changing your aim. That is to launch an offensive against the enemy."

A defensive cannot defeat an enemy; this can only be done by an offensive. A defensive action serves temporarily to prepare and await the correct time for the offensive.

As is explained above, we will be forced to stage a temporary defensive since the

From Abdul Haris Nasution, *Fundamentals of Guerilla Warfare* (New York, 1965), pp. 16-17, 26-28. Reprinted by permission of Frederick A. Praeger, Inc.

enemy has attacked us first. So if we are not able to come forward with an equal force, or when our numbers are less, it will happen that the enemy will gradually succeed in seizing part of our territory. The most that we can control is what we can secure behind our front line. In the territory occupied by the enemy our regular war stops, and the enemy is able to control all important centres and communications. The only thing left for us to do is to make pockets between the enemy's positions. It is here that guerilla warfare can best be used by the remnants of the main army or by partisans from the people. A guerilla war, sufficiently active behind the front line of the enemy, can engage an enemy ten to thirty times its number. Thus the enemy becomes exhausted and is forced to decrease the number of troops used in the actual front line and whom we have to fight with our regular army. At the right time this army can go over to the offensive in order to destroy and annihilate the enemy's army as a result of the guerilla's activities carried out by army units and partisans behind the enemy's frontline.

* * *

5. Guerilla war does not mean that all the people are fighting. As has been explained, the guerilla fighter is a champion of the people's ideological struggle which lives in the hearts of the people. If the ideological foundation and roots are not there, there will be no support for a guerilla war. The guerilla soldier is rooted completely in the soul of the people, and therefore, the guerilla movement can only prosper if the people serve as its foundation.

Our leaders always compare the guerillas to fish and the people to the water, using the example from Mao Tse-tung's teachings. The Chinese leader has explained that the "water" must be nourished in its natural political and socio-economic climate to ensure the proper development of the guerilla fighter who "swims" in it.

Therefore, it is very important for the guerilla soldier, being a leader of the peo-

ple's fight for freedom, to maintain that favourable "climate" with the people. Since he is fighting for the people, his actions must have the immediate appreciation and approval of the people. We cannot profess to be fighting in the people's interest when in practice our actions consist of annoying or hurting the people. The relationship in regard to the people must be kept as perfect as possible. The guerilla soldier should not be allowed to have a special position above the people, as often happens in the case of so-called fighters with whom we have had experience in the past.

In other words, guerilla war is a people's war; the guerilla is born and bred in the midst of the fighting people, the guerilla fights with the help, care and protection of the people. The guerilla is a loyal soldier of the people.

It is not necessary, however, that all the people should actively participate in guerilla warfare in its special sense. In its general meaning, a guerilla war is a total people's war, a military, political, socio-economic and psychological war. For specialized active guerilla services to hit the enemy with armed attacks and sabotage, according to Lawrence, only two percent are guerillas and ninety-eight percent are people sympathetic to the cause; two percent do the fighting and ninety-eight percent give assistance; two percent are active and ninety-eight percent passive guerilla fighters.

Of importance also is the quality of the guerilla fighters. One group consisting of brave, spirited guerilla soldiers, skillful in their task although small in number, are more useful than an armed mob. In the Boer War in South Africa guerilla troops were able to hold off the English army which was thirty times larger. Five to six thousand Red guerillas in Malaya were able to engage a hundred thousand British soldiers and police. We have seen ourselves, how the RMS (Republik Maluku Selatan) guerillas were able to fight TNI (Tentara Nasional Indonesia) troops at an average of one platoon against one or two battalions. In the revolt in the South Moluccas one battalion of rebel troops engaged eight battalions of our Republic's troops, but they could not be annihilated, even though they were pursued until we tired of chasing them.

One small guerilla party equipped with light weapons but trained intensively can effectively engage a force ten to thirty times larger and can compel it to disperse, rendering it impotent.

In the history of our fight there were many suggestions of an "armed people" and "revolt of the masses." These slogans must be understood as slogans, because it would be wrong to think that we were aiming at making all the people active guerilla fighters, something which is not possible, not necessary, in addition to being inefficient. Revolutions by armed masses are usually unsuccessful in defending themselves. It is true that it is quite easy to agitate the masses to become violent, but it is equally true that a mob tends to break and become easily confused so that it becomes difficult to lead. A single success can quickly ignite the spirit of the masses but one failure can cause this spirit to tumble and can even break it entirely. The masses are easily confused by rumours.

Generally our armed mass revolts in the big cities did not result in military gains. Armed mass movements took place in Djakarta, Bandung, Semarang and Surabaja. Only the one in Surabaja had any historical importance. In all the other instances we were badly beaten and ultimately driven out of those cities. By operating systematically the enemy could gradually master a situation, while we were forced to flee, leaving behind men and material of immeasurable value for our guerilla activities which took place later. The above cited examples of upheavals of masses first of all have psychological meaning, showing our willingness to fight as a nation. However, the leadership failed to organize those skilled fighters into a nucleus to fight the long guerilla war which was required.

A guerilla war also needs economic implementation. Therefore a people engaged in a guerilla war must adapt their organization [to existing conditions] by assigning duties to each guerilla, the number of active guerilla fighters being decided by the situation and the ability to equip them.

IV. *Imperialism in a Postcolonial World: 1955-1965*

The dissolution of nearly all the European overseas empires in the two decades since World War II has not brought an end to the role of imperialism as an idea and a force in international politics. For the former colonial territories anticolonialism remains a major theme of both internal national unity and the formation of international blocs. For the western powers, now led by the United States, foreign policy is still shaped by commitments which can be traced to former colonial interests and are thus subject to indictment as "neocolonialism."

That group of non-European countries variously referred to as "new nations," "underdeveloped" or "developing" countries, or the "Third World" has as one of its defining characteristics a history of previous colonial relationships with Europe. Consciousness of this definition is evidenced most clearly in the politics of the Afro-Asian bloc of nations, first officially assembled at the Bandung Conference of 1955 (1). Latin America, with its more European cultural tradition and avoidance of nineteenth century paternalist colonization, has generally shunned political identification with the Third World. In economic terms, however, leaders of Latin American, African, and Asian countries acknowledge a common need to emulate the industrialism of Europe and the United States in order to escape a continuing state of informal dependency (2). At a more intimate level, Third World intellectuals have had to confront the two facets of their colonial heritage, one, an experience of degradation and violence (3), the other an initiation into alien techniques indispensable for the attainment of nationalist ends (4).

The continuing anti-imperialist stance of spokesmen for the Third World is premised at least in part upon the belief that the struggle against colonialism is not yet completed. Such views received reinforcement in 1956 when Britain and France attempted to protect their interest in the Suez Canal by means of military action against Egypt (5). With far greater success, the colonial regimes of Southern Africa have prevented the indigenous majorities of this entire area from attaining self-rule (6). And in Latin America—particularly the Caribbean—the United States continues to work against regimes which it considers overly leftist (7).

On a larger world scale, most discussions of imperialism focus on the obvious position of the United States as the leading contemporary international power (8). Defenders of direct United States involvement in the suppression of foreign guerilla revolutionary movements claim that such efforts do not perpetuate colonialism but rather ward off communist subversion (9). To the Chinese sector of the communist camp, such guerilla wars do, in fact, represent a universal historical process directed simultaneously against imperialism and capitalism (10). Even writers with less dogmatic views of capitalism feel impelled to criticize America's global political commitments under a somewhat revised rubric of imperialism (11).

THE EX-COLONIALS SEEK AN IDENTITY

1. THE BANDUNG ASIAN-AFRICAN CONFERENCE, 1955

A conference held at Bandung, Indonesia, in April 1955 brought together for the first time representatives of nations virtually all of whom had recently been or were in the process of being liberated from some form of colonialism. Shortly afterwards a liberalization of United Nations membership rules offered the Conference members an important arena for confronting the rest of the world. At the same time the actual organization established at Bandung, now known as the Afro-Asian Solidarity Conference, has come increasingly to be identified with Communist Chinese tutelage. Moreover the general unity of the Afro-Asian bloc on matters other than imperialism and the need for development aid has been severely impaired by regionalism, ideological rifts, and internecine territorial disputes.

SPEECH BY PRESIDENT SUKARNO AT THE OPENING OF THE ASIAN-AFRICAN CONFERENCE April 18, 1955

Your Excellencies, Ladies and Gentlemen, Sisters and Brothers!

*   *   *

As I survey this hall and the distinguished guests gathered here, my heart is filled with emotion. This is the first intercontinental conference of coloured peoples in the history of mankind! I am proud that my country is your host. I am happy that you were able to accept the invitations extended by the five Sponsoring Countries.

But also I cannot restrain feelings of sadness when I recall the tribulations through which many of our peoples have so recently passed, tribulations which have exacted a heavy toll in life, in material things, and in the things of the spirit.

I recognise that we are gathered here today as a result of sacrifices. Sacrifices made by our forefathers and by the people of our own and younger generations. For me, this hall is filled not only by the leaders of the nations of Asia and Africa; it also contains within its walls the undying, the indomitable, the invincible spirit of those who went before us. Their struggle and sacrifice paved the way for this meeting of the highest rep-

George McTurnan Kahin, *The Asian-African Conference* (Ithaca, Cornell University Press, 1956), 39-41, 76-84, with omissions.

resentatives of independent and sovereign nations from two of the biggest continents of the globe.

It is a new departure in the history of the world that leaders of Asian and African peoples can meet together in their own countries to discuss and deliberate upon matters of common concern. Only a few decades ago it was frequently necessary to travel to other countries and even other continents before the spokesmen of our peoples could confer.

I recall in this connection the Conference of the "League Against Imperialism and Colonialism" which was held in Brussels almost thirty years ago. At that Conference many distinguished Delegates who are present here today met each other and found new strength in their fight for independence.

But that was a meeting place thousands of miles away, amidst foreign people, in a foreign country, in a foreign continent. It was not assembled there by choice, but by necessity.

Today the contrast is great. Our nations and countries are colonies no more. Now we are free, sovereign and independent. We are again masters in our own house. We do not need to go to other continents to confer.

Already there have been important meetings of Asian States in Asia itself.

If we look for the forerunner of this great gathering, we must look to Colombo, capital of independent Çri Lanka, [Ceylon] and to the Conference of the five Prime Ministers which was held there in 1954. And the Bogor Conference in December of 1954 showed that the road ahead was clear for Asian-African solidarity, and the Conference to which I have the honour of welcoming you today is the realisation of that solidarity.

Indeed, I am proud that my country is your host.

But my thoughts are not wholly of the honour which is Indonesia's today. No. My mind is for a part darkened by other considerations.

You have not gathered together in a world of peace and unity and co-operation. Great chasms yawn between nations and groups of nations. Our unhappy world is torn and tortured, and the peoples of all countries walk in fear lest, through no fault of theirs, the dogs of war are unchained once again.

And if, in spite of all that the peoples may do, this should happen, what then? What of our newly-recovered independence then? What of our culture, what of our spiritual heritage, what of our ancient civilisation? What of our children and our parents?

The burden of the delegates to this Conference is not a light one, for I know that these questions — which are questions of the life or death of humanity itself — must be on your minds, as they are on mine. And the nations of Asia and Africa cannot, even if they wish to, avoid their part in finding solutions to these problems.

For that is part of the duties of independence itself. That is part of the price we gladly pay for our independence. For many generations our peoples have been the voiceless ones in the world. We have been the un-regarded, the peoples for whom decisions were made by others whose interests were paramount, the peoples who lived in poverty and humiliation. Then our nations demanded, nay fought for independence, and achieved independence, and with that independence came responsibility. We have heavy responsibilities to ourselves, and to the world, and to the yet unborn generations. But we do not regret them.

In 1945, the first year of our national revolution, we of Indonesia were confronted with the question of what we were going to do with our independence when it was finally attained and secured — we never questioned that it would be attained and secured. We knew how to oppose and destroy. Then we were suddenly confronted with the necessity of giving content and meaning to our independence. Not material content and meaning only, but also ethical and moral content, for independence without ethics and without morality would be indeed a poor imitation of what we sought. The responsibilities and burdens, the rights and duties and privileges of independence must be seen as part of the ethical and moral content of independence.

Indeed, we *welcome* the change which places new burdens upon us, and we are all resolved to exert all our strength and courage in carrying these burdens.

FINAL COMMUNIQUE OF THE
ASIAN-AFRICAN CONFERENCE

The Asian-African Conference, convened upon the invitation of the Prime Ministers of Burma, Ceylon, India, Indonesia and Pakistan met in Bandung from the 18th to the 24th April, 1955. In addition to the sponsoring countries the following 24 countries participated in the conference:

1. Afghanistan
2. Cambodia
3. People's Republic of China
4. Egypt
5. Ethiopia
6. Gold Coast
7. Iran
8. Iraq
9. Japan
10. Jordan
11. Laos
12. Lebanon
13. Liberia
14. Libya
15. Nepal
16. Philippines
17. Saudi Arabia
18. Sudan
19. Syria
20. Thailand
21. Turkey
22. Democratic Republic of Vietnam
23. State of Vietnam
24. Yemen

The Asian-African Conference considered problems of common interest and concern to countries of Asia and Africa and discussed ways and means by which their people could achieve fuller economic, cultural and political cooperation.

A. *Economic Cooperation*

1. The Asian-African Conference recognized the urgency of promoting economic development in the Asian-African region. There was general desire for economic cooperation among the participating countries on the basis of mutual interest and respect for national sovereignty. The proposals with regard to economic cooperation within the participating countries do not preclude either the desirability or the need for cooperation with countries outside the region, including the investment of foreign capital. It was further recognized that the assistance being received by certain participating countries from outside the region, through international or under bilateral arrangements, had made a valuable contribution to the implementation of their development programmes.

2. The participating countries agreed to provide technical assistance to one another, to the maximum extent practicable, in the form of: experts, trainees, pilot projects and equipment for demonstration purposes; exchange of know-how and establishment of national, and where possible, regional training and research institutes for imparting technical knowledge and skills in cooperation with the existing international agencies.

3. The Asian-African Conference recommended: the early establishment of the Special United Nations Fund for Economic Development; the allocation by the International Bank for Reconstruction and Development of a greater part of its resources to Asian-African countries; the early establishment of the International Finance Corporation which should include in its activities the undertaking of equity investment, and encouragement to the promotion of joint ventures among Asian-African countries in so far as this will promote their common interest.

4. The Asian-African Conference recognized the vital need for stabilizing commodity trade in the region. The principle of enlarging the scope of multilateral trade and payments was accepted. However, it was

recognized that some countries would have to take recourse to bilateral trade arrangements in view of their prevailing economic conditions.

5. The Asian-African Conference recommended that collective action be taken by participating countries for stabilizing the international prices of and demand for primary commodities through bilateral and multilateral arrangements, and that as far as practicable and desirable, they should adopt a unified approach on the subject in the United Nations Permanent Advisory Commission on International Commodity Trade and other international forums.

6. The Asian-African Conference further recommended that: Asian-African countries should diversify their export trade by processing their raw material, wherever economically feasible, before export; intraregional trade fairs should be promoted and encouragement given to the exchange of trade delegations and groups of businessmen; exchange of information and of samples should be encouraged with a view to promoting intra-regional trade and normal facilities should be provided for transit trade of land-locked countries.

* * *

C. Human Rights and Self-determination

1. The Asian-African Conference declared its full support of the fundamental principles of Human Rights as set forth in the Charter of the United Nations and took note of the Universal Declaration of Human Rights as a common standard of achievement for all peoples and all nations.

The Conference declared its full support of the principles of self-determination of peoples and nations as set forth in the Charter of the United Nations and took note of the United Nations resolutions on the rights of peoples and nations to self-determination, which is a pre-requisite of the full enjoyment of all fundamental Human Rights.

2. The Asian-African Conference deplored the policies and practices of racial segregation and discrimination which form the basis of government and human relations in large regions of Africa and in other parts of the world. Such conduct is not only a gross violation of human rights, but also a denial of the fundamental values of civilization and the dignity of man.

The Conference extended its warm sympathy and support for the courageous stand taken by the victims of racial discrimination, especially by the peoples of African and Indian and Pakistani origin in South Africa; applauded all those who sustain their cause, re-affirmed the determination of Asian-African peoples to eradicate every trace of racialism that might exist in their own countries; and pledged to use its full moral influence to guard against the danger of falling victims to the same evil in their struggle to eradicate it.

D. Problems of Dependent Peoples

1. The Asian-African Conference discussed the problems of dependent peoples and colonialism and the evils arising from the subjection of peoples to alien subjugation, domination and exploitation.

The Conference is agreed:

(a) in declaring that colonialism in all its manifestations is an evil which should speedily be brought to an end;

(b) in affirming that the subjection of peoples to alien subjugation, domination and exploitation constitutes a denial of fundamental human rights, is contrary to the Charter of the United Nations and is an impediment to the promotion of world peace and cooperation;

(c) in declaring its support of the cause of freedom and independence for all such people; and

(d) in calling upon the powers concerned to grant freedom and independence to such peoples.

2. In view of the unsettled situation in North Africa and of the persisting denial to the peoples of North Africa of their right to self-determination, the Asian-African Conference declared its support of the rights of the people of Algeria, Morocco and Tunisia to self-determination and independence

and urged the French Government to bring about a peaceful settlement of the issue without delay.

* * *

F. Promotion of World Peace and Cooperation

1. The Asian-African Conference, taking note of the fact that several States have still not been admitted to the United Nations, considered that for effective cooperation for world peace, membership in the United Nations should be universal, called on the Security Council to support the admission of all those States which are qualified for membership in terms of the Charter. In the opinion of the Asian-African Conference, the following among participating countries, viz: Cambodia, Ceylon, Japan, Jordan, Libya, Nepal, a unified Vietnam were so qualified.

The Conference considered that the representation of the countries of the Asian-African region on the Security Council, in relation to the principle of equitable geographical distribution, was inadequate. It expressed the view that as regards the distribution of the non-permanent seats, the Asian-African countries which, under the arrangement arrived at in London in 1946, are precluded from being elected, should be enabled to serve on the Security Council, so that they might make a more effective contribution to the maintenance of international peace and security.

2. The Asian-African Conference having considered the dangerous situation of international tension existing and the risks confronting the whole human race from the outbreak of global war in which the destructive power of all types of armaments, including nuclear and thermo-nuclear weapons, would be employed, invited the attention of all nations to the terrible consequences that would follow if such a war were to break out.

The Conference considered that disarmament and the prohibition of the production, experimentation and use of nuclear and thermonuclear weapons of war are imperative to save mankind and civilization from the fear and prospect of wholesale destruction. It considered that the nations of Asia and Africa assembled here have a duty towards humanity and civilization to proclaim their support for disarmament and for the prohibition of these weapons and to appeal to nations principally concerned and to world opinion, to bring about such disarmament and prohibition.

The Conference considered that effective international control should be established and maintained to implement such disarmament and prohibition and that speedy and determined efforts should be made to this end.

Pending the total prohibition of the manufacture of nuclear and thermo-nuclear weapons, this Conference appealed to all the powers concerned to reach agreement to suspend experiments with such weapons.

The Conference declared that universal disarmament is an absolute necessity for the preservation of peace and requested the United Nations to continue its efforts and appealed to all concerned speedily to bring about the regulation, limitation, control and reduction of all armed forces and armaments, including the prohibition of the production, experimentation and use of all weapons of mass destruction, and to establish effective international control to this end.

G. Declaration on the Promotion of World Peace and Cooperation

The Asian-African Conference gave anxious thought to the question of world peace and cooperation. It viewed with deep concern the present state of international tension with its danger of an atomic world war. The problem of peace is correlative with the problem of international security. In this connection, all States should cooperate, especially through the United Nations, in bringing about the reduction of armaments and the elimination of nuclear weapons under effective international control. In this way international peace can be promoted and nuclear energy may be used exclusively for peaceful purposes. This would help answer the needs particularly of Asia and Africa, for what they urgently require are social progress and better standards of life in larger freedom. Freedom and peace are interdependent. The right of self-determination must be enjoyed by all peoples, and freedom and independence must be granted, with the least possible delay, to those who are still dependent peoples. Indeed, all nations should have the right freely to choose their own political and economic systems and their own way of life, in conformity with the purposes and principles of the Charter of the United Nations. . . .

2. GENEVA, 1964: THE SOLIDARITY OF ECONOMIC NEED

The most consistently "colonial" aspect of the Third World nations today is their continuing economic dependence upon the western powers. This condition — which prevails in Latin America as much as in Africa and Asia — is expressed most directly by the need for foreign aid but has its deepest roots in the disadvantageous trading position of tropical and semitropical countries as producers of primary rather than manufactured goods. The Geneva Conference on Trade and Development, sponsored by the United Nations, brought together one hundred twenty states representing all sectors of the world. Preliminary attempts were made to devise aid policies which would help overcome the disparities between industrialized and nonindustrialized nations.

JOINT DECLARATION

[Afghanistan, Algeria, Argentina, Bolivia, Brazil, Burma, Burundi, Cambodia, Cameroon, Central African Republic, Ceylon, Chad, Chile, Colombia, Congo (Brazzaville), Congo (Leopoldville), Costa Rica, Cyprus, Dahomey, Dominican Republic, Ecuador, El Salvador, Ethiopia, Gabon, Ghana, Guatemala, Guinea, Haiti, Honduras, India, Indonesia, Iran, Iraq, Jamaica, Jordan, Kenya, Kuwait, Laos, Lebanon, Liberia, Libya, Madagascar, Malaysia, Mali, Mauritania, Mexico, Morocco, Nepal, Nicaragua, Niger, Nigeria, Pakistan, Panama, Paraguay, Peru, Philippines, Republic of Korea, Republic of Viet-Nam, Rwanda, Saudi Arabia, Senegal, Sierra Leone, Somalia, Sudan, Syria, Thailand, Togo, Trinidad and Tobago, Tunisia, Uganda, United Arab Republic, United Republic of Tanganyika and Zanzibar, Upper Volta, Uruguay, Venezuela, Yemen and Yugoslavia].

I

1. The developing countries named above recognize the United Nations Conference on Trade and Development as a significant step towards creating a new and just world economic order. They regard this Conference as the fruition of sustained efforts which found expression in the Cairo Declaration, the Alta Gracia Charter, the Resolutions of Brasilia, Addis Ababa, Niamey, Manila and Teheran and, above all, in the Joint Declaration of the seventy-five countries made at the eighteenth session of the General Assembly of the United Nations. These efforts helped to forge the unity of the seventy-five — the outstanding feature

Proceedings of the United Nations Conference on Trade and Development (Geneva, March 23–June 16, 1964) Volume I, Annex B.

of the entire Conference and an event of historic significance.

II

2. The basic premises of the new order were enumerated in these earlier declarations and in the report of the Secretary-General of the Conference. In brief, they involve a new international division of labour oriented towards the accelerated industrialization of developing countries. The efforts of developing countries to raise the living standards of their peoples, which are now being made under adverse external conditions, should be supplemented and strengthened by constructive international action. Such action should establish a new framework of international trade that is wholly consistent with the needs of accelerated development.

3. The several themes of a new and dynamic international policy for trade and development, including the question of transit trade of land-locked countries, found concrete expression in specific programmes and proposals presented by the developing countries to this Conference as a united expression of objectives and measures in all major fields. The developing countries consider it an achievement that this Conference has provided a basis for the fullest discussion of these programmes and proposals by the entire international community. They are confident that the deliberations of this Conference will be of assistance in the formulation of new policies by the Governments of both developed and developing countries in the context of a new awareness of the needs of developing countries.

III

4. The developing countries declare, however, that they consider the final recommendations of the Conference as only an initial step towards an international endorsement of a new trade policy for development. They do not consider that the progress that has been registered in each of the major fields of economic development has been adequate or commensurate with their essential requirements. There has not, for instance, been an adequate appreciation of the problem of the "trade gap" of developing countries. Only the most limited approaches were made regarding trade in primary commodities, and of preferences for exports of manufactures. Similarly, only preliminary steps were possible relating to schemes for compensatory financing to meet long-term deterioration in the terms of trade. The developing countries have, nevertheless, accepted the results of this Conference in the hope that these results would lay the foundation for more substantial progress in the period ahead. They have also accepted these resolutions in recognition of the need for a co-operative effort in the international field. To this end they have chosen to arrive at the widest measure of agreements possible, rather than to register their aspirations by majority decisions.

IV

5. The developing countries attach singular importance to the establishment of international machinery in the field of trade and development. It is vitally necessary that this new machinery should be an effective instrument for the discussion of issues, the formulation of policies, the review of results, and for taking such operational measures as are needed in the sphere of international economic relations.

6. The developing countries recognize the value of the general agreement attained regarding the establishment of continuing machinery. They note that some important issues pertaining to such machinery have been held over for decision by the General Assembly. In this connexion, it is their view that there should be ample scope for reaching workable agreement on substantial issues. But, they categorically declare that no arrangements designed for this purpose should derogate from the ultimate right of the proposed Board and the Conference to adopt recommendations on any point of substance by a simple majority vote in the case of the Board and two-thirds majority vote in the case of the Conference. The developing countries attach cardinal impor-

tance to democratic procedures which afford no position of privilege in the economic and financial, no less than in the political spheres. Furthermore, the developing countries would stress the need for continued evolution in the institutional field, leading not merely to the progressive strengthening of the machinery that is now contemplated, but also to the ultimate emergence of a comprehensive international trade organization.

V

7. The developing countries regard their own unity, the unity of the seventy-five, as the outstanding feature of this Conference. This unity has sprung out of the fact that facing the basic problems of development they have a common interest in a new policy for international trade and development. They believe that it is this unity that has given clarity and coherence to the discussions of this Conference. Their solidarity has been tested in the course of the Conference and they have emerged from it with even greater unity and strength.

8. The developing countries have a strong conviction that there is a vital need to maintain, and further strengthen, this unity in the years ahead. It is an indispensable instrument for securing the adoption of new attitudes and new approaches in the international economic field. This unity is also an instrument for enlarging the area of co-operative endeavour in the international field and for securing mutually beneficent relationships with the rest of the world.

Finally, it is a necessary means for co-operation amongst the developing countries themselves.

9. The seventy-five developing countries, on the occasion of this declaration, pledge themselves to maintain, foster and strengthen this unity in the future. Towards this end they shall adopt all possible means to increase the contacts and consultations amongst themselves so as to determine common objectives and formulate joint programmes of action in international economic co-operation. They consider that measures for consolidating the unity achieved by the seventy-five countries during the Conference and the specific arrangements for contacts and consultations should be studied by government representatives during the nineteenth session of the United Nations General Assembly.

VI

10. The United Nations Conference on Trade and Development marks the beginning of a new era in the evolution of international co-operation in the field of trade and development. Such co-operation must serve as a decisive instrument for ending the division of the world into areas of affluence and intolerable poverty. This task is the outstanding challenge of our times. The injustice and neglect of centuries need to be redressed. The developing countries are united in their resolve to continue the quest for such redress and look to the entire international community for understanding and support in this endeavour.

Frantz Fanon

3. PURIFICATION THROUGH ANTICOLONIAL VIOLENCE

Frantz Fanon (1925-1961), a French-speaking Black West Indian psychiatrist, took an active part in the Algerian revolution against French rule, a guerilla war which became his model for decolonization. Historically, it would be difficult to apply Fanon's ideas to all anticolonial nationalisms, particularly those in tropical Africa. As ideology, nevertheless, his views have had considerable resonance in the Third World as well as in the Black community of the United States.

National liberation, national renaissance, the restoration of nationhood to the people, commonwealth: whatever may be the headings used or the new formulas introduced, decolonisation is always a violent phenomenon. At whatever level we study it—relationships between individuals, new names for sports clubs, the human admixture at cocktail parties, in the police, on the directing boards of national or private banks—decolonisation is quite simply the replacing of a certain "species" of men by another "species" of men. Without any period of transition, there is a total, complete and absolute substitution. It is true that we could equally well stress the rise of a new nation, the setting up of a new State, its diplomatic relations, and its economic and political trends. But we have precisely chosen to speak of that kind of *tabula rasa* which characterises at the outset all decolonisation. Its unusual importance is that it constitutes, from the very first day, the minimum demands of the colonised. To tell the truth, the proof of success lies in a whole social structure being changed from the bottom up. The extraordinary importance of this change is that it is willed, called for, demanded. The need for this change exists in its crude state, impetuous and compelling, in the consciousness and in the lives of the men and women who are colonised. But the possibility of this change is equally experienced in the form of a terrifying future in the consciousness of another "species" of men and women: the colonisers.

Decolonisation, which sets out to change the order of the world, is, obviously, a programme of complete disorder. But it cannot come as a result of magical practices, nor of a natural shock, nor of a friendly understanding. Decolonisation, as we know, is a historical process: that is to say that it cannot be understood, it cannot become intelligible nor clear to itself except in the exact measure that we can discern the movements which give it historical form and content. Decolonisation is the meeting of two forces, opposed to each other by their very nature, which in fact owe their originality to that sort of substantification which results from and is nourished by the situation in the colonies. Their first encounter was marked by violence and their existence together—that is to say the exploitation of the native by the settler—was carried on by dint of a great

From Frantz Fanon, *The Wretched of the Earth* (N. Y., 1965), pp. 29-31, 73-83. Translated from the French by Constance Farrington. Reprinted by permission of Grove Press, Inc. and MacGibbon & Kee Limited. Copyright © 1963 by Presence Africaine.

array of bayonets and cannon. The settler and the native are old acquaintances. In fact, the settler is right when he speaks of knowing "them" well. For it is the settler who has brought the native into existence and who perpetuates his existence. The settler owes the fact of his very existence, that is to say his property, to the colonial system.

Decolonisation never takes place unnoticed, for it influences individuals and modifies them fundamentally. It transforms spectators crushed with their inessentiality into privileged actors, with the grandiose glare of history's floodlights upon them. It brings a natural rhythm into existence, introduced by new men, and with it a new language and a new humanity. Decolonisation is the veritable creation of new men. But this creation owes nothing of its legitimacy to any supernatural power; the "thing" which has been colonised becomes man during the same process by which it frees itself.

In decolonisation, there is therefore the need of a complete calling in question of the colonial situation. If we wish to describe it precisely, we might find it in the well-known words: "The last shall be first and the first last." Decolonisation is the putting into practice of this sentence. That is why, if we try to describe it, all decolonisation is successful.

The naked truth of decolonisation evokes for us the searing bullets and bloodstained knives which emanate from it. For if the last shall be first, this will only come to pass after a murderous and decisive struggle between the two protagonists. That affirmed intention to place the last at the head of things, and to make them climb at a pace (too quickly, some say) the well-known steps which characterise an organised society, can only triumph if we use all means to turn the scale, including, of course, that of violence.

You do not turn any society, however primitive it may be, upside-down with such a programme if you are not decided from the very beginning, that is to say from the actual formulation of that programme, to

overcome all the obstacles that you will come across in so doing. The native who decides to put the programme into practice, and to become its moving force, is ready for violence at all times. From birth it is clear to him that this narrow world, strewn with prohibitions, can only be called in question by absolute violence.

The colonial world is a world divided into compartments. It is probably unnecessary to recall the existence of native quarters and European quarters, of schools for natives and schools for Europeans; in the same way we need not recall Apartheid in South Africa. Yet, if we examine closely this system of compartments, we will at least be able to reveal the lines of force it implies. This approach to the colonial world, its ordering and its geographical lay-out will allow us to mark out the lines on which a decolonised society will be reorganised.

The colonial world is a world cut in two. The dividing line, the frontiers are shown by barracks and police stations. In the colonies it is the policeman and the soldier who are the official, instituted go-betweens, the spokesmen of the settler and his rule of oppression. In capitalist societies the educational system, whether lay or clerical, the structure of moral reflexes handed down from father to son, the exemplary honesty of workers who are given a medal after fifty years of good and loyal service, and the affection which springs from harmonious relations and good behaviour—all these esthetic expressions of respect for the established order serve to create around the exploited person an atmosphere of submission and of inhibition which lightens the task of policing considerably. In the capitalist countries a multitude of moral teachers, counsellors and "bewilderers" separate the exploited from those in power. In the colonial countries, on the contrary, the policeman and the soldier, by their immediate presence and their frequent and direct action maintain contact with the native and advise him by means of rifle-butts and napalm not to budge. It is obvious here that the agents of government speak the language of pure force. The intermediary does not lighten the oppression, nor seek to hide the domination; he shows them up and puts them into practice with the clear conscience of an upholder of the peace; yet he is the bringer of violence into the home and into the mind of the native.

* * *

The mobilisation of the masses, when it arises out of the war of liberation, introduces into each man's consciousness the ideas of a common cause, of a national destiny and of a collective history. In the same way the second phase, that of the building-up of the nation, is helped on by the existence of this cement which has been mixed with blood and anger. Thus we come to a fuller appreciation of the originality of the words used in these under-developed countries. During the colonial period the people are called upon to fight against oppression; after national liberation, they are called upon to fight against poverty, illiteracy and under-development. The struggle, they say, goes on. The people realise that life is an unending contest.

We have said that the native's violence unifies the people. By its very structure, colonialism is separatist and regionalist. Colonialism does not simply state the existence of tribes; it also re-inforces it and separates them. The colonial system encourages chief-taincies and keeps alive the old Marabout confraternities. Violence is in action all-inclusive and national. It follows that it is closely involved in the liquidation of regionalism and of tribalism. Thus the national parties show no pity at all towards the caids and the customary chiefs. Their destruction is the preliminary to the unification of the people.

At the level of individuals, violence is a cleansing force. It frees the native from his inferiority complex and from his despair and inaction; it makes him fearless and restores his self-respect. Even if the armed struggle has been symbolic and the nation is demobilised through a rapid movement of decolonisation, the people have the time

to see that the liberation has been the business of each and all and that the leader has no special merit. From thence comes that type of aggressive reticence with regard to the machinery of protocol which young governments quickly show. When the people have taken violent part in the national liberation they will allow no one to set themselves up as "liberators." They show themselves to be jealous of the results of their action and take good care not to place their future, their destiny or the fate of their country in the hands of a living god. Yesterday they were completely irresponsible; today they mean to understand everything and make all decisions. Illuminated by violence, the consciousness of the people rebels against any pacification. From now on the demagogues, the opportunists and the magicians have a difficult task. The action which has thrown them into a hand-to-hand struggle confers upon the masses a voracious taste for the concrete. The attempt at mystification becomes, in the long run, practically impossible.

VIOLENCE IN THE INTERNATIONAL CONTEXT

We have pointed out many times in the preceding pages that in under-developed regions the political leader is forever calling on his people to fight: to fight against colonialism, to fight against poverty and under-development, and to fight against sterile traditions. The vocabulary which he uses in his appeals is that of a chief of staff: "mass mobilisation"; "agricultural front"; "fight against illiteracy"; "defeats we have undergone"; "victories won." The young independent nation evolves during the first years in an atmosphere of the battlefield, for the political leader of an under-developed country looks fearfully at the huge distance his country will have to cover. He calls to the people and says to them: "Let us gird up our loins and set to work," and the country, possessed by a kind of creative madness, throws itself into a gigantic and disproportionate effort. The programme consists not only of climbing out of the morass but also of catching up with the other nations using the only means at hand. They reason that if the European nations have reached that stage of development, it is on account of their efforts: "Let us therefore," they seem to say, "prove to ourselves and to the whole world that we are capable of the same achievements." This manner of setting out the problem of the evolution of under-developed countries seems to us to be neither correct nor reasonable.

The European states achieved national unity at a moment when the national middle-classes had concentrated most of the wealth in their hands. Shopkeepers and artisans, clerks and bankers monopolised finance, trade and science in the national framework. The middle class was the most dynamic and prosperous of all classes. Its coming to power enabled it to undertake certain very important speculations: industrialisation, the development of communications and soon the search for outlets overseas.

In Europe, apart from certain slight differences (England, for example was some way ahead) the various states were at a more or less uniform stage economically when they achieved national unity. There was no nation which by reason of the character of its development and evolution caused affront to the others.

Today, national independence and the growth of national feeling in under-developed regions take on totally new aspects. In these regions, with the exception of certain spectacular advances, the different countries show the same absence of infrastructure. The mass of the people struggle against the same poverty, flounder about making the same gestures and with their shrunken bellies outline what has been called the geography of hunger. It is an under-developed world, a world inhuman in its poverty; but also it is a world without doctors, without engineers and without administrators. Confronting this world, the European nations sprawl, ostentatiously opulent. This European opulence is literally scandalous, for it has been founded on slav-ery, it has been nourished with the blood of slaves and it comes directly from the soil and from the subsoil of that under-developed world. The well-being and the progress of Europe have been built up with the sweat and the dead bodies of Negroes, Arabs, Indians and the yellow races. We have decided not to overlook this any longer. When a colonialist country, embarrassed by the claims for independence made by a colony, proclaims to the nationalist leaders: "If you wish for independence, take it, and go back to the middle ages," the newly-independent people tend to acquiesce and to accept the challenge; in fact you may see colonialism withdrawing its capital and its technicians and setting up around the young State the apparatus of economic pressure. The apotheosis of independence is transformed into the curse of independence, and the colonial power through its immense resources of coercion condemns the young nation to regression. In plain words, the colonial power says: "Since you want independence, take it and starve." The nationalist leaders have no other choice but to turn to their people and ask from them a gigantic effort. A regime of austerity is imposed on these starving men; a disproportionate amount of work is required from their atrophied muscles. An autarkic regime is set up and each state, with the miserable resources it has in hand, tries to find an answer to the nation's great hunger and poverty. We see the mobilisation of a people which toils to exhaustion in front of a suspicious and bloated Europe.

Other countries of the Third World refuse to undergo this ordeal and agree to get over it by accepting the conditions of the former guardian power. These countries use their strategic position—a position which accords them privileged treatment in the struggle between the two *blocs*—to conclude treaties and give undertakings. The former dominated country becomes an economically dependent country. The ex-colonial power, which has kept intact and sometimes even reinforced its colonialist trade channels agrees to provision the budget of the independent nation by small injections. Thus we see that the accession to independence of the colonial countries places an important question before the world, for the national liberation of colonised countries unveils their true economic state and makes it seem even more unendurable. The fundamental duel which seemed to be that between colonialism and anticolonialism, and indeed between capitalism and socialism, is already losing some of its importance. What counts today, the question which is looming on the horizon is the need for a re-distribution of wealth. Humanity must reply to this question, or be shaken to pieces by it.

It might have been generally thought that the time had come for the world, and particularly for the Third World, to choose between the capitalist and socialist systems. The under-developed countries, which have used the fierce competition which exists between the two systems in order to assure the triumph of their struggle for national liberation, should however refuse to become a factor in that competition. The Third World ought not to be content to define itself in the terms of values which have preceded it. On the contrary, the under-developed countries ought to do their utmost to find their own particular values and methods and a style which shall be peculiar to them. The concrete problem we find ourselves up against is not that of a choice, cost what it may, between socialism and capitalism as they have been defined by men of other continents and of other ages. Of course we know that the capitalist regime, in so far as it is a way of life, cannot leave us free to perform our work at home, nor our duty in the world. Capitalist exploitation and cartels and monopolies are the enemies of under-developed countries. On the other hand the choice of a socialist regime, a regime which is completely orientated towards the people as a whole and based on the principle that man is the most precious of all possessions will allow us to go forward more quickly and more harmoniously, and thus make impossible that caricature of society where all economic and political power is held in the hands of a few who regard the nation as a whole with scorn and contempt.

But in order that this regime may work to good effect so that we can in every instance respect those principles which were our inspiration, we need something more than human output. Certain under-developed countries expend a huge amount of energy in this way. Men and women, young and old undertake enthusiastically what is in fact forced labour, and proclaim themselves the slaves of the nation. The gift of oneself, and the contempt for every preoccupation which is not in the common interest, bring into being a national *morale* which comforts the heart of man, gives him fresh confidence in the destiny of mankind and disarms the most reserved observers. But we cannot believe that such an effort can be kept up at the same frenzied pace for very long. These young countries have agreed to take up the challenge after the unconditional withdrawal of the ex-colonial countries. The country finds itself in the hands of new managers; but the fact is that everything needs to be reformed and everything thought out anew. In reality the colonial system was concerned with certain forms of wealth and certain resources only—precisely those which provisioned her own industries. Up to the present no serious effort had been made to estimate the riches of the soil or of mineral resources. Thus the young independent nation sees itself obliged to use the economic channels created by the colonial regime. It can, obviously, export to other countries and other currency areas, but the basis of its exports is not fundamentally modified. The colonial regime has carved out certain channels and they must be maintained or catastrophe will threaten. Perhaps it is necessary to begin everything all over again: to change the nature of the country's exports, and not simply their destination, to re-examine the soil and mineral resources, the rivers, and—why not?—the sun's productivity. Now, in order to do all this other things are needed over and above human output—capital of all

147

kinds, technicians, engineers, skilled mechanics, and so on. Let's be frank: we do not believe that the colossal effort which the under-developed peoples are called upon to make by their leaders will give the desired results. If conditions of work are not modified, centuries will be needed to humanise this world which has been forced down to animal level by imperial powers.

The truth is that we ought not to accept these conditions. We should flatly refuse the situation to which the western countries wish to condemn us. Colonialism and imperialism have not paid their score when they withdraw their flags and their police forces from our territories. For centuries the capitalists have behaved in the underdeveloped world like nothing more than war criminals. Deportations, massacres, forced labour, and slavery have been the main methods used by capitalism to increase its wealth, its gold or diamond reserves, and to establish its power. Not long ago Nazism transformed the whole of Europe into a veritable colony. The governments of the various European nations called for reparations and demanded the restitution in kind and money of the wealth which had been stolen from them: cultural treasures, pictures, sculptures, and stained glass have been given back to their owners. There was only one slogan in the mouths of Europeans on the morrow of the 1945 V-day: "Germany must pay." Herr Adenauer, it must be said, at the opening of the Eichmann trial, and in the name of the German people, asked once more for forgiveness from the Jewish people. Herr Adenauer has renewed the promise of his people to go on paying to the state of Israel the enormous sums which are supposed to be compensation for the crimes of the Nazis.

In the same way we may say that the imperialist states would make a great mistake and commit an unspeakable injustice if they contented themselves with withdrawing from our soil the military cohorts, and the administrative and managerial services whose function it was to discover the wealth of the country, to extract it and to send it off to the mother countries. We are not blinded by the moral reparation of national independence; nor are we fed by it. The wealth of the imperial countries is our wealth too. On the universal plane this affirmation, you may be sure, should on no account be taken to signify that we feel ourselves affected by the creations of Western arts or techniques. For in a very concrete way Europe has stuffed herself inordinately with the gold and raw materials of the colonial countries: Latin America, China and Africa. From all these continents, under whose eyes Europe today raises up her tower of opulence, there has flowed out for centuries towards that same Europe diamonds and oil, silk and cotton, wood and exotic products. Europe is literally the creation of the Third World. The wealth which smothers her is that which was stolen from the under-developed peoples. The ports of Holland, the docks of Bordeaux and Liverpool were specialised in the Negro slave-trade, and owe their renown to millions of deported slaves. So when we hear the head of a European state declare with his hand on his heart that he must come to the help of the poor under-developed peoples, we do not tremble with gratitude. Quite the contrary; we say to ourselves: "It's a just reparation which will be paid to us." Nor will we acquiesce in the help for under-developed countries being a programme of "sisters of charity." This help should be the ratification of a double realisation: the realisation by the colonised peoples that *it is their due,* and the realisation by the capitalist powers that in fact *they must pay.* For if, through lack of intelligence (we won't speak of lack of gratitude) the capitalist countries refuse to pay, then the relentless dialectic of their own system will smother them. It is a fact that young nations do not attract much private capital. There are many reasons which explain and render legitimate this reserve on the part of the monopolies. As soon as the capitalists know—and of course they are the first to know—that their government is getting ready to decolonise, they hasten to withdraw all their capital from the colony in question. The spectacular flight of capital is one of the most constant phenomena of decolonisation.

Private companies, when asked to invest in independent countries, lay down conditions which are shown in practice to be inacceptable or unrealizable. Faithful to the principle of immediate returns which is theirs as soon as they go "over-seas," the capitalists are very chary concerning all long-term investments. They are unamenable and often openly hostile to the prospective programmes of planning laid down by the young teams who form the new government. At a pinch they willingly agree to lend money to the young States, but only on condition that this money is used to buy manufactured products and machines: in other words, that it serves to keep the factories in the mother-country going.

In fact the cautiousness of the Western financial groups may be explained by their fear of taking any risk. They also demand political stability and a calm social climate which are impossible to obtain when account is taken of the appalling state of the population as a whole immediately after independence. Therefore, vainly looking for some guarantee which the former colony cannot give, they insist on garrisons being maintained or the inclusion of the young state in military or economic pacts. The private companies put pressure on their own governments to at least set up military bases in these countries for the purpose of assuring the protection of their interests. In the last resort these companies ask their government to guarantee the investments which they decide to make in such-and-such an underdeveloped region.

It happens that few countries fulfill the conditions demanded by the trusts and monopolies. Thus capital, failing to find a safe outlet, remains blocked in Europe, and is frozen. It is all the more frozen because the capitalists refuse to invest in their own countries. The returns in this case are in fact negligible and treasury control is the despair of even the boldest spirits.

In the long run the situation is cata-strophic. Capital no longer circulates, or else its circulation is considerably diminished. In spite of the huge sums swallowed up by military budgets, international capitalism is in desperate straits.

But another danger threatens it as well. Insofar as the Third World is in fact abandoned and condemned to regression or at least to stagnation by the selfishness and wickedness of Western nations, the underdeveloped peoples will decide to continue their evolution inside a collective autarky. Thus the Western industries will quickly be deprived of their overseas markets. The machines will pile up their products in the warehouses and a merciless struggle will ensue on the European market between the trusts and the financial groups. The closing of factories, the paying off of workers and unemployment will force the European working-class to engage in an open struggle against the capitalist regime. Then the monopolies will realise that their true interests lie in giving aid to the under-developed countries — unstinted aid with not too many conditions. So we see that the young nations of the Third World are wrong in trying to make up to the capitalist countries. We are strong in our own right, and in the justice of our point of view. We ought on the contrary to emphasise and explain to the capitalist countries that the fundamental problem of our time is not the struggle between the socialist regime and them. The Cold War must be ended, for it leads nowhere. The plans for nuclearising the world must stop, and large-scale investments and technical aid must be given to under-developed regions. The fate of the world depends on the answer that is given to this question.

Moreover, the capitalist regime must not try to enlist the aid of the socialist regime over "the fate of Europe" in face of the starving multitudes of coloured peoples. The exploit of Colonel Gargarin doesn't seem to displease General de Gaulle, for is it not a triumph which brings honour to Europe? For some time past the statesmen of the capitalist countries have adopted an equivocal attitude towards the Soviet Union. After having united all their forces to abolish the socialist regime, they now realise that they'll have to reckon with it. So they look as pleasant as they can, they make all kinds of advances, and they remind the Soviet people the whole time that they "belong to Europe."

They will not manage to divide the progressive forces which mean to lead mankind towards happiness by brandishing the threat of a Third World which is rising like the tide to swallow up all Europe. The Third World does not mean to organise a great crusade of hunger against the whole of Europe. What it expects from those who for centuries have kept it in slavery is that they will help it to rehabilitate mankind, and make man victorious everywhere, once and for all. But it is clear that we are not so naive as to think that this will come about with the co-operation and the good will of the European governments. This huge task which consists of re-introducing mankind into the world, the whole of mankind, will be carried out with the indispensable help of the European peoples, who themselves must realise that in the past they have often joined the ranks of our common masters where colonial questions were concerned. To achieve this, the European peoples must first decide to wake up and shake themselves, use their brains, and stop playing the stupid game of the Sleeping Beauty.

A. L. Adu

4. REVOLUTIONARY POLITICS VERSUS ADMINISTRATIVE CONTINUITY

While political leadership in the Third World is based upon a reaction against imperialism, another portion of the new elite in colonized areas had been trained to maintain the structures of European rule. For this indigenous civil service class, both described and represented by the author of the following selection, the transition to independence has posed a serious dilemma. Adu makes specific reference to the often overwhelming technical problem of meeting vastly increased expectations with a sometimes diminished professional capacity. Strongly suggested here is the even more critical issue of ideological conflict between the prophets of dramatic decolonization and the priests of orderly modernization. Adu himself has found it advantageous to avoid such a confrontation by pursuing an administrative career outside his native Ghana. Within Ghana, as in various other African states, friction between party cadres and European-trained professionals of both the civil service and the armed forces have resulted in military coups and a return, in many respects, to the antipolitical paternalism of colonial days.

Much has been said in earlier chapters about the role of the Civil Service in African States and its relations with the Government. Perhaps no more need really be said about this matter, but on the other hand it would be most convenient to put in a summary form in the concluding chapter the main objectives which it has been intended all along to put across. Unless the Civil Service and Civil Servants form a proper appreciation of the part they have to play in the revolution now taking place in contemporary Africa, they run the risk of forfeiting their right to survive in the form in which the service now exists and is likely to develop in the future.

The Civil Service in present-day Africa is faced with tasks and responsibilities which were not envisaged only a few years ago. Certainly, no one contemplated, before 1939, that there would be this rapid postwar acceleration of constitutional development. It caught the Civil Service completely unawares. The service was therefore not easily adjustable to the rapidly changing conditions. As stated earlier, the old colonial administrations and technical departments were concerned with such matters as maintenance of law and order, local administration, the provision of a moderate level of social services, elementary communications networks and the husbanding of natural resources. There were no five or ten year development plans, no major policies on industrialization, no talk of providing economic infrastructure services, nor any

From A. L. Adu, *The Civil Service in the New African States* (New York, 1965), pp. 226-232, 235-236. Reprinted by permission of Frederick A. Praeger, Inc. and George Allen & Unwin Ltd.

full development of the economy, no balance of payment difficulties, no talk of deficit financing policies, no central banking nor the creation of money markets, and no external relations problems whether political, economic or commercial.

Now, however, all African States have got to concern themselves with major matters and problems of a variety and complexity that would test the abilities of the most mature Civil Servants of any country. All African governments promise to work for the raising of the standard of life of their peoples and they all, as a matter of priority, embark on the preparation and carrying out of comprehensive development plans. The preparation of such plans, which shall provide for balanced development in economic, social and cultural fields, so that the increase in the national income and therefore government revenue is able to pay for the non-productive services, is a very complicated matter and requires a degree of sophisticated economic, statistical and professional knowledge not easily available to African countries. Coupled with this programme of economic and social development planning is the need to establish a system for the regulation of the economic and financial structure of the particular State. This implies the modernization of budgeting policies and procedures, the creation of a central banking institution, the establishment of legislation, institutions or machinery to favour industrial and agricultural development, and the setting up of planning organizations or units, including machinery for manpower planning.

Closely related is the accelerated expansion of social and socio-economic services in such fields as health and nutrition, education, social development and community development. These used to be regarded as social services only, which should be maintained and expanded when the economic services could pay for them. It is now recognized that they have their significant contributions to make to economic development. Obviously for instance, the provision of health services and better nutrition in areas which are populated with men whose health is below the normal level, and who suffer from food deficiencies, would be bound to result in healthier workers and therefore higher productivity. It is recognized also that the educational system is the main instrument for the training of manpower and that social and community development provides positive means for mobilizing local available resources — including local manpower resources for tackling some of the more immediate social and economic problems of the local areas. This recognition of the role of social and socio-economic services in the improvement of the well-being of the people has come at a time when new African governments are taking over. Even expatriate Civil Servants of ripe experience generally would have found it difficult to adjust their ideas to this new approach.

Furthermore, the establishment of external relations policies and organizations is something completely new to the experience of all who exercise some responsibilities for the affairs of government in African States. It is natural that external or foreign relations should come to new countries at the time of their independence, since only independent States could organize Ministries of External or Foreign Affairs, diplomatic services and diplomatic missions abroad. New policies in relation to the United Nations, the Afro-Asian bloc, apartheid, colonialism, the European Common Market, disarmament, the "cold war" and other external matters have to be formulated, bearing in mind the safeguarding of the national interest. Policies and organizations have also to accommodate the rise of African politics and Pan-Africanism and moves towards the achievement of a political union of African States.

Again, there is the problem of the creation of a nation out of a conglomeration of tribes and communities and, in some instances races, who reside within the national boundaries. These were brought together and held together by the imperial power in the pre-independence days. The task before the new States is to create a national consciousness among these various peoples and a feeling of belonging to one nation whose interests should transcend all others, including tribal and communal interests. This is not an easy task to perform, and the objective of achieving a sense of nationhood by which citizenship is the best qualification for consideration in all national matters rather than tribe or religion or race is a hard one to attain.

All these matters — economic development planning, the provision of social and socio-economic services, the establishment of economic and financial services, external relations, African politics and the integration of all tribes, religions, communities and races into a sense of nationhood — are formidable matters for any Government to handle. They are even more formidable when they have to be tackled by governments whose members are new to these problems and whose Civil Services are being rapidly Africanized. Such men are carried forward into doing the best they can, under the circumstances, because of an almost missionary zeal which impels them to attempt to bring progress, prosperity and happiness to their peoples. Enthusiasm operates where experience is lacking or is insufficient. In most African States, Ministers and other members of the government have had comparatively recent experience of matters of policy of this nature. Certainly, a rapidly changing Civil Service which is being Africanized at an accelerated rate could not claim to have the experience for tackling these formidable programmes and problems. They could not have acquired this experience from their former expatriate colleagues since these themselves had not been through this experience, which is a function of independence.

The new African Civil Service has therefore the task of not only building itself up and placing itself as rapidly as possible on an indigenous basis but also of adapting itself to assist Ministers in tackling the major matters and problems mentioned above, as well as others not included. To this should be added the need to reform the orientation and structure of the Civil Service so that it is able to function in consonance with the government's political systems and policies. It should be emphasized that these responsibilities are either very new to the African situation or else they have to be discharged under conditions vastly different from those prevailing before independence. The experience that rested in the old Civil Service was therefore either irrelevant in some cases or else had to be considerably adapted to the contemporary situation. This adaptation and this orientation have to take place at a time when the service itself is going through a period of rapid turnover in personnel brought about by accelerated Africanization policies, and when inevitably there are lacking in the officials a wealth of ripe experience and adequate maturity. In the circumstances, therefore, it is most encouraging to find that there is a great awareness among African Civil Servants that they have a role to play in the contemporary African situation which must match the increased range of responsibilities that now devolve on them. In most cases, they have succeeded in providing, in understanding and enthusiasm, what they might have lacked in experience and maturity. There is no disguising the fact, however, that on the whole, the African Civil Service has not been prepared for its new role, through no fault of its own, and has therefore not been able to meet adequately, and in all respects, the challenge of the new age.

The task of the Civil Service has been made more difficult by a number of other factors which might account for the fact that the service has to go through a much longer period of adjustment before it settles down to the responsibilities thrust upon it. Far too often, African governments and their Ministers do not understand and appreciate the relative roles of themselves and the Civil Service. They either expect too much and are disappointed if they do not have performance matching up to expectations, or else they endeavour to by-pass their Civil Servants, which further complicates matters.

153

This situation arises from a number of reasons. Ministers are impatient to get on with the programmes they have set before them in their election manifestos and Party pronouncements. Their people expect quick results and they themselves are anxious to demonstrate that independence means action for progress and the alleviation of some of the burdens and impediments of the past. They find, in the circumstances, that the Civil Service machinery is too ponderous for their purpose and too deliberate in its procedures for examining and implementing policies. They make no allowances for the fact that by their own policies, comparatively inexperienced persons have been placed in the key positions of Permanent Secretaries and Heads of Departments and that, even though these men are working long hours and with all their ability to keep up with the pile of responsibilities which confront them, they would necessarily take a much longer time to get through their tasks, since they have to work most things out from first principles and only a few can take things in the stride of experience. In such circumstances, patience and understanding is called for from both sides and this is not always forthcoming.

The situation is further complicated by attempts by Ministers to control or influence appointments, promotions and discipline in the Civil Service. This is an understandable desire since a Minister's responsibility for the management of the services and policies within his portfolio cannot be entirely divorced from those aspects of this management concerning the personnel executing these services and policies. This matter has been discussed at some length earlier but there is a tendency for Ministers to go beyond the point that is reasonable and they make it difficult to create the conditions for the establishment of those healthy conventions that are essential for ensuring morale, security and discipline in the Civil Service.

An aspect of this improper intervention in appointments and promotions is the intrusion of political appointments into the Civil Service. Where these are competent, they present no problem and in fact they might result in a net gain since, in the early stages of Africanization at any rate, there is normally so much vacant room that the interests of career Civil Servants are not at any serious risk. Very often, however, the main qualification of a political appointee is party political zeal and he does not have the ability, experience or competence to discharge the responsibilities of the post to which he is appointed. This sort of situation is bound to undermine confidence and efficiency in the service. The situation is worse where politically appointed officers are placed above career Civil Servants of greater experience and ability. A relevant example is the appointment of politicians to district administrative positions as District or Area Commissioners, in some cases over the heads of graduates or officials with long field experience.

Another factor in the situation is that all African governments adopt the policy of a welfare state in some form or other. This policy very often takes the form of socialism — African or democratic socialism, Nkrumahism or Ujamaa.* Whether it is termed socialism or not, all new governments adopt a policy of State intervention and participation in the major economic and social programmes of development so as to accelerate the economic and social betterment of the people. They further endeavour to influence the political, social and cultural outlook of the people, particularly of the youth, as part of the programme for the transformation of the society into one which is indigenously based, whilst taking advantage of existing or future developments from overseas which would help to bring indigenous society into the modern world. This is an additional factor in making the task of the Civil Service more complex than it would normally be.

It is not surprising, therefore, that in nearly all the African States, the Civil Service no more has the initiative in the formu-

*Swahili term used to designate "African Socialism" in Tanzania.

lation of operational policies. It is, it has already been made clear, the responsibility of the Ministers to determine political policy but the programming of such policies should normally be left to the Civil Service. It is the usual situation nowadays, however, to see Ministers working out their own detailed programmes, supervising the execution of these programmes and generally carrying out functions which should properly be discharged by their officials. Admittedly there is nothing sacrosanct about the pattern of the past or the conventions in the relationship between Ministers and officials established elsewhere; it is entirely proper that African States should wish to establish their own patterns or conventions. But local and appropriate patterns and conventions have to be established and stabilized so that the Civil Service is in the position to form an appreciation of its role and to exercise full initiative within it. The object should be that operational policy is defined as the responsibility of the Civil Service, leaving political and broad policy to Ministers. In between there is always room for Civil Servants to assist Ministers with their policy formulation responsibilities and for Ministers to give clear indications, whenever necessary or appropriate, on how they wish particular policies to be carried out.

To recapture the initiative in exercising the right to formulate operational policy, and even to provide the lead in most of the major, sometimes political, policies, does mean both the establishment of the proper pattern or conventions in the relations between Minister and officials, and imagina tive planning for the education and orientation of the Civil Service. The policies and detailed programmes required for these would vary from State to State according to the circumstances. But some or all of the programmes which will now be discussed would apply.

*   *   *

Fundamental to all these programmes is the endeavour to inculcate in Civil Servants the right ideas on the role of their service in the welfare state — or socialist state, as some would prefer to call it. This is necessary if they are to be effective as the executive arm of the government and, for those in the higher ranks, if they are to be in the position to help, counsel and advise their Governments in the formidable task of shaping the policies and hence the destiny, of the nation. The scope of this process of orientation is wide and embraces an appreciation and study of such matters as political science, economics, sociology, social psychology, law, and international relations in combinations as necessary for the particular situation. The process of orientation should also not only lay emphasis on professional training, efficient working methods and training in objectivity and analysis, but should also provide synthesis, common sense, power of judgement and reason and the ability to find out practical and positive solutions to various administrative problems.

The programmes discussed above do not by any means exhaust all the possibilities. They are given as some examples of the means by which the Civil Service, in the contemporary situation of the Africa of today and tomorrow, can prepare itself to play a positive role in the affairs of the State and to accept and retain the initiative in determining operational policies that are designed to match the political, economic and social policies of the government. The Civil Service in its life and work should effectively and positively respond to a nation's will and be able to act in consonance with the urgency of the political situation of all new countries. It should work to earn the trust and confidence of the government and the people so that it is enabled to establish itself as the permanent and stabilizing force necessary for orderly progress in the State and towards the well-being of the people.

5. UNITED NATIONS INTERVENTION IN THE SUEZ CRISIS

The events leading to the British and French invasion of Egypt in 1956 cover more than a century and a half of imperialist history, including not only the strategic role of the Canal itself, which had been seized from its European owners earlier in the same year by Egyptian President Gamal Abdel Nasser, but also the founding in Palestine of a Jewish state which, since 1947, has been in various forms of official warfare with its Arab neighbors. United States pressure on Britain, France, and Israel forced all three powers to withdraw from Egypt, and a new precedent for settling such questions was established by using the United Nations as both an arena of deliberation and a supplier of neutral forces for occupying disputed zones on the border between Israel and Egypt. Similar deployment of U.N. forces in the Congo from 1960 to 1964 proved somewhat less successful. Moreover, with the removal of U.N. troops from the Middle East in 1967, a new war broke out between Israel and the Arab states, and the Suez Canal was once again closed.

UNITED NATIONS RESOLUTIONS ADOPTED
WITHOUT REFERENCE TO A COMMITTEE

Question considered by the Security Council at its 749th and 750th meetings, held on 30 October 1956.

RESOLUTION 997 (ES-1)

The General Assembly,

Noting the disregard on many occasions by parties to the Israel-Arab armistice agreements of 1949 of the terms of such agreements, and that the armed forces of Israel have penetrated deeply into Egyptian territory in violation of the General Armistice Agreement between Egypt and Israel of 24 February 1949,

Noting that armed forces of France and the United Kingdom of Great Britain and Northern Ireland are conducting military operations against Egyptian territory,

Noting that traffic through the Suez Canal is now interrupted to the serious prejudice of many nations,

Expressing its grave concern over these developments,

1. *Urges* as a matter of priority that all parties now involved in hostilities in the area agree to an immediate cease-fire and, as part thereof, halt the movement of military forces and arms into the area;

2. *Urges* the parties to the armistice agreements promptly to withdraw all forces behind the armistice lines, to desist from raids across the armistice lines into neighbouring territory, and to observe scrupulously the provisions of the armistice agreements;

3. *Recommends* that all Member States refrain from introducing military goods in the area of hostilities and in general refrain from any acts which would delay or prevent the implementation of the present resolution;

4. *Urges* that, upon the cease-fire being effective, steps be taken to reopen the Suez Canal and restore secure freedom of navigation;

Official Records of the General Assembly, First Emergency Special Session, Supplement No. 1 (A/3354).

5. *Requests* the Secretary-General to observe and report promptly on the compliance with the present resolution to the Security Council and to the General Assembly, for such further action as they may deem appropriate in accordance with the Charter;

6. *Decides* to remain in emergency session pending compliance with the present resolution.

562nd plenary meeting,
2 November 1956.

RESOLUTION 998 (ES-1)

The General Assembly,

Bearing in mind the urgent necessity of facilitating compliance with its resolution 997 (ES-I) of 2 November 1956,

Requests, as a matter of priority, the Secretary-General to submit to it within forty-eight hours a plan for the setting up, with the consent of the nations concerned, of an emergency international United Nations Force to secure and supervise the cessation of hostilities in accordance with all the terms of the aforementioned resolution.

563rd plenary meeting,
4 November 1956.

RESOLUTION 999 (ES-1)

The General Assembly,

Noting with regret that not all the parties concerned have yet agreed to comply with the provisions of its resolution 997 (ES-I) of 2 November 1956,

Noting the special priority given in that resolution to an immediate cease-fire and, as part thereof, to the halting of the movement of military forces and arms into the area,

Noting further that the resolution urged the parties to the armistice agreements promptly to withdraw all forces behind the armistice lines, to desist from raids across the armistice lines into neighbouring territory, and to observe scrupulously the provisions of the armistice agreements,

1. *Reaffirms* its resolution 997 (ES-I), and once again calls upon the parties immediately to comply with the provisions of the said resolution;

2. *Authorizes* the Secretary-General immediately to arrange with the parties concerned for the implementation of the cease-fire and the halting of the movement of military forces and arms into the area, and requests him to report compliance forthwith and, in any case, not later than twelve hours from the time of adoption of the present resolution;

3. *Requests* the Secretary-General, with the assistance of the Chief of Staff and the members of the United Nations Truce Supervision Organization, to obtain compliance of the withdrawal of all forces behind the armistice lines;

4. *Decides* to meet again immediately on receipt of the Secretary-General's report referred to in paragraph 2 of the present resolution.

563rd plenary meeting,
4 November 1956.

RESOLUTION 1000 (ES-1)

The General Assembly,

Having requested the Secretary-General, in its resolution 998 (ES-I) of 4 November 1956, to submit to it a plan for an emergency international United Nations Force, for the purposes stated,

Noting with satisfaction the first report of the Secretary-General on the plan, and having in mind particularly paragraph 4 of that report,

1. *Establishes* a United Nations Command for an emergency international Force to secure and supervise the cessation of hostilities in accordance with all the terms of General Assembly resolution 997 (ES-I) of 2 November 1956;

2. *Appoints*, on an emergency basis, the Chief of Staff of the United Nations Truce Supervision Organization, Major-General E. L. M. Burns, as Chief of the Command;

3. *Authorizes* the Chief of the Command immediately to recruit, from the observer

corps of the United Nations Truce Supervision Organization, a limited number of officers who shall be nationals of countries other than those having permanent membership in the Security Council, and further authorizes him, in consultation with the Secretary-General, to undertake the recruitment directly, from various Member States other than the permanent members of the Security Council, of the additional number of officers needed;

4. *Invites* the Secretary-General to take such administrative measures as may be necessary for the prompt execution of the actions envisaged in the present resolution.

565th plenary meeting,
5 November 1956.

RESOLUTION 1001 (ES-1)

The General Assembly,

Recalling its resolution 997 (ES-I) of 2 November 1956 concerning the cease-fire, withdrawal of troops and other matters related to the military operations in Egyptian territory, as well as its resolution 998 (ES-I) of 4 November 1956 concerning the request to the Secretary-General to submit a plan for an emergency international United Nations Force,

Having established by its resolution 1000(ES-I) of 5 November 1956 a United Nations Command for an emergency international Force, having appointed the Chief of Staff of the United Nations Truce Supervision Organization as Chief of the Command with authorization to him to begin the recruitment of officers for the Command, and having invited the Secretary-General to take the administrative measures necessary for the prompt execution of that resolution,

Noting with appreciation the second and final report of the Secretary-General on the plan for an emergency international United Nations Force as requested in General Assembly resolution 998 (ES-I), and having examined that plan,

1. *Expresses its approval* of the guiding principles for the organization and func-

tioning of the emergency international United Nations Force as expounded in paragraphs 6 to 9 of the Secretary-General's report;

2. *Concurs* in the definition of the functions of the Force as stated in paragraph 12 of the Secretary-General's report;

3. *Invites* the Secretary-General to continue discussions with Governments of Member States concerning offers of participation in the Force, toward the objective of its balanced composition;

4. *Requests* the Chief of the Command, in consultation with the Secretary-General as regards size and composition, to proceed forthwith with the full organization of the Force;

5. *Approves provisionally* the basic rule concerning the financing of the Force laid down in paragraph 15 of the Secretary-General's report;

6. *Establishes* an Advisory Committee composed of one representative from each of the following countries: Brazil, Canada, Ceylon, Colombia, India, Norway and Pakistan, and requests this Committee, whose Chairman shall be the Secretary-General, to undertake the development of those aspects of the planning for the Force and its operation not already dealt with by the General Assembly and which do not fall within the area of the direct responsibility of the Chief of the Command;

7. *Authorizes* the Secretary-General to issue all regulations and instructions which may be essential to the effective functioning of the Force, following consultation with the Committee aforementioned, and to take all other necessary administrative and executive action;

8. *Determines* that, following the fulfillment of the immediate responsibilities defined for it in operative paragraphs 6 and 7 above, the Advisory Committee shall continue to assist the Secretary-General in the responsibilities falling to him under the present and other relevant resolutions;

9. *Decides* that the Advisory Committee, in the performance of its duties, shall be empowered to request, through the usual

procedures, the convening of the General Assembly and to report to the Assembly whenever matters arise which, in its opinion, are of such urgency and importance as to require consideration by the General Assembly itself;

10. *Requests* all Member States to afford assistance as necessary to the United Nations Command in the performance of its functions, including arrangements for passage to and from the area involved.

567th plenary meeting,
7 November 1956.

RESOLUTION 1002 (ES-1)

The General Assembly,

Recalling its resolutions 997 (ES-I) of 2 November 1956, 998 (ES-I) and 999 (ES-I) of 4 November 1956 and 1000 (ES-I) of 5 November 1956, adopted by overwhelming majorities,

Noting in particular that the General Assembly, by its resolution 1000 (ES-I), established a United Nations Command for an emergency international Force to secure and supervise the cessation of hostilities in accordance with all the terms of its resolution 997 (ES-I),

1. *Reaffirms* the above-mentioned resolutions;

2. *Calls once again upon* Israel immediately to withdraw all its forces behind the armistice lines established by the General Armistice Agreement between Egypt and Israel of 24 February 1949;

3. *Calls once again upon* the United Kingdom and France immediately to withdraw all their forces from Egyptian territory, consistently with the above-mentioned resolutions;

6. RHODESIA: COLONIAL SURVIVAL IN SOUTHERN AFRICA

If the rapid decolonization of Africa, long considered the most backward of the world's major population centers, set the seal on the main phase of western imperialism, it is also in Africa that imperialism has been able to preserve a last bastion. The southern tier of the continent contains two territories still under direct Portuguese rule, Angola and Moçambicque, and two states dominated by white-settler minorities, Rhodesia and the Republic of South Africa. Rhodesia, where the proportion of whites to blacks is particularly small and where Great Britain, up until 1965, retained a measure of constitutional control, seemed the most likely of these areas to come under African rule. In response to British pressures for enfranchising the African majority, however, white Rhodesians elected an extremely conservative government whose Prime Minister, Ian Smith, finally committed himself to a Unilateral Declaration of Independence, the text of which, with Smith's official commentary, is printed below. Attempts on the part of Britain and other powers to apply economic sanctions against Rhodesia have largely been thwarted by the import of supplies via Moçambicque and South Africa.

Nov. 12, 1965

Your Government have issued the following proclamation, which I will read to you.

A PROCLAMATION

Whereas, in the course of human affairs, history has shown that it may become necessary for a people to resolve the political affiliations which have connected them with another people and to assume among other nations the separate and equal status to which they are entitled, and

Whereas, in such event, a respect for the opinions of mankind requires them to declare to other nations the causes which impel them to assume full responsibility for their own affairs,

Now Therefore, we the Government of Rhodesia, do hereby declare:

That it is an indisputable and accepted historic fact that since 1923 the Government of Rhodesia have exercised the powers of self-government and have been responsible for the progress, development and welfare of their people.

That the people of Rhodesia, having demonstrated their loyalty to the Crown and to their kith and kin in the United Kingdom and elsewhere throughout two world wars and having been prepared to shed their blood and give of their substance in what they believed to be a mutual interest of freedom-loving people, now see all that they have cherished about to be shattered on the rocks of expediency.

That the people of Rhodesia have witnessed a process which is destructive of those very precepts upon which civilization in a primitive country has been built; they have seen the principles of Western democracy and responsible government and moral standards crumble elsewhere; nevertheless they have remained steadfast.

Declaration by Ian Smith in the *New York Times*, November 12, 1965. © 1965 by The New York Times Company. Reprinted by permission.

That the people of Rhodesia fully support the request of their Government for sovereign independence and have witnessed the consistent refusal of the Government of the United Kingdom to accede to their entreaties.

That the Government of the United Kingdom have thus demonstrated that they are not prepared to grant sovereign independence to Rhodesia on terms acceptable to the people of Rhodesia, thereby persisting in maintaining an unwarrantable jurisdiction over Rhodesia, obstructing laws and treaties with other states in the conduct of affairs with other nations and refusal of assent to necessary laws for the public good, all this to the detriment of the future peace, prosperity and good government of Rhodesia.

That the Government of Rhodesia have for a long period patiently and in good faith negotiated with the Government of the United Kingdom for the removal of the remaining limitations placed upon them and for the grant of sovereign independence.

That in the belief that procrastination and delay strike at and injure the very life of the nation, the Government of Rhodesia consider it essential that Rhodesia should obtain without delay sovereign independence, the justice of which is beyond question.

Now Therefore we, the Government of Rhodesia, in humble submission to Almighty God, who controls the destiny of nations, conscious that the people of Rhodesia have always shown unswerving loyalty and devotion to Her Majesty the Queen and earnestly praying that we the people of Rhodesia will not be hindered in our determination to continue exercising our undoubted right to demonstrate the same loyalty and devotion in seeking to promote the common good so that the dignity and freedom of all men may be assured, do by this proclamation adopt, enact and give to the people of Rhodesia the Constitution annexed hereto.

God save the Queen!

PRIME MINISTER'S REMARKS

Now, if I may, I would like to say a few words to you. Today, now that the final stalemate in negotiations has become evident, the end of the road has been reached.

It has become abundantly clear that it is the policy of the British Government to delay us along, with no real intention of arriving at a solution which we could possibly accept. Indeed, in the latest verbal and confidential message delivered to me last night, we find that on the main principle which is in dispute, the two Governments have moved further apart.

I promised the people of this country that I would continue to negotiate to the bitter end, and that I would leave no stone unturned in my endeavors to secure an honorable and mutually accepted settlement.

It now falls to me to tell you that negotiations have come to an end. No one could deny that we have striven with might and main and at times leaned over backwards to bridge the gap which divides us from the British Government.

My ministers and I have not arrived at this decision without the deepest heart-searching. We have sat for days in ceaseless conference, trying to find any possible way of achieving negotiated independence, as we undertook to the country we would do.

But I would be failing in my duty to all of you who live in Rhodesia if I was to permit this country to drift in the present paralyzing state of uncertainty. The bitter lesson of the federation [Northern Rhodesia, Southern Rhodesia and Nyasaland] is constantly in the forefront of my mind. In that case, matters were permitted to drift and plans for action were formulated too late to prevent the destruction of this noble concept of racial harmony.

However, Rhodesia has not rejected the possibility of racial harmony in Africa. The responsibility for the break-up of the federation was Great Britain's alone. Their experiment failed, and they are now trying to foist the same dogma onto Rhodesia.

161

We are determined that the same will never be allowed to happen here. Let no one believe that this action today marks a radical departure from the principles by which we have lived, or be under any misconception that now the Constitution will be torn up and that the protection of the rights of all peoples, which are enshrined in that Constitution, will be abrogated and discarded.

Neither let it be thought that this event marks a diminution in the opportunities which our African people have to advance and prosper in Rhodesia. Far from this being the case, it is our intention, in consultation with the chiefs, to bring them into the Government and Administration as the acknowledged leaders of the African people on a basis acceptable to them.

* * *

There can be no solution to our racial problems while African nationalists believe that provided they stir up sufficient trouble they will be able to blackmail the British Government into bringing about a miracle on their behalf by handing the country over to irresponsible rule.

There can be no happiness in this country while the absurd situation continues to exist where people such as ourselves, who have ruled ourselves with an impeccable record for over 40 years, are denied what is freely granted to other countries, who have ruled themselves in some cases for no longer than a year.

There can never be long-term prosperity — which is so necessary for the nurturing of our endeavors, to improve the standard of living and increase the happiness and better the lot of all our people — while the present uncertainty exists.

No businessman could ever seriously contemplate massive long-term investment in a country in which chaos and confusion will always be future possibilities.

Whatever the short-term economic disadvantages may be, in the long term steady economic progress could never be achieved unless we are masters in our own house.

To those of you who fear the short-term effect of economic sanctions, I would say that while we in no way minimize the possible hardship and inconvenience they may bring about, nonetheless we are firmly convinced that in the long run, because of our natural resources and the enterprise of our people, there will be brought about a prosperous and better future for everyone.

Week after week, we have seen businessmen passing through here on their way to South Africa, who with few exceptions say that while this state of uncertainty continues, they will not even contemplate a serious investigation of the possibility of investment.

However, they also say that once we have solved our constitutional difficulties and are independent, then they will be very interested in undertaking serious investigation and inquiries with a view to investing.

That some economic retributions will be visited upon us, there is no doubt. Those who seek to damage us do not have any great concern for the principles to which they endlessly pay lip service for if they really believed in these principles, which they ceaselessly proclaim, then they could not possibly deny the many disasters which have been brought about by the premature withdrawal of European influence from countries in Africa and Asia who were nowhere near ready for it.

There is no doubt that the talk of threats and sanctions is no more than appeasement to the United Nations, the Afro-Asian bloc and certain members of the Commonwealth, and undoubtedly some action will be taken.

But I cannot conceive of a rational world uniting in an endeavor to destroy the economy of this country, knowing as they undoubtedly do that in many cases the hardest hit will be the very people on whose behalf they would like to believe they are invoking these sanctions. We, for our part, will never do anything in the nature of taking revenge on any neighboring African state for what other countries may do to us.

*   *   *

I call upon all of you in this historic hour to support me and my Government in the struggle in which we are engaged. I believe that we are a courageous people and history has cast us in a heroic role. To us has been given the privilege of being the first Western nation in the last two decades to have the determination and fortitude to say "so far and no further."

We may be a small country, but we are a determined people who have been called upon to play a role of worldwide significance.

We Rhodesians have rejected the doctrinaire philosophy of appeasement and surrender. The decision which we have taken today is a refusal by Rhodesians to sell their birthright. And, even if we were to surrender, does anyone believe that Rhodesia would be the last target of the Communists in the Afro-Asian bloc?

We have struck a blow for the preservation of justice, civilization and Christianity; and in the spirit of this belief, we have thus assumed our sovereign independence.

God bless you all!

Fidel Castro

7. UNITED STATES IMPERIALISM

The United States has maintained its position of dominance in the Western Hemisphere by a policy more analogous to British "informal empire" of the earlier nineteenth century than through direct administration of alien territory. Immediate threats to interests of the United States—particularly in the Caribbean—have been met by military intervention or the manipulation of local political forces. The most dramatic recent case of such a reaction was when forces opposed to Cuba's self-styled Communist dictator, Fidel Castro, landed with U.S. assistance at the Bay of Pigs (Playa Girón) in April 1961. The failure of either internal Cuban uprisings or U.S. combat forces to support the invasion led to its rapid defeat and a strengthening of Castro's position as the champion of radical revolution throughout Latin America.

FIDEL CASTRO EXPLAINS THE INVASION

Speech at the People's University
April 23, 1961

We can give some idea of the general type of the entire enemy plan as well as its form and the manner in which the Revolutionary [Cuban Government] plan was developed in the zone of operations.

In the first place it was known before this time, almost a year before, that an expeditionary force was being formed in order to attack our country. Since the triumph of the Revolution we have been living in the midst of a series of threats, perils, and risks; that is to say, the Revolution always needed to ward off successive external attacks.

There existed a series of variations on the part of the enemies of the Revolution, that is to say, on the part of imperialism, which is

Playa Girón: Derrota del Imperialismo (Havana, 1962), Vol. II.

the only enemy possessing force and the only enemy capable of organizing this type of attack. And several distinct types of action were always planned by the enemy; first, a type of indirect aggression, which is, by and large, the type which finally took place, although not so indirect—it was a type of indirect aggression in regard to the human personnel participating in the invasion, and a direct type insofar as this personnel attacked with instructions received in camps organized by the North Americans, with naval and aviation equipment supplied by the North Americans; and furthermore, the invasion forces were escorted by North American naval units and, still more, the participation of the North American Air Force in the decisive moment. This is an important point.

Therefore this aggressiveness was not a typical indirect aggression, it was a mixture of indirect aggression, or of the strategy of indirect attack, and direct aggression, carried out directly by the marines, with their planes and military forces; nor was it an indirect aggression. . . . They basically organized it using mercenaries as a foundation and supported it quite directly with marines and airplanes.

That is to say, the following types of action were always contemplated as possibilities: an indirect attack, an attack via the Organization of American States, or a direct attack.

* * *

The policies of capitalism and imperialism cannot maintain themselves in a normal situation because they are progressing towards a crisis. It is not like the case of a socialist regime which has its economy perfectly organized, perfectly planned in accord with its needs, estimating a growth of 10% per annum . . . while the increase of the United States is 1% per annum, more or less, and a large part of the factories in North America are paralyzed. Why? Because it is not a planned economy, because it does not produce for the needs of the country nor for the needs of the world, but it

is a system based on the control of national interests by groups whose interests are completely divorced from the national interest, from the interests of the State and of the people.

Therefore the system leads to crises of overproduction, of underutilization of natural resources, of underutilization of the existing industrial capacity. And thus, they use genuine wars as "horse doctor cures," that is to say, cures by means of transient crises through which they can reinvigorate the economy on the basis of demands for war materials. . . .

That is to say, they cannot use all of this capacity devoted to the benefit of the United States and of humanity; their own economic system prevents them from using their natural resources and industrial capacity for peaceful ends. And as a consequence of this, a vast amount of energy, industrial plant, and natural resources is wasted; it is only made to function by warfare.

* * *

No one could have launched greater boasts and threats into the world than those of Hitler; the speeches and threats of Kennedy bear great resemblance to the speeches and threats of Hitler. Hitler lived by threatening neighboring peoples and small neighboring countries which he set out to invade, into which he sent his tanks and "panzer" divisions. Kennedy likewise lives by threatening Cuba, this small neighboring country which he is going to invade and where he can intervene, since his patience is exhausted. . . . Very well! Let his patience exhaust itself! And how much patience have we needed to withstand economic aggression, suspensions of quotas, aerial attacks, mercenary attacks, the bombing of our towns, destruction of metropolitan centers, sugar fields, stores, and establishments, and we have had to be infinitely patient to withstand all this, simply because they are the carnages and aggressions imposed upon a people as a result of being governed by an international bully who takes upon himself the right to all these things—murder, bombing, assaults, and the perpetration of invasions. Then afterwards, they say that their patience has come to an end, but the fact is that they have come to the end of their patience because of our resistance, because the plans laid by them have collapsed; the economic blockade plan has collapsed; the Latin American plan has collapsed; the mercenary plan has collapsed. Finally, in desperation, they seek another which will not collapse: they are thinking of their own forces without realizing that this may be the ultimate collapse [*Applause*], not one more collapse . . . the attack on Cuba can represent the final collapse of imperialism.

We do not want them to attack us; we do not want them to commit suicide on our shores. We wish that they would reflect; that they would think it over; that they would realize that they have brought this problem upon themselves through their own guilt . . . that they consider that the only correct and intelligent path is to leave our country in peace. Only to be left in peace, which is our right and their obligation.

If they want to ignore the lesson of Cuba, then the attack on Cuba is going to lead to more lessons, is going to cause more irritation, is going to reveal itself before the world and is going to provoke further revolutionary spirits in Latin America.

W. W. Rostow

8. COUNTERINSURGENCY AS INSURANCE FOR FREEDOM

The United States' position as successor to the European powers in defending order throughout the world is perhaps most intimately symbolized by the role of the Special Forces, the "Green Berets," presently engaged in combating national communist guerillas in the very country, Viet-Nam, where an earlier defeat had taught the French to develop such counterinsurgency tactics. Here a group of newly trained Special Forces is lectured on the relation of their tasks to wider U.S. policies by W. W. Rostow, key advisor to Presidents Kennedy and Johnson and previously an economic historian at Massachusetts Institute of Technology.

ADDRESS TO THE GRADUATING CLASS
AT THE U.S. ARMY SPECIAL WARFARE SCHOOL
Fort Bragg, June, 1961

It does not require much imagination to understand why President Kennedy has taken the problem of guerrilla warfare seriously. When this Administration came to responsibility it faced four major crises: Cuba, the Congo, Laos, and Viet-Nam. Each represented a successful Communist breaching—over the previous two years—of the Cold War truce lines which had emerged from the Second World War and its aftermath. In different ways each had arisen from the efforts of the international Communist movement to exploit the inherent instabilities of the underdeveloped areas of the non-Communist world, and each had a guerrilla warfare component.

Cuba, of course, differed from the other cases. The Cuban revolution against Batista was a broad-based national insurrection. But that revolution was tragically captured from within by the Communist apparatus; and now Latin America faces the

"Guerilla Warfare in Underdeveloped Areas" in Marcus G. Raskin and Bernard B. Fall, *The Viet-Nam Reader* (N. Y., Random House, 1965), 108-116.

danger of Cuba's being used as the base for training, supply, and direction of guerrilla warfare in the hemisphere.

More than that, Mr. Khrushchev, in his report to the Moscow conference of Communist parties (published January 6, 1961), had explained at great length that the Communists fully support what he called wars of national liberation and would march in the front rank with the peoples waging such struggles. The military arm of Mr. Khrushchev's January, 1961, doctrine is, clearly, guerrilla warfare.

Faced with these four crises, pressing in on the President from day to day, and faced with the candidly stated position of Mr. Khrushchev, we have, indeed, begun to take the problem of guerrilla warfare seriously.

To understand this problem, however, one must begin with the great revolutionary process that is going forward in the southern half of the world; for the guerrilla warfare problem in these regions is a product of that revolutionary process and the Communist effort and intent to exploit it.

What is happening throughout Latin America, Africa, the Middle East, and Asia is this: Old societies are changing their ways in order to create and maintain a national personality on the world scene and to bring to their peoples the benefits modern technology can offer. This process is truly revolutionary. It touches every aspect of the traditional life — economic, social, and political. The introduction of modern technology brings about not merely new methods of production but a new style of family life, new links between the villages and the cities, the beginnings of national politics, and a new relationship to the world outside.

Like all revolutions, the revolution of modernization is disturbing. Individual men are torn between the commitment to the old familiar way of life and the attractions of a modern way of life. The power of old social groups — notably the landlord, who usually dominates the traditional society — is reduced. Power moves toward those who command the tools of modern technology, including modern weapons.

Men and women in the villages and the cities, feeling that the old ways of life are shaken and that new possibilities are open to them, express old resentments and new hopes.

This is the grand arena of revolutionary change which the Communists are exploiting with great energy. They believe that their techniques of organization — based on small disciplined cadres of conspirators — are ideally suited to grasp and to hold power in these turbulent settings. They believe that the weak transitional governments that one is likely to find during this modernization process are highly vulnerable to subversion and to guerrilla warfare. And whatever Communist doctrines of historical inevitability may be, Communists know that their time to seize power in the underdeveloped areas is limited. They know that, as momentum takes hold in an underdeveloped area — and the fundamental social problems inherited from the traditional society are solved — their chances to seize power decline.

It is on the weakest nations, facing their most difficult transitional moments, that the Communists concentrate their attention. They are the scavengers of the modernization process. They believe that the techniques of political centralization under dictatorial control — and the projected image of Soviet and Chinese Communist economic progress — will persuade hesitant men, faced by great transitional problems, that the Communist model should be adopted for modernization, even at the cost of surrendering human liberty. They believe that they can exploit effectively the resentments built up in many of these areas against colonial rule and that they can associate themselves effectively with the desire of the emerging nations for independence, for status on the world scene, and for material progress.

This is a formidable program; for the history of this century teaches us that communism is not the long-run wave of the future toward which societies are naturally drawn. But, on the contrary it is one particular form of modern society to which a nation may fall prey during the transitional process. Communism is best understood as a disease of the transition to modernization.

What is our reply to this historical conception and strategy? What is the American purpose and the American strategy? We, too, recognize that a revolutionary process is under way. We are dedicated to the proposition that this revolutionary process of modernization shall be permitted to go forward in independence, with increasing degrees of human freedom. We seek two results: first, that truly independent nations shall emerge on the world scene; and, second, that each nation will be permitted to fashion, out of its own culture and its own ambitions, the kind of modern society it wants. The same religious and philosophical beliefs which decree that we respect the uniqueness of each individual make it natural that we respect the uniqueness of each national society. Moreover, we Americans are confident that, if the independence of this process can be maintained over the coming years and decades, these societies will choose their own version of what we would recognize as a democratic, open society.

These are our commitments of policy and of faith. The United States has no interest in political satellites. Where we have military pacts we have them because governments feel directly endangered by outside military action and we are prepared to help protect their independence against such military action. But, to use Mao Tse-tung's famous phrase, we do not seek nations which "lean to one side." We seek nations which shall stand up straight. And we do so for a reason: because we are deeply confident that nations which stand up straight will protect their independence and move in their own ways and in their own time toward human freedom and political democracy.

Thus our central task in the underdeveloped areas, as we see it, is to protect the independence of the revolutionary process now going forward. This is our mission, and it is our ultimate strength. For this is

not—and cannot be—the mission of communism. And in time, through the fog of propaganda and the honest confusions of men caught up in the business of making new nations, this fundamental difference will become increasingly clear in the southern half of the world. The American interest will be served if our children live in an environment of strong, assertive, independent nations, capable, because they are strong, of assuming collective responsibility for the peace.

The diffusion of power is the basis for freedom within our own society, and we have no reason to fear it on the world scene. But this outcome would be a defeat for communism—not for Russia as a national state, but for communism. Despite all the Communist talk of aiding movements of national independence, they are driven in the end, by the nature of their system, to violate the independence of nations. Despite all the Communist talk of American imperialism, we are committed, by the nature of our system, to support the cause of national independence. And the truth will out.

The victory we seek will see no ticker-tape parades down Broadway, no climactic battles, nor great American celebrations of victory. It is a victory which will take many years and decades of hard work and dedication—by many peoples—to bring about. This will not be a victory of the United States over the Soviet Union. It will not be a victory of capitalism over socialism. It will be a victory of men and nations which aim to stand up straight, over the forces which wish to entrap and to exploit their revolutionary aspirations of modernization. What this victory involves, in the end, is the assertion by nations of their right to freedom as they understand it. And we deeply believe this victory will come—on both sides of the Iron Curtain.

If Americans do not seek victory in the usual sense, what do we seek? What is the national interest of the United States? Why do we Americans expend our treasure and assume the risks of modern war in this global struggle? For Americans the reward of victory will be, simply, this: It will permit American society to continue to develop along the old humane lines which go back to our birth as a nation—and which reach deeper into history than that—back to the Mediterranean roots of Western life. We are struggling to maintain an environment on the world scene which will permit our open society to survive and to flourish.

To make this vision come true places a great burden on the United States at this phase of history. The preservation of independence has many dimensions.

The United States has the primary responsibility for deterring the use of nuclear weapons in the pursuit of Communist ambitions. The United States has a major responsibility to deter the kind of overt aggression with conventional forces which was launched in June, 1950, in Korea.

The United States has the primary responsibility for assisting the economies of those hard-pressed states on the periphery of the Communist bloc, which are under acute military or quasimilitary pressure which they cannot bear from their own resources; for example, South Korea, Viet-Nam, Taiwan, Pakistan, Iran. The United States has a special responsibility of leadership in bringing not merely its own resources but the resources of all the free world to bear in aiding the long-run development of those nations which are serious about modernizing their economy and their social life. And, as President Kennedy has made clear, he regards no program of his Administration as more important than his program for long-term economic development, dramatized, for example, by the Alliance for Progress in Latin America. Independence cannot be maintained by military measures alone. Modern societies must be built, and we are prepared to help build them.

Finally, the United States has a role to play—symbolized by your presence here and by mine—in learning to deter guerrilla warfare, if possible, and to deal with it, if necessary.

I do not need to tell you that the primary responsibility for dealing with guerrilla warfare in the underdeveloped areas cannot be American. There are many ways in which we can help—and we are searching our minds and our imaginations to learn better how to help; but a guerrilla war must be fought primarily by those on the spot. This is so for a quite particular reason. A guerrilla war is an intimate affair, fought not merely with weapons but fought in the minds of the men who live in the villages and in the hills, fought by the spirit and policy of those who run the local government. An outsider cannot, by himself, win a guerrilla war. He can help create conditions in which it can be won, and he can directly assist those prepared to fight for their independence. We are determined to help destroy this international disease; that is, guerrilla war designed, initiated, supplied, and led from outside an independent nation.

Although as leader of the free world the United States has special responsibilities which it accepts in this common venture of deterrence, it is important that the whole international community begin to accept its responsibility for dealing with this form of aggression. It is important that the world become clear in mind, for example, that the operation run from Hanoi against Viet-Nam is as clear a form of aggression as the violation of the 38th Parallel by the North Korean armies in June, 1950.

In my conversations with representatives of foreign governments, I am sometimes lectured that this or that government within the free world is not popular; they tell me that guerrilla warfare cannot be won unless the peoples are dissatisfied. These are, at best, half-truths. The truth is that guerrilla warfare, mounted from external bases—with rights of sanctuary—is a terrible burden to carry for any government in a society making its way toward modernization. As you know, it takes anywhere between ten and twenty soldiers to control one guerrilla in an organized operation. Moreover, the guerrilla force has this advantage: its task is merely to destroy, while the government must build and protect what it is building. A guerrilla war mounted from outside a transitional nation is a crude act of international vandalism. There will be no peace in the world if the international community accepts the outcome of a guerrilla war, mounted from outside a nation, as tantamount to a free election.

The sending of men and arms across international boundaries and the direction of guerrilla war from outside a sovereign nation is aggression; and this is a fact which the whole international community must confront and whose consequent responsibilities it must accept. Without such international action those against whom aggression is mounted will be driven inevitably to seek out and engage the ultimate source of the aggression they confront.

I suspect that in the end the real meaning of the conference on Laos at Geneva will hinge on this question: It will depend on whether or not the international community is prepared to mount an International Control Commission which has the will and the capacity to control the borders it was designed to control.

In facing the problem of guerrilla war, I have one observation to make as a historian. It is now fashionable — and I daresay for you it was compulsory — to read the learned works of Mao Tse-tung and Che Guevara on guerrilla warfare. This is, indeed, proper. One should read with care and without passion into the minds of one's enemies. But it is historically inaccurate and psychologically dangerous to think that these men created the strategy and tactics of guerrilla war to which we are now responding. Guerrilla warfare is not a form of military and psychological magic created by the Communists. There is no rule or parable in the Communist texts which was not known at an earlier time in history. The operation of Marion's men in relation to the Battle of Cowpens in the American Revolution was, for example, governed by rules which Mao merely echoes. Che Guevara knows nothing of this business that T. E. Lawrence did not

know or was not practiced, for example, in the Peninsular Campaign during the Napoleonic wars, a century earlier. The orchestration of professional troops, militia and guerrilla fighters is an old game whose rules can be studied and learned.

My point is that we are up against a form of warfare which is powerful and effective only when we do not put our minds clearly to work on how to deal with it. I, for one, believe that with purposeful efforts most nations which might now be susceptible to guerrilla warfare could handle their border areas in wars which would make them very unattractive to the initiation of this ugly game. We can learn to prevent the emergence of the famous sea in which Mao Tse-tung taught his men to swim. This requires, of course, not merely a proper military program of deterrence but programs of village development, communications, and indoctrination. The best way to fight a guerrilla war is to prevent it from happening. And this can be done.

Similarly, I am confident that we can deal with the kind of operation now under way in Viet-Nam. It is an extremely dangerous operation, and it could overwhelm Viet-Nam if the Viet-namese — aided by the free world — do not deal with it. But it is an unsubtle operation by the book, based more on murder than on political or psychological appeal.

When Communists speak of wars of national liberation and of their support for "progressive forces," I think of the systematic program of assassination now going forward in which the principal victims are health, agriculture, and education officers in the Viet-Nam villages. The Viet-Cong are not trying to persuade the peasants of Viet-Nam that communism is good; they are trying to persuade them that their lives are insecure unless they co-operate with them. With resolution and confidence on all sides and with the assumption of international responsibility for the frontier problem, I believe we are going to bring this threat to the independence of Viet-Nam under control.

My view is, then, that we confront in guerrilla warfare in the underdeveloped areas a systematic attempt by the Communists to impose a serious disease on those societies attempting the transition to modernization. This attempt is a present danger in Southeast Asia. It could quickly become a major danger in Africa and Latin America. I salute in particular those among you whose duty it is — along with others — to prevent that disease, if possible, and to eliminate it where it is imposed.

As I understand the course you are now completing, it is designed to impress on you this truth: You are not merely soldiers in the old sense. Your job is not merely to accept the risks of war and to master its skills. Your job is to work with understanding with your fellow citizens in the whole creative process of modernization. From our perspective in Washington you take your place side by side with those others who are committed to help fashion independent, modern societies out of the revolutionary process now going forward. I salute you as I would a group of doctors, teachers, economic planners, agricultural experts, civil servants, or those others who are now leading the way in the whole southern half of the globe in fashioning new nations and societies that will stand up straight and assume in time their rightful place of dignity and responsibility in the world community; for this is our common mission.

Each of us must carry into his day-to-day work an equal understanding of the military and the creative dimensions of the job. I can tell you that those with whom I have the privilege to work are dedicated to that mission with every resource of mind and spirit at our command.

Henry A. Kissinger

9. NEUTRALISM VERSUS UNITED STATES LEADERSHIP

The following selection does not deal directly with the question of imperialism but rather argues that the United States must avoid overreacting against the charge of behaving imperialistically. The Congo Crisis of 1960-1961 with which the author documents his argument is a classic case of American movement into a power vacuum created by decolonization. In the period alluded to here actual responsibility for restoring order in the Congo—which virtually fell apart within months of receiving independence from Belgium—was delegated to the United Nations and its energetic Secretary General, Dag Hammerskjöld. The presence of U.N. forces (largely financed by the U.S.) proved little more than an interim solution and, since 1964, the United States has taken a more direct role in supporting a series of Congolese governments. For a view of the Congo situation directly opposing this one, see Conor Cruise O'Brien (selection 11 below). Henry A. Kissinger moved in 1968 from the faculty of Harvard University to a post as chief foreign policy advisor in the Nixon administration.

THE NEW COUNTRIES AND INTERNATIONAL RELATIONS

The problems of political and economic development would be difficult enough in their own right. They are complicated by the fact that the new nations find themselves drawn into international affairs to an unprecedented degree. While building a state and seeking to realize the most elementary aspirations of their people, they are being wooed, asked to form judgments or to assume international responsibilities. Whether they have joined political or military groupings or remained neutral, the contest for their favor has continued to rage. The result has been a diversion of the energies of the new states and a demoralization of international relations.

The United States approach to the new nations has not helped matters. As in most other fields of policy we have been going from one extreme to the other. For a time we acted as if the only political significance of the new nations was as potential military allies in the Cold War. The quest for neutrality was officially condemned. Great efforts were made to induce new nations to join security pacts. Within the space of a few years this policy has been replaced by its precise opposite. Instead of castigating neutrality we have been almost exalting it. Instead of seeking to create security pacts, we have conducted ourselves in a manner which may make allies, at least those outside the North Atlantic area, doubt the wisdom of close association with the United States. The oversimplification which could

pp. 229-239 from *The Necessity For Choice* by Henry A. Kissinger. Copyright © 1960, 1961 by Henry A. Kissinger. Reprinted by permission of Harper & Row, Publishers and Chatto and Windus Ltd.

see no political role for the new nations outside the Cold War has been replaced by another oversimplification based on the premise that the "real" contest is for the allegiance of the uncommitted. We sometimes act as if we and the Communists were engaged in a debate in the Oxford Union, with the uncommitted nations acting as moderators and awarding a prize after hearing all arguments.

The questions arise, however, whether the exaltation of non-commitment is not as pernicious as the previous period of alliance-building and whether there is not an inconsistency between the desire of the new nations to be neutrals and their desire to be arbiters.

To begin with, there is a certain ambivalence, if not disingenuousness, in the sudden deference paid to neutrality. The impression is sometimes overwhelming that the difference between the approach to the new nations identified with Mr. Dulles and that which urges America "to respect neutrality" is primarily one of method as to how to win over the uncommitted areas. Both are designed to bring the new nations somehow to our side. Mr. Dulles thought the way to do so was to castigate their neutralism. Many of those who see in the new countries the arbiters of international relations imply that the way to win their friendship is to respect their desire for non-involvement. Both assuptions are based on an illusion.

For it is highly doubtful whether on a great variety of issues dividing the world *any* policy can win the support of the uncommitted. There is a tacit assumption in much of American discussion that the non-commitment of the new nations is due in large part to our failure to "present our case properly" or to the fact that the new nations have certain positive views which we have failed to take into account. But this line of reasoning fails to do justice to a complicated situation. On most issues, except those affecting them most directly, the new nations will take a position somewhere between the contenders regardless of their view of the intrinsic merit of a given dispute. Neutrality seems more important than any particular dispute because the new nations' image of themselves as well as their bargaining position depends on maintaining it: "Neither side has won us," said an African diplomat during the 1960 session of the General Assembly, "and we are determined that neither side will."

America, of all countries, should be sympathetic to this state of mind. In the first 150 years of our existence no conceivable British policy could have led to an American alliance or even to American support on policies outside the Western Hemisphere. Our desire not to become involved was stronger than any views we may have had on international issues, save those affecting the Western Hemisphere most urgently. Nothing Britain could have said or done would have induced us formally to take sides. Throughout, we would have resented being asked to assume responsibilities and our predisposition would have been to invent reasons for not doing so. And if Britain had sought to meet our criticisms we would have invented new ones. The desire to remain aloof from world affairs was stronger than any views we might have had on the disputed issues.

There is no question, then, that we ought to respect the desire of the new nations to remain aloof from world affairs. The problem arises when the laudable view that we should *accept* their neutrality is transformed into an *exaltation* of non-commitment. Whatever the wisdom of such groupings as the South East Asia Treaty Organization (SEATO) when they were formed — and it would probably have been wiser to avoid them — it is surely going too far to seem to pay greater attention to neutrals than to allies. The correct attitude that we should not press the new nations to join alliances must not be carried to the extreme of discouraging those who have made a different choice. When non-commitment becomes a cult, slogans such as "appealing to world opinion" can easily turn into excuses for inaction or irresponsibility.

Again, our national experience can serve as a guide to understanding the problem. If Great Britain in 1914 or 1939 had made its resistance to German aggression dependent on American support (not to speak of that of other powers) the course of history would have been radically different. Neither the invasion of Belgium nor the attack on Poland seemed to Americans at the time to involve our interests sufficiently to justify giving up our neutrality. And no British policy, however respectful of our neutrality, could have induced us to forego this role.

It is no different with many of the new nations. They will take a stand against dangers which seem to them to affect their vital interests. They will not take a stand on problems which seem to them far away, or, if they do, it may make the situation worse rather than better, as will be seen below. The Chinese brutality in Tibet made an impression in India, whereas the equally brutal Soviet repression in Hungary did not. Despite all moralistic protestations to the contrary, the reason for the difference in attitude was practical and not theoretical. Chinese pressure on India's borders was a concrete danger and the events in Hungary simply were not. Though it is true that our policies with respect to the new nations have often been maladroit, it does not follow that different policies can change their non-alignment.

To be sure, the new nations sometimes create the opposite impression because their own attitude toward non-commitment is at least as ambivalent as ours. All too often, they couple insistence on respect for their neutrality with an attempt to play the arbiter's role in international affairs. But the arbiter's role implies that they will support one of the parties if they can be convinced of the correctness of its position. It is an invitation to a courtship. It encourages the pressure which is said to be resented.

Many of the leaders of the new states want the best of two worlds: of neutrality and of judging all disputes. They are flattered by the rewards that fall to the uncommitted in the competition of the major powers. For many of them, playing a role on the international scene seems more dramatic and simpler than the complex job of domestic construction. Many domestic problems are intractable. Almost all of them require patient, detailed efforts and their results are frequently long delayed. Domestically, each action has a price. But on the international scene, it is possible to be the center of attention simply by striking a pose. Here ambitious men can play the dramatic role so often denied to them at home and so consistent with their image of the role of a national leader.

Unfortunately, the same factors that make entry on the international arena so tempting —the possibility of being wooed, the chance of escaping from complicated domestic problems—also militate against the seriousness of the effort. It is the symbolic quality of international forums that is most attractive to many of the leaders of the new nations. They welcome an opportunity to declaim on the general maxims which never seem to apply quite so simply at home or to the foreign policy problems in which the uncommitted nation is directly concerned. But they are much less willing to assume substantive responsibilities, particularly in areas not directly related to their immediate interests.

If the new nations are encouraged to arbitrate all disputes, the impact on international relations will have to be demoralizing. Non-commitment will thereby defeat its own object. It will be merely another reason for occupying a place at the center of all disputes.

The utility of common action for carrying out tasks on which a real world opinion already exists is not at issue. For example, long ago we ought to have taken the lead in fostering a substantial economic assistance program through the United Nations. But it is essential to recognize that on many of the most difficult international problems there is no such thing as a meaningful world opinion. It is simply asking too much of the new nations which barely have achieved independence to help settle disputes of the

173

technical complexity of disarmament.

The result of gearing all policy to the presumed wishes of the uncommitted is that many issues are falsified and many problems are evaded. Abstract declarations substitute for concrete negotiations. Diplomacy is reduced to slogans. Pressure for confrontations of heads of state is not accompanied by any detailed program. There are many demands for peace in the abstract, but much less attention is given to defining the conditions which can alone make peace meaningful.

Far from aiding the diplomatic progress which is so insistently demanded, such a process tends to thwart it. Far from "strengthening the United Nations," it may ultimately undermine it. Soviet negotiators will lose any incentive for making responsible proposals, since they will be constantly tempted by opportunities for cheap propaganda victories. The West will grow increasingly frustrated when it finds itself incapable of enlisting the support of the new nations no matter how moderate or reasonable its program. And the new nations will be induced to take positions on issues on which the very act of non-commitment proclaims their disinterest and with respect to which their judgment is often highly erratic. It is not clear why nations said to be in need of assistance in almost all aspects of their national life, many of which have difficulty organizing their own countries, should be presumed to be able to act with more wisdom in relation to the whole gamut of international problems.

Indeed, when neutrality becomes an end in itself, it can lead the uncommitted unwittingly to add their pressure to that of the Communist bloc. The tendency to seek a position separate from the two big blocs can be used by skillful Communist diplomacy to drive back the West step by step.

When countries as varied as India, Yugoslavia, Indonesia, Ghana and the United Arab Republic form a "bloc," they are united above all by two motives: to stay aloof from the disputes of the major powers and to magnify their own influence. This desire is understandable. But it must not lead us to believe that they can be swayed by the logic of our argument or of our proposals. The internal requirements of a neutral bloc will prevent this, apart from domestic and Communist pressures. Individual neutralist nations will not easily separate themselves from their partners even should they disagree with them on specific measures. The tone of the whole neutral bloc can thus easily be set by the most irresponsible of its members. While we should have patience with these attitudes, we must understand also that on any given issue most of the new nations will seek a position somewhere between the two contenders regardless of the merits of the disputes.

As a result, a premium will be placed on Soviet intransigence. When Mr. Khrushchev spoke to the General Assembly in September, 1960, a considerable portion of the American press claimed that he "had overplayed his hand," that he had "alienated the uncommitted." His intemperance was contrasted with the sobriety and statesmanship of President Eisenhower. There is no doubt that Mr. Khrushchev was intemperate. It is less clear, however, whether in the long run his actions will not prove of considerable advantage to the U.S.S.R. The very violence of the attack on Mr. Hammarskjöld served as a warning to the new nations of the fate awaiting them should they displease the Communist countries too much. In any given crisis, therefore, the urgings of the new nations may be directed against us, not because they disagree with our position but because opposition to us carries few risks. Conversely, the virulence of Communist reaction to any criticism causes the uncommitted to behave with great circumspection in opposing Communist policies.

The speeches in the General Assembly of 1960 by such leaders as Nasser, Sukarno, Nkrumah or even Nehru illustrate this point. The attacks on the West were pointed and direct; those on the Communist bloc circumspect and highly ambiguous. Almost every speech by these leaders castigated Western imperialism. Not a single reference was made to the unprovoked Soviet threat against Berlin—not to speak of other Soviet policies in Eastern Europe. Nor did the uncommitted nations which were supposed to have been alienated by Mr. Khrushchev rush to the defense of the Secretary General.

Moreover, if one considers Soviet relations with the neutrals from the point of view of bargaining technique, Communist belligerence may not have been nearly as foolish as was often alleged. Since the new nations are not likely to support the position of either side completely, regardless of what arguments are presented, it may in fact be good negotiating tactics to start from extreme proposals. Then even if the new nations support Communist demands only partially, the Soviets can in effect add the pressure of the uncommitted to their own to realize at least part of their program. The requirements of maintaining formal neutrality force many leaders who have opposed the Soviet Union on one issue to support them on another. Thus at the 1960 session of the General Assembly, Mr. Nehru failed to support Mr. Khrushchev's proposal for change in the U.N. Charter with respect to the Secretary General. In return, he proposed organizational changes whose practical consequence came very close to meeting Mr. Khrushchev's aims. The danger then exists that Soviet brutality, coupled with the desire of the uncommitted to remain neutral above all else, can import into the United Nations the familiar Soviet diplomatic "rules," according to which the only changes of the status quo which prove acceptable are those which magnify the influence of Communism.

Conversely, by seeking to meet all the presumed wishes of the new nations we may force them to move away from us to demonstrate their independence. It would be ironical indeed if in seeking to approach them too closely we drove them in the direction of the Communist position.

World opinion is not something abstract which our diplomats must seek to discover and to which we then have to adjust. We have a duty not only to discover but to shape it. World opinion does not exist in a vacuum. It is compounded of many factors, including the imagination and decisiveness of our own policy. Many a leader from the uncommitted areas may well prefer a clear and firm United States position which gives him an opportunity to demonstrate his neutrality both internationally and at home to the almost desperate attempt to make him share responsibility for our actions.

This is not to say, of course, that independent action is desirable in itself. And like many dictators before him, Mr. Khrushchev may well overplay his hand. It does suggest, however, that when we are convinced of the correctness of our course we should pursue it, even if it does not gain the immediate approval of the uncommitted— particularly in fields such as disarmament and European policy, which are remote from the understanding or the concern of the new nations. If the uncommitted are to act as intermediaries there must be a position to mediate. Any other course throws on them or on the United Nations a responsibility which they will not be able to bear.

The crisis in the Congo illustrates this. Our objective of keeping the Cold War out of Central Africa was unexceptionable. But the measures adopted to achieve it were highly questionable. "Keeping the Cold War out of Africa" is an abstraction which must be given concrete application if it is to be meaningful. It could not possibly succeed without at least tacit agreement on some ground rules between us and the U.S.S.R. Instead of throwing all the responsibility on Mr. Hammarskjöld we should have come forward with a concrete charter of what we understood by the independence, the development and the neutrality of the Congo. This could then have been negotiated with the neutrals and the Communists. Instead we advanced vague resolutions which we left for the Secretary General to interpret, putting him into the position of assuming personal responsibility.

Though in this manner we achieved temporary tactical gains, we may well have mortgaged the future position of the Secretary General as well as that of the Congo. The motto of "Let Dag do it" became an evasion of a responsibility, at least part of which was ours. It may be argued, of course, that the Soviet Union was not interested in stability and would therefore not have accepted our charter. But quite apart from the fact that it would have been useful to make this evident, the course adopted forced the Secretary General to attempt to impose on the Communist countries a course of action highly distasteful to them. It was against all reason to expect them to accept from Mr. Hammarskjöld what we thought they would not even consider if made by us as a formal proposal.

Moreover, by not defining our position, we deprived the Secretary General of any real bargaining power. Rather than seeking to adjust conflicting views, he was forced to develop his own definition of stability. This had the practical consequence of bringing him into direct conflict with the Communist states and with some of the African countries as well. It is clear that the office of the Secretary General cannot survive the determined opposition of the Communist bloc together with its sympathizers among the neutrals, and it should therefore never be put into a position of seeming to be the sole originator of policy. This policy also encourages the African states to use the United Nations to extend their own influence—the Ghanese and Guinean troops in effect have taken advantage of the mantle of the United Nations to pursue their own national policies in the Congo.

In short, in a situation where a great deal depended on the ability to be concrete, our approach was uncertain, vague, and abstract. We proclaimed stability in circumstances where all criteria of judging it had evaporated, and we offered no others to take their place. The chief result was to sharpen the contest for Africa rather than to ameliorate it and to raise issues about the structure and operation of the United Nations which would have better remained muted. The slogan "strengthening the United Nations" can become a means for weakening the world organization.

In short, our role in relation to the new countries is much more complicated than engaging in a popularity contest for their favor. We must show sympathy and support for their efforts to realize their economic aspirations—to an extent considerably beyond our current contribution. We must respect their desire to stand aloof from many of the disputes which divide the world. On many issues we can work closely with the new nations and on all issues they are entitled to understanding and sympathy. But we must not build our policies on illusions. Neither economic assistance nor respect for neutrality should imply the expectation of short-term political support—nor the hidden motive that the way to win the new nations over to our side is to make a cult of their non-commitment. Painful as it may be, *some* situations are conceivable where we may have a duty to act without the support of the new nations, and perhaps even with some of them opposing us.

Though we of course prefer to be popular, we cannot gear all our policies to an attempt to curry the favor of the new nations. We cannot undermine our security for illusory propaganda victories, because the safety of even the uncommitted depends on our unimpaired strength—whether they realize it or not. As for the uncommitted, they cannot eat their cake and have it too. They cannot ask us to respect their neutrality unless they respect our commitment. They cannot remain uncommitted and seek to act as arbiters of all disputes at the same time.

We thus face two contradictory dangers: we can demoralize the new nations by drawing them into the political relationships of the Cold War. But we can demoralize them also by making a cult of their non-commitment and acting as if only incorrect United States policies kept them from taking sides. And the latter danger may be the more insidious because it is more subtle. We have to face the fact that in major areas of the world constructive programs as well as defense depend largely on us. Many tasks, if not accomplished by us, will not be carried out at all. Compassion, understanding and help for the new nations must not be confused with gearing all policy to their pace. A cult of non-commitment will doom freedom everywhere.

As the strongest and most cohesive nation in the free world we have an obligation to lead and not simply depend on the course of events. History will not hand us our deepest desires on a silver platter. A leader does not deserve the name unless he is willing occasionally to stand alone. He cannot content himself simply with registering prevailing attitudes. He must build consensus, not merely exploit it.

There is involved here a question of style as well as of substance. Moderation, generosity, self-restraint are all desirable qualities in our relations with the new nations. But if we seem forever on the defensive, frantically striving to stave off disaster, we will have great difficulty convincing others that our measures were motivated by these qualities. Generosity and moderation and self-restraint are meaningful, after all, only if it is believed that another choice is available. As long as our measures seem to be the consequence of our fears, our policy will seem to be the result of panic rather than of sober thought. Our constant defensiveness and our erratic behavior may merely convince the new nations that we are doomed regardless of what they may think of the individual measures. Even more important than a change in policy, then, is a change in attitude. We will finally be judged not so much by the cleverness of our arguments as by the purposefulness and conviction, indeed the majesty, of our conduct.

Lin Piao

10. WARS OF LIBERATION

China, forced since the early nineteenth century to yield concessions to western powers but never subjugated to direct colonial rule, has emerged in the middle of the twentieth century as the source of the most violent attacks upon American international policy. Because the Chinese Communist Revolution achieved success through guerilla warfare, "Maoist" Marxism has always stressed the importance of popular rural forces in bringing about the overthrow of world capitalism. Lin Piao, currently Chinese Defense Minister, a leader of the Great Cultural Revolution, and heir apparent to Mao Tse-tung, achieved particular notoriety among western policymakers for the following speech. It should be noted, however, that far from threatening Chinese intervention in foreign revolutions, Lin emphasizes the need for each national liberation movement to rely mainly upon its own resources.

The people's armed forces led by our Party independently waged people's war on a large scale and won great victories without any material aid from outside, both during the more than eight years of the anti-Japanese war and during the more than three years of the People's War of Liberation.

Comrade Mao Tse-tung has said that our fundamental policy should rest on the foundation of our own strength. Only by relying on our own efforts can we in all circumstances remain invincible.

The peoples of the world invariably support each other in their struggles against imperialism and its lackeys. Those countries which have won victory are duty bound to support and aid the peoples who have not yet done so. Nevertheless, foreign aid can only play a supplementary role.

In order to make a revolution and to fight a people's war and be victorious, it is imperative to adhere to the policy of self-reliance, rely on the strength of the masses in one's own country and prepare to carry on the fight independently even when all material aid from outside is cut off. If one does not operate by one's own efforts, does not independently ponder and solve the problems of the revolution in one's own country and does not rely on the strength of the masses, but leans wholly on foreign aid — even though this be aid from socialist countries which persist in revolution — no victory can be won, or be consolidated even if it is won.

* * *

War is the product of imperialism and the system of exploitation of man by man. Lenin said that "war is always and everywhere begun by the exploiters themselves, by the ruling and oppressing classes." So long as imperialism and the system of exploitation of man by man exist, the imperi-

Lin Piao, *Long Live the Victory of the People's War* (Peking, September 3, 1965), 41-42, 44-58, with omissions.

alists and reactionaries will invariably rely on armed force to maintain their reactionary rule and impose war on the oppressed nations and peoples. This is an objective law independent of man's will.

In the world today, all the imperialists headed by the United States and their lackeys, without exception, are strengthening their state machinery, and especially their armed forces. U.S. imperialism, in particular, is carrying out armed aggression and suppression everywhere.

What should the oppressed nations and the oppressed people do in the face of wars of aggression and armed suppression by the imperialists and their lackeys? Should they submit and remain slaves in perpetuity? Or should they rise in resistance and fight for their liberation?

* * *

In the last analysis, whether one dares to wage a tit-for-tat struggle against armed aggression and suppression by the imperialists and their lackeys, whether one dares to fight a people's war against them, means whether one dares to embark on revolution. This is the most effective touchstone for distinguishing genuine from fake revolutionaries and Marxist-Leninists.

In view of the fact that some people were afflicted with the fear of the imperialists and reactionaries, Comrade Mao Tse-tung put forward his famous thesis that "the imperialists and all reactionaries are paper tigers." He said,

> All reactionaries are paper tigers. In appearance, the reactionaries are terrifying, but in reality they are not so powerful. From a long-term point of view, it is not the reactionaries but the people who are really powerful.

The history of people's war in China and other countries provides conclusive evidence that the growth of the people's revolutionary forces from weak and small beginnings into strong and large forces is a universal law of development of class struggle, a universal law of development of people's war. A people's war inevitably meets with many difficulties, with ups and downs and setbacks in the course of its development, but no force can alter its general trend towards inevitable triumph.

Comrade Mao Tse-tung points out that we must despise the enemy strategically and take full account of him tactically.

To despise the enemy strategically is an elementary requirement for a revolutionary. Without the courage to despise the enemy and without daring to win, it will be simply impossible to make revolution and wage a people's war, let alone to achieve victory.

It is also very important for revolutionaries to take full account of the enemy tactically. It is likewise impossible to win victory in a people's war without taking full account of the enemy tactically, and without examining the concrete conditions, without being prudent and giving great attention to the study of the art of struggle, and without adopting appropriate forms of struggle in the concrete practice of the revolution in each country and with regard to each concrete problem of struggle.

Dialectical and historical materialism teaches us that what is important primarily is not that which at the given moment seems to be durable and yet is already beginning to die away, but that which is arising and developing, even though at the given moment it may not appear to be durable, for only that which is arising and developing is invincible.

Why can the apparently weak new-born forces always triumph over the decadent forces which appear so powerful? The reason is that truth is on their side and that the masses are on their side, while the reactionary classes are always divorced from the masses and set themselves against the masses.

* * *

Comrade Mao Tse-tung's theory of people's war solves not only the problem of daring to fight a people's war, but also that of how to wage it.

Comrade Mao Tse-tung is a great statesman and military scientist, proficient at directing war in accordance with its laws. By the line and policies, the strategy and tactics he formulated for the people's war, he led the Chinese people in steering the ship of the people's war past all hidden reefs to the shores of victory in most complicated and difficult conditions.

It must be emphasized that Comrade Mao Tse-tung's theory of the establishment of rural revolutionary base areas and the encirclement of the cities from the countryside is of outstanding and universal practical importance for the present revolutionary struggles of all the oppressed nations and peoples, and particularly for the revolutionary struggles of the oppressed nations and peoples in Asia, Africa and Latin America against imperialism and its lackeys.

Many countries and peoples in Asia, Africa and Latin America are now being subjected to aggression and enslavement on a serious scale by the imperialists headed by the United States and their lackeys. The basic political and economic conditions in many of these countries have many similarities to those that prevailed in old China. As in China, the peasant question is extremely important in these regions. The peasants constitute the main force of the national-democratic revolution against the imperialists and their lackeys. In committing aggression against these countries, the imperialists usually begin by seizing the big cities and the main lines of communication, but they are unable to bring the vast countryside completely under their control. The countryside, and the countryside alone, can provide the broad areas in which the revolutionaries can manoeuvre freely. The countryside, and the countryside alone, can provide the revolutionary bases from which the revolutionaries can go forward to final victory. Precisely for this reason, Comrade Mao Tse-tung's theory of establishing revolutionary base areas in the rural districts and encircling the cities from the countryside is attracting more and more attention among the people in these regions.

Taking the entire globe, if North America and Western Europe can be called "the cities of the world," then Asia, Africa and Latin America constitute "the rural areas of the world." Since World War II, the proletarian revolutionary movement has for various reasons been temporarily held back in the North American and West European capitalist countries, while the people's revolutionary movement in Asia, Africa and Latin America has been growing vigorously. In a sense, the contemporary world revolution also presents a picture of the encirclement of cities by the rural areas. In the final analysis, the whole cause of world revolution hinges on the revolutionary struggles of the Asian, African and Latin American peoples who make up the overwhelming majority of the world's population. The socialist countries should regard it as their internationalist duty to support the people's revolutionary struggles in Asia, Africa and Latin America.

The October Revolution opened up a new era in the revolution of the oppressed nations. The victory of the October Revolution built a bridge between the socialist revolution of the proletariat of the West and the national-democratic revolution of the colonial and semi-colonial countries of the East. The Chinese revolution has successfully solved the problem of how to link up the national-democratic with the socialist revolution in the colonial and semi-colonial countries.

Comrade Mao Tse-tung has pointed out that, in the epoch since the October Revolution, anti-imperialist revolution in any colonial or semi-colonial country is no longer part of the old bourgeois, or capitalist world revolution, but is part of the new world revolution, the proletarian-socialist world revolution.

Comrade Mao Tse-tung has formulated a complete theory of the new-democratic revolution. He indicated that this revolution, which is different from all others, can only be, nay must be, a revolution against imperialism, feudalism and bureaucrat-capitalism waged by the broad masses of the people under the leadership of the proletariat.

This means that the revolution can only be, nay must be, led by the proletariat and the genuinely revolutionary party armed with Marxism-Leninism, and by no other class or party.

* * *

Comrade Mao Tse-tung made a correct distinction between the two revolutionary stages, *i.e.*, the national-democratic and the socialist revolutions; at the same time he correctly and closely linked the two. The national-democratic revolution is the necessary preparation for the socialist revolution, and the socialist revolution is the inevitable sequel to the national-democratic revolution. There is no Great Wall between the two revolutionary stages. But the socialist revolution is only possible after the completion of the national-democratic revolution. The more thorough the national democratic revolution, the better the conditions for the socialist revolution.

The experience of the Chinese revolution shows that the tasks of the national-democratic revolution can be fulfilled only through long and tortuous struggles. In this stage of revolution, imperialism and its lackeys are the principal enemy. In the struggle against imperialism and its lackeys, it is necessary to rally all anti-imperialist patriotic forces, including the national bourgeoisie and all patriotic personages. All those patriotic personages from among the bourgeoisie and other exploiting classes who join the anti-imperialist struggle play a progressive historical role; they are not tolerated by imperialism but welcomed by the proletariat.

It is very harmful to confuse the two stages, that is, the national-democratic and the socialist revolutions. Comrade Mao Tse-tung criticized the wrong idea of "accomplishing both at one stroke," and pointed out that this utopian idea could only weaken the struggle against imperialism and its lackeys, the most urgent task at that time.

* * *

The Khrushchev revisionists are now actively preaching that socialism can be built without the proletariat and without a genuinely revolutionary party armed with the advanced proletarian ideology, and they have cast the fundamental tenets of Marxism-Leninism to the four winds. The revisionists' purpose is solely to divert the oppressed nations from their struggle against imperialism and sabotage their national-democratic revolution, all in the service of imperialism.

* * *

Ours is the epoch in which world capitalism and imperialism are heading for their doom and socialism and communism are marching to victory. Comrade Mao Tse-tung's theory of people's war is not only a product of the Chinese revolution, but has also the characteristics of our epoch. The new experience gained in the people's revolutionary struggles in various countries since World War II has provided continuous evidence that Mao Tse-tung's thought is a common asset of the revolutionary people of the whole world. This is the great international significance of the thought of Mao Tse-tung.

DEFEAT U.S. IMPERIALISM AND ITS LACKEYS BY PEOPLE'S WAR

Since World War II, U.S. imperialism has stepped into the shoes of German, Japanese and Italian fascism and has been trying to build a great American empire by dominating and enslaving the whole world. It is actively fostering Japanese and West German militarism as its chief accomplices in unleashing a world war. Like a vicious wolf, it is bullying and enslaving various peoples, plundering their wealth, encroaching upon their countries' sovereignty and interfering in their internal affairs. It is the most rabid aggressor in human history and the most ferocious common enemy of the people of the world. Every people or country in the world that wants revolution, independence and peace cannot but direct the spearhead of its struggle against U.S. imperialism.

Just as the Japanese imperialists' policy of subjugating China made it possible for the Chinese people to form the broadest possible united front against them, so the U.S. imperialists' policy of seeking world domination makes it possible for the people throughout the world to unite all the forces that can be united and form the broadest possible united front for a converging attack on U.S. imperialism.

At present, the main battlefield of the fierce struggle between the people of the world on the one side and U.S. imperialism and its lackeys on the other is the vast area of Asia, Africa, and Latin America. In the world as a whole, this is the area where the people suffer worst from imperialist oppression and where imperialist rule is most vulnerable. Since World War II, revolutionary storms have been rising in this area, and today they have become the most important force directly pounding U.S. imperialism. The contradiction between the revolutionary peoples of Asia, Africa and Latin America and the imperialists headed by the United States is the principal contradiction in the contemporary world. The development of this contradiction is promoting the struggle of the people of the whole world against U.S. imperialism and its lackeys.

Since World War II, people's war has increasingly demonstrated its power in Asia, Africa and Latin America. The peoples of China, Korea, Viet Nam, Laos, Cuba, Indonesia, Algeria and other countries have waged people's wars against the imperialists and their lackeys and won great victories. The classes leading these people's wars may vary, and so may the breadth and depth of mass mobilization and the extent of victory, but the victories in these people's wars have very much weakened and pinned down the forces of imperialism, upset the U.S. imperialist plan to launch a world war, and become mighty factors defending world peace.

* * *

U.S. imperialism is stronger, but also more vulnerable, than any imperialism of the past. It sets itself against the people of the whole world, including the people of the United States. Its human, military, material and financial resources are far from sufficient for the realization of its ambition of dominating the whole world. U.S. imperialism has further weakened itself by occupying so many places in the world, overreaching itself, stretching its fingers out wide and dispersing its strength, with its rear so far away and its supply lines so long. As Comrade Mao Tse-tung has said, "Wherever it commits aggression, it puts a new noose around its neck. It is besieged ring upon ring by the people of the whole world."

* * *

Everything is divisible. And so is this colossus of U.S. imperialism. It can be split up and defeated. The peoples of Asia, Africa, Latin America and other regions can destroy it piece by piece, some striking at its head and others at its feet. That is why the greatest fear of U.S. imperialism is that people's wars will be launched in different parts of the world, and particularly in Asia, Africa and Latin America, and why it regards people's war as a mortal danger.

U.S. imperialism relies solely on its nuclear weapons to intimidate people. But these weapons cannot save U.S. imperialism from its doom. Nuclear weapons cannot be used lightly. U.S. imperialism has been condemned by the people of the whole world for its towering crime of dropping two atom bombs on Japan. If it uses nuclear weapons again, it will become isolated in the extreme. Moreover, the U.S. monopoly of nuclear weapons has long been broken; U.S. imperialism has these weapons, but others have them too. If it threatens other countries with nuclear weapons, U.S. imperialism will expose its own country to the same threat. For this reason, it will meet with strong opposition not only from the people elsewhere but also inevitably from the people in its own country. Even if U.S. imperialism brazenly uses nuclear weapons, it cannot conquer the people, who are indomitable.

However highly developed modern weapons and technical equipment may be and however complicated the methods of modern warfare, in the final analysis the outcome of a war will be decided by the sustained fighting of the ground forces, by the fighting at close quarters on battlefields, by the political consciousness of the men, by their courage and spirit of sacrifice. Here the weak points of U.S. imperialism will be completely laid bare, while the superiority of the revolutionary people will be brought into full play. The reactionary troops of U.S. imperialism cannot possibly be endowed with the courage and the spirit of sacrifice possessed by the revolutionary people. The spiritual atom bomb which the revolutionary people possess is a far more powerful and useful weapon than the physical atom bomb.

Viet Nam is the most convincing current example of a victim of aggression defeating U.S. imperialism by a people's war. The United States has made South Viet Nam a testing ground for the suppression of people's war. It has carried on this experiment for many years, and everybody can now see that the U.S. aggressors are unable to find a way of coping with people's war. On the other hand, the Vietnamese people have brought the power of people's war into full play in their struggle against the U.S. aggressors. The U.S. aggressors are in danger of being swamped in the people's war in Viet Nam. They are deeply worried that their defeat in Viet Nam will lead to a chain reaction. They are expanding the war in an attempt to save themselves from defeat. But the more they expand the war, the greater will be the chain reaction. The more they escalate the war, the heavier will be their fall and the more disastrous their defeat. The people in other parts of the world will see still more clearly that U.S. imperialism can be defeated, and that what the Vietnamese people can do, they can do too.

History has proved and will go on proving that people's war is the most effective weapon against U.S. imperialism and its lackeys. All revolutionary people will learn to wage people's war against U.S. imperialism and its lackeys. They will take up arms, learn to fight battles and become skilled in waging people's war, though they have not done so before. U.S. imperialism like a mad bull dashing from place to place, will finally be burned to ashes in the blazing fires of the people's wars it has provoked by its own actions.

Conor Cruise O'Brien

11. A NON-MARXIST ASSESSMENT OF AMERICAN IMPERIALISM

The author of the following essay, presently Schweitzer Professor of Humanities
at New York University, has been in the past an historian, a member of the Republic of Ireland's diplomatic corps, a United Nations representative in the Congo, and Vice-Chancellor of the University of Ghana. In the latter two posts he
came into conflict first with what he considers manipulation of the United Nations by the United States and, second, with the leftist dictatorship of Kwame
Nkrumah. The critique presented here may therefore be considered a particularly
articulate example of current liberal anti-imperialism.

We know that when J. A. Hobson found
the economic tap-root of imperialism in the
workings of the capitalist system at a given
stage, several conditions applied which no
longer apply today. Apart from the question
of the validity of his economic analysis as
applying to the conditions of his own day
. . . and apart from the great technological
and economic changes which the past sixty
years have brought, there have also been
political changes of such a character and on
such a scale as to transform the whole discussion. In Hobson's day—and Lenin's—
there could be no doubt, on any side, about
the relevance and usefulness of the term
"imperialism." There were then British and
French and Russian empires, openly labelled as such, and there were many men,
and important men, who not merely defended but gloried in the existence of these
empires. There were also influential men
who openly preached the doctrine of America's imperial destiny. These men could
properly be called "imperialists" and their
doctrine "imperialism"; they and their increasingly vocal critics had at least these

basic words and concepts in common. There
was also something else in common: since
all the powerful states of the early twentieth
century—with the partial exception of a
Russia in transition—were capitalist states,
it was natural, and indeed inevitable, that
contemporary imperialism should be discussed as a function or outgrowth of capitalism.

Two world wars and two major revolutions have changed that landscape out of
recognition. The old empires seem to have
disappeared; if they have not entirely disappeared, they have at least lost the name of
empire. A new vocabulary has arisen—
Commonwealth, Communauté, Union—
"imperialist" is in popular present use
solely as a term of abuse. Of the five great
powers, recognized as such in the Charter of
the United Nations by permanent seating
on the Security Council, two now have
Communist governments—a situation only
flimsily disguised by the insertion of an
American satellite delegation in China's
place. None of the five great powers would
admit to having today anything resembling

"Contemporary Forms of Imperialism," *Studies on the Left*, VI, No. 4 (1965).

an empire; all officially are against imperialism or deny its existence, although France's conversion from open imperial practice is so recent that the vocabulary of her spokesmen is still under repair. Imperialism, in the Hobsonian sense, can have no economic tap-root in those powers which have ceased to be capitalist; as for the capitalist countries, these claim to have overcome the supposedly inbuilt Hobsonian compulsion and to have divested themselves of their empires and of any thought of acquiring empires.

Yet the term imperialism has not only survived the overt phenomena which it was used to designate in Hobson's day; it has acquired new life and is in far more frequent international use today than it was in the heyday of the empires. Why should this be? Is it, as some maintain, that the term has become purely emotive, of propaganda value only? Or has it still rational relevance, as a general descriptive term grouping sets of relations still existing, though officially unacknowledged, and continuing certain crucial patterns of the old imperial systems and ambitions? It is obvious that the most frequent uses of the term are operational, that is to say propagandist, and that it is thus used by both sides in the cold war. The Communist side, or rather the Communist sides, have used it most persistently and aggressively, concentrating in recent years on "American imperialism" especially in Latin America, the Near East, Southeast Asia and the Congo. Western spokesmen have retorted by attacks on "Soviet imperialism" in Eastern Europe and "Chinese imperialism" in Tibet, Southeast Asia and the Indian border, and Chinese imperial ambitions towards Indonesia, Africa, etc. The peoples of the newly independent countries are warned from time to time, mainly by American writers and speakers, to be careful not to fall under the sway of a far more cruel form of imperialism than that which they have just shaken off. There has, however, been something half-hearted and ineffective about Western propaganda on these lines; it remains a *tu quoque* and an

intellectual gimmick rather than a driving force as Communist anti-imperialism is. The peoples addressed—Africans, Asians, Latin Americans—find it impossible, on the basis of their historical experience, to believe in the sincerity of Western anti-imperialism, and many non-Communist Westerners also find such propaganda distasteful. Many Englishmen and Frenchmen dislike hearing Americans tell the peoples of Ghana or Guinea that Russian rule will be "even more oppressive" than English or French rule was. And many feel—though they do not say—that the rule of more advanced over less advanced people is part of the law of nature and that if the Russians and Chinese were genuinely imperialists, and only imperialists, it would be possible to reach agreement with them. At bottom the West objects to Communists not in so far as they may be imperialists, but in so far as they are revolutionaries.

?

Western propaganda on "Communist imperialism" lines also errs when it assumes that African and Asian governments necessarily shrink in horror from the thought of the domination of one people over another. Most of these governments are themselves the instruments of such rule over "minority" peoples—and most of them feel that unless they are ready when necessary to take repressive action against minorities, or against refractory elements among the minorities, their states will break up and collapse. Thus many of these states were sympathetic to the Chinese action in Tibet, when this action was presented to them in the light of bringing a dissident peripheral minority to heel—which is of course how the Chinese government envisaged the action. Again Asian and African governments are impressed when an Asian nation like China—or formerly Japan—shows the capacity to act as a great power acts, even in ways which would be stigmatized as imperialist if used by a Western power against Africans or Asians. In such contexts even left-wing African spokesmen are themselves liable to use the classic language of imperialism. Thus I have heard an African

185

delegate, speaking against the inclusion of the question of Tibet on the agenda of the U.N. General Assembly in 1958, argue that the Chinese action was justifiable because Tibetan society was archaic, stagnant and monk-ridden, and the Chinese would bring roads, medicine and education. There was truth in much of what he said, but every argument he used could have been—and was—used to justify, say, Mussolini's conquest of Ethiopia. The man who spoke thus at the U.N. was the delegate of Ethiopia.

Not unnaturally such contradictions have enabled some Western and other spokesmen to pour scorn on the moral position of African and Asian governments, and to deny to these governments any moral right to challenge Western imperialism, or colonialism or the actions of white settler governments. It was the practice of Mr. Eric Louw, representing South Africa when that country still defended its practices in the U.N. General Assembly, to rattle the bones of all the minority skeletons in the U.N. cupboard—caste discrimination in India, oppression by Ethiopia of its Moslem subjects, by Sudan of its non-Muslim subjects and so on. Again there was truth in much of what he said, but he left his audience at best indifferent. Outside a few Western delegations, no one felt that the treatment of minorities in some independent African and Asian countries was seriously comparable to *apartheid*.

White domination over non-white has been after all an almost universally experienced reality. South Africa is a symbol of the continuance of this reality. It is not surprising that the non-white peoples, guilty though some of them are of particular and local acts of aggression, should resent the symbol of their universal bondage. In their reaction to pictures from South Africa or Dixie, the Moslem from Khartoum and his rebellious subject the pagan from Southern Sudan would be at one. It is quite true that the moral altitude from which African and Asian governments criticize the West is often less elevated than those governments assume; such governments are not wiser or

nicer than other governments, only weaker, and therefore more limited in the scale of their depredations. But the consensus of non-white opinion which they reflect is important and it is this consensus, and not the morals of those through whom it finds expression, that Western policy-makers should take into account. Western policy should—and hopefully must—ultimately be based on the values professed in the West, including that of consent of the governed, and not on, say, the example of Baghdad's treatment of the Kurds. Yet some Western commentators write as if the policies of Baghdad, Khartoum, etc., constitute a vindication of Western imperialism.

In the propaganda battle over "imperialism" the West has been the losing side; the Western nations, and in particular the United States, are still widely regarded as the imperialists and have generally failed in their efforts to pin this label on to the Communist countries. Is this due to resentments arising from past history, including the deep resentments generated by white color-consciousness? Or has the fear of Western imperialism an objective referent in the present? When we are discussing the reactions of many thousands of people, representing in some fashion hundreds of millions of others, the answer to the first question has necessarily to be a qualified one. On personal observation, however, I would say that the role of resentment of *past* wrongs is less than it is often represented to be, and in many of the countries concerned is no more than a latent factor, which in normal circumstances does not become manifest at all. No country is more militantly anti-imperialist in its language than Ghana, yet it is almost impossible to find a Ghanaian who has any really bitter memories of British rule; villagers everywhere respond with spontaneous friendliness to the sight of a white face; the products of the secondary schools and University who man the civil service, the embassies and the U.N. delegation are pro-British to a degree which seems to an Irishman even a little mawkish. It is true that the class in between villager and elite, the class of those whose education stopped at primary level, is a somewhat embittered body, as well as an important one, and not disposed to be sentimental about the benefits of British rule. The real bitterness however is directed against the Ghanaian elite, who have enjoyed secondary and higher education; the anti-Western attitudes of the "Standard VII" boys are principally directed, not so much against the West as such as against a native elite which happens to be, on the whole, pro-Western. A similar problem, though at present with greater dominance of pro-Western elites, prevails in Nigeria. Combinations of this kind, whether with a "Nigerian" or "Ghanaian" balance, are to be found throughout all those territories of the former British—and with some qualification French—empires which were not burdened with settlers from the metropolis. (The Belgian Congo, exposed within living memory to the most ferocious and unbridled form of colonial rapacity, is of course quite a different matter.) I find it hard to believe, therefore, that among most of the newly independent countries, resentment of *past* wrongs is a really live factor, actively and independently inspiring present choices. But past experience illuminates contemporary events. Most Algerians, for example, are far too preoccupied with the pressing problems of the present to waste much time in brooding over the wrongs inflicted on them by the French. But when Algerians hear on the radio, from a Western source, that peasants in certain parts of Vietnam are being brought together in special villages for their protection against terrorists, it is inevitable that these Algerians should think of the French regroupment camps and of the realities which underlay the French army's claim that it was protecting villagers from terror. From this it is a short step to concluding that America's war in Vietnam, like France's in Algeria, is in reality an imperialist war accompanied by mendacious slogans. As this is just what the Communist press and radio say it is, the net effect for so many people, will be to

strengthen confidence in the Communist picture of world events, while deepening scepticism about the picture presented by the Western media; this scepticism extends of course to stories of Soviet and Chinese imperialism. (Similarly, those who have lived under people like Trujillo or Batista are not likely to be roused to free world enthusiasm by news of the emergence of another anti-Communist strong man in say, the Congo.) Algeria is, of course, an extreme example, but even those—like, say, the English-speaking West Africans—whose recent experience of colonial rule has been on the whole a benign one, are sensitized by their past history in such a way as to be repelled by much in the present conduct of the Western powers. Even the benevolent generations of British rulers carried with them their racial exclusiveness and assumptions of superiority, and even the most pro-Western Ghanaian or Nigerian is necessarily affected by corresponding doubts and suspicions—which normally he will seek to repress—about white attitudes towards non-white peoples. These doubts and suspicions can be fanned into hostility by certain news and above all news pictures. An African who has just seen pictures of white Americans using dogs and cattle prods against black men is not psychologically prepared to believe that the white Americans who land in Vietnam have come to help the yellow man. And the more closely he follows the news from Vietnam the less he will be disposed to accept the American official version.

One may note here, to the credit of the American system, how ill-adapted that system is, in certain respects, to the successful waging of a colonial-type war. The French in Algeria did not distribute to the world pictures of their harkis torturing prisoners; British reporters covering Mau Mau had plenty to say about Mau Mau atrocities but little or nothing about atrocities committed by the suppressors of Mau Mau. But American wire services do distribute to the world pictures of "Viet Cong suspects" being tortured by America's Vietnamese allies;

American reporters tell of indiscriminate shooting, including the shooting of children, by American marines. Critics of American imperialism can buttress their case with abundant and horrifying detail supplied by impeccable American sources. No corresponding facilities are available to critics of Soviet or Chinese policies and activities.

It seems fair, then, to conclude that the hostility of the newly independent countries to Western imperialism derives not so much from past resentments as from the actual flow of world news, interpreted, as we all must interpret news—in the light of personal and community experience. That news, so interpreted makes up a pattern in which the Western whites, who control almost all the physical resources of the non-Communist world, seek also with a high degree of success to control its non-white peoples, indirectly and by guile where possible, directly and by force where necessary. This is what is meant by "Western imperialism" today.

How far is this picture valid? Personally I believe that it is substantially accurate, and it is meaningful to speak of Western imperialism, in this sense, as one of the greatest and most dangerous forces in the world today. Those who would deny or minimize its existence assert, with some degree of truth, that the Hobsonian version of imperialism no longer applies if ever it did apply, and that there is no adequate economic motive for imperialist activities. Thus, if France, for example, has a powerful say in the political life of Upper Volta, this is not because she needs the resources or the market—both of them almost non-existent—of that desolate and destitute country, but on the contrary, because France annually makes up the deficit in the Upper Volta budget. This might be defined as *un*economic imperialism. Such examples can easily be multiplied, by writers like Mr. Brian Crozier, to bring into ridicule the idea of economic imperialism and, implicitly, of *all* forms of Western imperialism. I have heard Barbara Ward explain to a Ghanaian audience that the advanced countries of the West have no longer any serious need either for the markets or the resources of the underdeveloped countries generally, and consequently have no economic need either to control or to develop these countries; without the underdeveloped countries, according to this thesis, the advanced countries will continue to progress while, without the advanced countries, the underdeveloped are doomed to continue to stagnate. . . . The Ward thesis, at least as understood and here summarized by me, itself seems open to some question. I find it hard to believe that Britain is so indifferent to the resources of Kuwait, the United States to those of Venezuela, or Belgium to those of Katanga, as this thesis seems to suggest. Nor does the thesis seem to take sufficient account of the overseas interests of particular groups in the advanced countries. It is uneconomic for France to pay prices higher than world market prices for Ivory Coast *robusta* coffee, but this practice is highly economic for those Frenchmen who own Ivory Coast coffee plantations. Political leverage of interested groups (Standard Oil, United Fruit, etc.) has done much to create, through the mass media, the pattern of anti-Communist public opinion and, by now, anti-Communist *reflexes*. One may, however, agree with the Ward thesis to the extent that economic motives are not in *themselves* sufficient to account for a world-wide effort by the Western countries and especially by the United States to control the politics of the underdeveloped countries generally.

That such an effort exists, is, I think, undeniable. It is a declared goal of the United States, not merely to prevent Soviet and Chinese territorial expansion, but to check the spread of a political doctrine: Communism. This cannot be done without close surveillance of the internal politics of all countries deemed vulnerable to Communism—including all underdeveloped countries—without discreet guidance of these politics when necessary, without economic pressure and without in the penultimate resort intervention by all the methods prac-

ticed by all secret services including brib-
ery, blackmail and political assassination.
The Congo is an obvious case in point. I
have myself heard a senior and responsible
American official state that it was not America's responsibility to prevent the Congolese from massacring each other, but it *was*
America's responsibility to keep Communism out of the Congo. In practice, American officials, some employed by the C.I.A.
and at least one by the United Nations, actively intervened in Congolese politics in
order to bring about the downfall of Lu-
mumba and the triumph of his enemies; his
subsequent murder and the murder of his
principal associates at the hands of these
enemies were then regarded as an internal
Congolese affair.

* * *

The Congo in some ways is an extreme
case, a *cas limité*, and the limit it stands for,
in the eyes of many Africans and Asians, is
the limit to their own freedom. From this
example they see that if their government
shows what are, in the eyes of U.S. officials,
Communist tendencies the diplomatic, political, secret service, and financial resources
of the greatest of world powers may be
turned against them and that a political re-
ceiver nominated by Western interests — a
Tshombe — may be put in charge of their
affairs. They know further that if they withstand the political shock — which few of
them indeed feel strong enough to do — they
may have to face actual military intervention, as those other *cas limités*, Santo Domingo and Vietnam, have demonstrated. If
there are sizeable Western business interests in their territory they will know that
their position in relation to these interests is
less than that of a fully sovereign state, for
their dealings with these interests will be
among the criteria of their non-Commu-
nism, that is to say of their continued existence. But even if they have little or nothing,
like many of the so-called French-speaking
African territories, this does not exempt
them from Western surveillance, for even
these wastelands form part of that "reser-

voir of strategic space" which is Africa in
the eyes of such competent Western observers as Professor Hans Morgenthau. The position of these countries, with backward
economies, often dependent on the export
of a single raw material, would be weak in
any case in relation to the advanced countries, agreement of whose nationals sets the
price of the commodities. When to these
structural conditions of dependence is
added the latent, and sometimes overt, tutelage implied in the doctrine of "containing
Communism" it is not surprising that many
people in the poor countries should feel
their present independence is little more
than a facade, and that in reality they still
form part of a sort of Western empire, which
is not the less real, economically and politically, for having no legal existence. If the
Communist parties have taken up the slogan of "the struggle against neo-colonial-
ism" — a word not of their coinage according
to Professor I. I. Potekhin — it is that they see
in this situation, and in the resentments
generated by it, the point of departure for
revolutionary change. In other words the
application of the American policy of "containing Communism" is regarded by Communists themselves as a principal generator
of Communism. This is of course especially
so in those "end-games" where, as in Indo-
China, the Congo and much of Latin America, the "containment" process, working by
elimination, has thrown up, as "friends of
the West" and holders of power, discredited
and parasitic groups with little or no unpaid
support within their own countries.

The policy of "containing Communism,"
which is both the mainspring and the justification of contemporary Western forms of
imperialism, has a number of points in
common with Stalin's policies in post-war
Europe. The anti-Communists, like Stalin,
seem to envisage their policies as essentially
defensive; like Stalin they prefer to work
through stooges, reserving military action
for the last resort; like Stalin they describe
the state of affairs which results from their
maneuvers as "freedom," and like Stalin
they are in fact adept at the manufacture of

satellite states. More adept than he, indeed, for every member of the United Nations which, in a critical vote, accepts the "whip" of the Soviet Union, there are at least five members which will follow the "whip" of the United States. In part as a result of this, and in part because of other pressures, the United Nations on most important matters and at every level—Security Council, Assembly and Secretariat—is preponderantly influenced by United States policy. The delegation seated as representing China is symbolic of this preponderant influence.

If indeed it is to remain the settled and official policy of the United States to prevent the spread of Communism, the quasi-imperial involvement of the United States in the domestic affairs of every country in the "free world" becomes inevitable. There is no way of being sure of "stopping Communism" without interfering, by force if necessary, in the internal affairs of every country in which Communism may appear. What such interference means in the penultimate resort we have seen in the Congo. What it means in the last resort we are seeing in Vietnam. There seems to be no doubt that, left to itself, Vietnam would go Communist; in the effort to prevent this, the United States has taken France's place as imperial power in Southeast Asia; the shadowy governments in Saigon disguise this fact, by now, even less effectively than France's role was disguised by the Emperor Bao Dai. It seems clear that the policy of "containing Communism" is likely to lead to other accretions of direct imperial responsibility—as distinct from indirect rule, as in the Congo—in other parts of the globe. And in an age of awakened nationalism, and of the existence of great powers outside the western system, imperial responsibilities are likely to involve wider resentments and greater bloodshed and infinitely greater risks than they did in the nineteenth century.

On a recent television program we saw the President and the Secretary of State defending their Vietnam policy. They gave three reasons for continuing the war: prestige, honor—meaning the necessity to abide by pledges—and the defense of the freedom of South Vietnam. The first two are contingent, that is to say that they are reasons which can be invoked for persisting in *any* policy, however bad; both were invoked in defense of France's Algerian war policy, until the time came when they had to be dropped. The only *substantive* reason invoked—and that briefly and skimpily—was the so-called defense of freedom. But what meaning can be assigned to the defense of freedom in South Vietnam? It is obvious that the people of South Vietnam do not enjoy freedom in any of the senses in which we so commonly understand the word; they are subject to the arbitrary will of juntas dependent on foreign military and economic support. "Freedom" here is a purely technical term, meaning the exclusion of Communists from power by force if necessary. Mr. James Reston, in a recent article in *The New York Times,* seemed puzzled by the failure of Asians to understand the fact that the U.S. championed their independence and nationalism. He himself failed to understand that the concepts of independence and nationalism are wholly vitiated by the qualifications which current U.S. policy attaches to them. In terms of that policy, independence must be non-Communist or it is not independence; nationalism must be non-Communist, or it is not nationalism. But what happens in a country where nationalists are Communists or pro-Communists, and where independence is thought of as being able to have one's own form of government, even if it should be a Communist form? What happens then is that an outside power, the United States, intervenes to impose its own doctrine of what independence and nationalism should constitute in the country concerned. This, it seems to me, constitutes the ideological mainspring of the most widespread form of contemporary "imperialism." The doctrine of the containment of Communism is necessarily an imperialist doctrine.

Suggestions for Reading

Even more than in most fields of modern history, the study of imperialism has up to now produced relatively few general works which can be enthusiastically recommended. Of the immense literature which does exist, a large part is polemical rather than scholarly, another segment is confined to constitutional and diplomatic issues, and very little offers the broad comparative scope which the subject demands.

One indication of this unfortunate situation is the absence of any up-to-date bibliographic work on imperialist studies. For limited samples of, and references to, such material the student can turn to several anthologies of secondary writings on imperialism such as George H. Nadel and Perry Curtis, *Imperialism and Colonialism* (New York, 1964); Louis L. Snyder, *The Imperialism Reader* (Princeton, 1962); and Harrison Wright, *The "New Imperialism"* (Boston, 1961). Good bibliographies are available for restricted aspects of European overseas expansion including a collection of essays edited by Robin W. Winks, *The Historiography of the British Empire-Commonwealth* (Durham, N. C., 1966) and a lengthy essay by Hartmut Pogge von Strandmann in W. R. Louis and Prosser Gifford (editors), *Imperial Rivalry and Colonial Rule: Britain and Germany in Africa* (New Haven, 1967). Similarly limited anthologies include George Bennett, *The Concept of* [British] *Empire* (London, 1962); Raymond F. Betts, *The Scramble for Africa* (Boston, 1966); Martin D. Lewis, *The British in India* (Boston, 1962); and Robin W. Winks, *British Imperialism* (New York, 1963).

Along with D. K. Fieldhouse (see selection 17 of Part II), recent attempts to survey the development of modern imperialism have been made by Stewart C. Easton, *The Rise and Fall of Western Colonialism* (New York, 1964) and in various chapters of *The New Cambridge Modern History*, volumes X–XII (1960–1962). Large portions of the subject are covered also in P. Duignan and L. H. Gann, *Burden of Empire* (New York, 1967), mainly on Africa; Ch.-A. Julien (editor), *Les Techniciens de la colonisation, Les Politiques d'expansion imperialiste* (Paris, 1947, 1949), collections of biographies; and William L. Langer, *European Alliances and Alignments, The Diplomacy of Imperialism* (New York, 1931, 1935), restricted to latter nineteenth century.

For more interpretive approaches to the general problems, there are Rupert Emerson, *From Empire to Nation* (Cambridge, Mass., 1960) and "Colonialism and Colonization in World History," *Journal of Economic History*, volume XXI, number 4 (December 1961); Richard Koebner and Helmut Dan Schmidt, *Imperialism* (Cambridge, United Kingdom, 1964); Robert Strauz-Hupe and Harry W. Hazard (editors), *The Idea of Colonialism* (New York, 1958); Immanuel Wallerstein (editor), *Social Change: The Colonial Situation* (New York, 1966); Earle M. Winslow, *The Pattern of Imperialism* (New York, 1948).

Most writing on modern overseas expansion is confined to the activities and policies of a single colonial power. Not surprisingly, the largest amount of this literature has been dedicated to the British Empire. The fullest, although now somewhat dated, survey remains *The Cambridge History of the British Empire* (eight volumes, 1927-1959). A handy account of the modern period is Robert A. Huttenback, *The British Imperial Experience* (New York, 1966). The key recent interpretive study is Ronald Robinson and John Gallagher, *Africa and the Victorians* (London, 1962).

French imperialism has received less thorough coverage, the most valuable survey still being Herbert I. Priestley, *France Overseas* (New York, 1938) along with S. H. Roberts, *A History of French Colonial Policy*, two volumes, (Chicago, 1929). A more recent effort at interpretation is Robert Brunschwig, *French Colonialism*, 1870-1914 (New York, 1966).

For German overseas expansion, the standard, Mary E. Townsend, *The Rise and Fall of Germany's Colonial Empire* (New York, 1930) and the brief W. O. Henderson, *Studies in German Colonialism* (London, 1962) should be supplemented by various essays in W. R. Louis and Prosser Gifford (editors), *Imperial Rivalry and Colonial Rule: Britain and Germany in Africa* (New Haven, 1967). The Belgian experience in the Congo is covered by Ruth Slade, *King Leopold's Congo* (London, 1962) and Roger Anstey, *King Leopold's Legacy* (London, 1966). Still the best survey of modern Dutch colonialism is B. H. M. Vlekke, *Nusantara: A History of Indonesia*, revised edition (The Hague, 1959). The Portuguese empire, slighted in this volume, can be studied through James Duffy, *Portugal in Africa* (Cambridge, Mass., 1962) and R. J. Hammond, *Portugal and Africa* (Stanford, 1966). For a survey of United States imperialism see Foster Rhea Dulles, *The Imperial Years* (New York, 1956). A more far-reaching and controversial account is presented in William Appleman Williams, *The Tragedy of American Diplomacy*, revised edition, (New York, 1962).

The view of imperialism from the perspective of the colonizing powers ought to be supplemented by an account of its impact upon the colonized peoples. Within the context of this bibliography, however, it is impossible to do justice to the vast output of recent writing on those non-European parts of the world whose entire modern history is inseparable from imperialist issues. The following summary works, mostly available in paperback, may also serve as guides to further literature concerning their respective areas: George Pendle, *A History of Latin America* (Baltimore, 1963); Roland Oliver and Antony Atmore, *Africa Sine 1800* (Cambridge, United Kingdom, 1967); Michael Edwardes, *Asia in the European Age* (London, 1961); George E. Kirk, *A Short History of the Middle East* (New York, 1964); Percival Spear, *A History of India*, volume II (Baltimore, 1965); Brian Harrison, *A Short History of Southeast Asia* (New York, 1966); John K. Fairbank, *The United States and China* (Cambridge, Mass., 1958); Richard Storry, *A Modern History of Japan* (Baltimore, 1960); C. Hartley Grattan, *The Southwest Pacific to 1900, The Southwest Pacific Since 1900* (Ann Arbor, 1963).

On the contemporary problems of development within the former colonial territories and their role in international relations, the literature is not only vast but also extremely difficult to reduce to any basic works. For development as such, C. E. Black, *The Dynamics of Modernization* (New York, 1966) offers a useful comparative framework and bibliographical essay. Paul E. Sigmund, *The Ideologies of the Developing Nations* (New York, 1963) and Peter Worsley, *The Third World* (London, 1964) offer helpful introductions, although the latter, like most works with such titles, omits Latin America.

1 2 3 4 5 6 7 8 9 10